In celebration of Rudy's
thoughtfulness and Spirit

Betty Wilson

Rudy!

The People's
Governor

Rudy!

The People's Governor

by

Betty Wilson

NODIN PRESS

Acknowledgements

Thanks to *Minneapolis Star* editors David Nimmer and
Deborah Howell who assigned me to cover the statehouse
starting in the 1970s and supported me through those years. It
was always a thrill to look up and see those golden horses—and
truly they were galloping during the Perpich years—and enter
that fascinating world of the Capitol. Thanks also to many
who have been especially helpful in writing this book: Vance
Opperman, Joe, Tony and Irene Perpich, Gwenyth Jones Spitz,
Alfred France, John Toren, Norton Stillman, Veda Ponikvar,
Judith Jones, Eric Eskola, Marshall Tannick, Rosalie Wahl, and
Gerry Nelson are just a few.

Photo Credits:

2, 9 Personal collection Tony Perpich, used with permission.
6, 19, 21 Personal collection Veda Ponikvar, used with permission.
39, 133, 178, 235, 244, 274 *Star Tribune* /Minneapolis-St. Paul.
65-Minnesota Historical Society, photo by Frank Frison.
100–Personal collection Rosalie Wahl, used with permission.
Cover photo, *Almanac*, April 19, 1985; used with permission.

ISBN - 1-932472-27-4

edited and designed by John Toren

Nodin Press is a division of Micawbers, Inc.
530 North Third Street
Suite 120
Minneapolis, MN 55401

Dedicated to Robert, Joseph,

Rodney, and Mark Wilson

Table of Contents

Foreword

by Rosalie Wahl

In broad strokes of black and white across the mid- to late-20th century landscape of Minnesota, Betty Wilson has brought to life Rudy Perpich, one of the most creative, constructive, colorful governors who has ever served this state and its people. Her lucid prose and matter-of-fact style uncover and illuminate Rudy's legacy even as the labors of Rudy's immigrant father, Anton Perpich, brought to light the rich red ore of the iron mines of "the Range." With meticulous detail gathered in her more than 30 years of reporting on the state capitol, bolstered by more recent research into events of that time, Wilson brings us the whole, indomitable, inimitable man.

Rudy Perpich, the "Hunkie from the Iron Range" who knew no English until he went to school, was a poor miner's son who was never quite accepted by the powers that be. Rudy Perpich validated, and still validates, the lives and dreams of immigrants and the children of immigrants, and all outsiders—on the Range and elsewhere. He gave them a seat at the table in the legislature where decisions that affected their lives are made, and for 12 years he gave them a seat at the governor's desk where policies for social, political, and economic reform are initiated.

It was clear to me that these people mattered to him when, on the cold, gray, January day in 1983, I, then Rudy's only appointee on the Minnesota Supreme Court, administered the oath of office to newly elected Governor Perpich before family and friends, teachers and students in the Hibbing High School auditorium. With the echo of Copland's "Fanfare for the Common Man" still lingering in the air, Rudy promised to insure for all Minnesota students an excellent education, strengthened by programs of foreign languages, computers, and science, so that they might better compete in the emerging "world marketplace." That shining moment was pictured the next day in the *New York Times*. Rudy was back in St. Paul working to make the dreams come true.

Rudy Perpich was a determined dreamer. His brilliant, curious mind threw off sparks of ideas like steel hitting a grindstone. The grindstone was Rudy's experience of the poverty on the Range, the frequent unemployment of his father and other miners, the unions through which the workers raised their voices, the failing farms, the dwindling small towns, and the desperate need for education and jobs in an increasingly globalized economy. Some of those flying sparks, those tremendous ideas, came to nothing, but others shaped initiatives and programs of reform that enhanced our common good and became so much a part of the landscape that we take them for granted.

A new generation is unaware that when Rudy Perpich was lieutenant governor, he marched and spoke out against the war in Vietnam and urged students to resist also. It is unaware of the doors he opened, especially for women and minorities. And those of us who stood with him, or walked through the doors he opened, tend to forget the political risks he took to make us full, participating members of our society. Rudy was not afraid of risks.

Rudy was not afraid of strong women, either. He was married to one; his mother was one. He was the first governor of Minnesota to choose a woman for his running mate. He appointed strong women to positions of power and influence in the executive and judicial branches of state government, never using his position on abortion as a litmus test for his appointments. He appointed the first woman to the Minnesota Supreme Court in 1977 and, on his last day in office, January 4, 1993, appointed the woman who would make a female majority on that court. He cared about women and children and the conditions under which they lived and worked. The governor who appointed Nina Rothchild to implement pay equity in state government was the Hibbing school board member two decades earlier who insisted that teachers be hired and paid on the basis of qualifications and experience, not on the basis of gender or marital status.

It's all here—the education governor, the environmental governor, the business-partnership governor, the can-do governor, the world-traveling, Minnesota-salesman governor, the people's governor. I found myself reading the book late into the night, drawn with increasing intensity along the roller coaster ride of the "Minnesota Massacre," the triumphal return, the great years of achievement, and an ending reminiscent of Greek tragedy. But nothing can cloud the brightness and hope and the better life Rudy Perpich brought to his beloved state and people.

Rudy!

The People's Governor

George, Rudy, and Tony Perpich

Chapter 1

Reaching for the American Dream

The village of Kriviput—"Crooked Path"—sits high in the mountains above the Adriatic Sea in a region that is now a part of the Republic of Croatia. It consists of little more than a few white-washed buildings, a town square, church steeples, houses, and barnyards. It was in this remote village where mountain tracks meet, during the era when the Austro-Hungarian Empire controlled the area, that Anton Russ Perpich was born on November 21, 1899.

The land was beautiful, but conditions were harsh, and Anton's parents struggled to raise seven sons and two daughters on their poor farm. Anton himself had to quit school after the fourth grade to help support his family, working on the farm in the summer and at lumber camps in the winter. At sixteen, he went to fight in World War I under the Austrians and was sent to the Russian front. He survived that brutal war, but he never forgot its horrors—the persistent lack of food, the relatives and friends lost in the fighting, and the traumatic moment when a friend fighting at his side was hit in the head by a rifle shot, and Anton was splattered with the poor youth's brains.

When Anton returned home from war, his parents told him he had no future there. As the youngest in the family, he was obliged to go to the United States and build a new life.[1] And so, in 1920, at the age of twenty-one, Anton Russ Perpich struck out for the New World, planning to earn $2,000 and then return to his beautiful mountain village. He paid $100 to a labor recruiter for U.S. mining companies to get him in the immigration quota and joined the waves of immigrants packing the boats from nearly every country in Europe.[2] He was on his way to join his older brother, Rudy, already working in the iron mines of Minnesota.

Anton traveled by train from Zagreb to Paris and Le Havre, then by boat to Southampton. There he boarded the *Empress of France*, landing six days later in St. John's, Newfoundland, and continued

3

by boat to Sault Ste. Marie in Ontario, Canada.[3] Traveling the rest of the way by train, he arrived on Christmas Day, 1920, in Hibbing, Minnesota, at the heart of the Mesabi Range.

Anton went to work in the iron mines, met and married Mary Vukelich and became a U.S. citizen at age thirty-two. He soon put aside his hopes of returning home to Kriviput, however. In fact, he spent the rest of his long life on the Range, and in the course of time he became the patriarch of one of the most extraordinary families in Minnesota's history.

The snake-like Mesabi Range—its Chippewa Indian name is commonly translated as "Sleeping Giant"—runs for a hundred miles across the forests and bogs of Northern Minnesota. When Anton arrived in Hibbing the Range was already churning with activity and excitement. Hibbing itself had originally been a lumber camp, but the Oliver Mining Company (a division of U.S. Steel Corporation) found that rich ore deposits lay under its streets, and in 1912 they began to relocate the north section and heart of Hibbing to get at the ore. Despite disputes and court injunctions against the controversial move, houses, stores, and even the Hibbing Hotel and the large Oliver Clubhouse, were mounted on log rollers and moved two miles to the south, and Old Hibbing became the site of a mammoth open-pit mine, three miles long, a mile across, and 350 feet deep. This Hull-Rust-Mahoning Mine was criss-crossed with seventy miles of railroad tracks. At one point in the 1940s, it produced as much as one-fourth of the ore mined in the U.S. Under the management of Oliver Mining Company, the major operator of the mine since 1901, more than 800 million gross tons of iron ore were shipped out of the complex. Hibbing boasted it was the Iron Ore Capital of the World, and the Hull-Rust mine was proudly labeled the largest open-pit mine in the world.

The story of the development of mining in northern Minnesota has been told many times. Anton's arrival in Hibbing was no different from that of thousands of other immigrants. The mine owners advertised all over Europe for workers. Multitudes of vigorous, hardworking laborers like Anton, contracted by labor agents, arrived seeking employment and to escape from political and economic hardship in their native countries, often with nothing but name-tags on their coats. The Range became a melting pot of many different ethnic backgrounds—Serbians, Croatians and other Eastern Europeans, Finns, Italians, Germans, and Irish. Trained mine workers came from the Michigan mines, while Cornishmen known as "Cousin Jacks" or "cousinjacks" came from Canada and the tin mines of Cornwall, England, and often assumed positions as mine bosses. Scandinavians and others switched over to the iron mines from the lumber industry. In 1900 half the Mesabi population was foreign-born. Once they had settled here, the new immigrants sent letters and money to folks back home, urging them to come over, too.

By the time Anton Perpich arrived, the frontier mining towns were already well-established—Biwabik, Virginia, Eveleth, Chisholm, Buhl, Kinney, Aurora, Embarrass, Nashwauk, Calumet, Keewatin, and Coleraine, to name a few. The new arrivals from diverse nationalities who settled in these towns shared little at times but a common goal—a better life for themselves and their children. And while most of the profits made by the mining companies went to Eastern investors, the companies supported the building of churches and schools, community buildings and parks, and other public improvements built to standards far beyond those of most Minnesota cities at the time. Range towns got about 90 percent of their incomes from taxes flowing in from the mining companies and were soon comparatively wealthy.

Mary Vukelich was born June 5, 1911, in Carson Lake, a mining "location," as those long-vanished, temporary communities were called.[5] Her immigrant parents had lived in the same Adriatic seacoast area as had Anton Perpich's family. Her father had come to the Iron Range about 1906 to work in the mines, and her mother came over in 1909. A leader in the community, Mary's father had traveled extensively and spoke five languages.

Mary and her father were very close in her early years. He told his extremely bright daughter that he expected her to get a good education and become a teacher, a remarkable goal for a girl on the Range in those days. Those dreams were dashed when Mary was twelve. Her father died in an underground mining accident when a tunnel collapsed. To help her widowed mother and her three younger siblings, Mary quit school after the eighth grade and went to work cleaning people's houses for a dollar a week. She cried when her best friend Margaret went to college, and she cried again when her friend became a teacher and married a teacher, and the two young women were separated. But Mary was determined that when she had children of her own, they would get the best education possible and live a better life, whatever sacrifice it took.

As a means of earning a livelihood Mary's mother began taking in boarders, many of whom worked in the open-pit mines.[6] Anton Perpich was one of them. Anton had known the Vukelich family in the old country, and when Anton and Mary decided to marry, the families considered it a suitable match. Family connections were very important to the Eastern European immigrants on the Range, as they had been in the Old World. Mary was sixteen and Anton was twenty-seven when they were married on August 14, 1927. Even after she was married, Mary continued to help her mother and brought meals to her when she became old.

Rudy as a toddler

Rudolph (Rudy) George Perpich, the first of Mary's and Anton's five children, was born in 1928, in the Perpiches' tiny, three-room home, one of about ninety look-alike frame houses in Carson Lake. Mary was seventeen at the time.

A daughter, Marion, nick-named Bunnie, was born a year later. Bunnie died tragically at the age of fourteen months. She had crawled behind the stove in the kitchen while her mother was doing housework and burned her hands in some scalding water. Mary took her baby to the hospital and was told the burns were not life-threatening, but Bunnie developed pneumonia and died. Mary Perpich was devastated, and she grieved for her only daughter for the rest of her life. She would say she never stopped hearing her young daughter's cries and seeing Bunnie with arms out waiting to be lifted up.[7]

In 1932, when Mary was twenty, a second son, Anton John (Tony) was born, and George Frank was born a year later. Mary was thirty when her youngest son, Joseph (Joe) George, was born in 1941. The Perpich family was very poor during those years, just as their friends and neighbors were, and when the Perpich children were young, they had no car, no hot water or indoor toilet, and almost no money. The three older boys, Rudy, Tony, and George, shared a bed in a bedroom in their little house before the birth of Joe, who escaped the worst of those hard times.

When he was employed, Anton would walk to work, up to ten miles a day, and in temperatures as cold as 40° F below zero. He worked a ten-hour day for $3 a day and would come home from work and fall asleep eating dinner while sitting and warming up at the edge of the coal-and-wood stove in the kitchen.[8] Up until World War II, he worked in the still profitable underground mines, digging out iron ore from small pockets. The miners would follow the ore veins, set off blasts of dynamite to break up the rock, and shovel it into a chain of six or seven small carts. The carts would then be hauled to the surface and moved to a loading area along tracks that were repeatedly re-laid along the terraced sides and bottoms of open pits; there the ore would be dumped into railroad cars and shipped to Duluth.

When a blast was set off, the mine would be filled with "punk," a dust-like substance from the dynamite. The harsh working conditions were made even worse by water seeping into the mines. Tony Perpich remembered watching his uncle and another miner sinking a new shaft about forty feet down. They were wearing rain suits such as firemen wear, with water pouring on top of them. He thought they looked like ants, shoveling dirt into a motorized bucket which carried it to the surface. Yet these were the highest-paying jobs in the mine, and workers fought to get them. There were even more hazardous jobs in the mines, and sometimes there was the dreaded sound of the siren signaling an accident. Though the record is fragmentary, it has been calculated that in the 10-year period between 1906 and 1916, more than 700 workers died in mining accidents on the Range.[9]

For the workers on the Iron Range survival was a constant struggle, but the ups and downs hardened people. If there was red iron ore dirt under their fingernails, there was steel in their backbones. Families gritted their teeth when the mines were closed and there were no jobs, and they worked even harder.

Rudy Perpich knew at an early age that when his father's lunch box was home on the shelf, Anton Perpich was out of work, and times were bad. Rudy vividly recalled the pain his parents endured during mine shutdowns. "We were born with that fear of losing jobs, and you used to lose them every year," he said.[10] When Anton Perpich wasn't working, he wouldn't talk for days, he'd be so angry about not working. Mary Perpich would cry all day.[11]

The Great Depression of the 1930s hit the Iron Range hard. An estimated 70 percent of the mine workers were unemployed. Mining companies issued "work slips" to school districts, counties, and municipalities to give out to needy people, authorizing them to work two or three days a week, enough for subsistence.[12]

One Christmas during the Depression, his parents sadly told a heartbroken Rudy, then six, that Santa Claus wasn't coming that year. Mary got her husband to go out anyhow on Christmas Eve to see if he could find Rudy a present. Anton went into a store just before closing time and saw a big red fire truck on the counter. But he had only twenty-five cents, not nearly enough. The store owner knew him, and since Christmas sales were over, sold him the truck for a quarter. The next morning a happy, excited Rudy found the truck and told his parents, "Santa did pay us a visit!"[13]

Anton and Mary retained Old World values while they pursued the American Dream, and hard work and thrift were the underpinnings of the family's daily routine. There were chores to do. They kept a cow for milk, and the cow also produced a calf every year that a neighbor butchered, providing meat for the family. The family raised hogs, and it was Tony's hated job during butchering to catch the blood in a pan which his mother later used to make blood sausage—sausage which he never ate.[14] They made lard from the fat rendered in boiling down the pork trimmings. Since there was no refrigerator, the pork was kept in a barrel of salt water. In the summer the boys had to hoe and weed their large garden and help their mother can hundreds of quarts of beans, peas, beets, and other vegetables, all on a wood-burning stove. They picked wild blueberries. In the fall they made sauerkraut, and the best heads of cabbage went for sarmas (a meat and sauerkraut dish). Mary was renowned for her potica[15] and strudel and made hundreds for weddings and celebrations. Anton made Slyvovitcia, a plum wine, as did many of his East European neighbors. If this was hard work for the Perpiches, it also was "togetherness" that bonded the close-knit family.

(left to right) Joseph, Mary, Rudy, George, Anton, Tony (and dog Pal) at the Carson Lake home

There was a winery in the area owned by John Fena. John's son Jack became a Hibbing lawyer, a state legislator, and Rudy Perpich's friend, while his nephew Thomas Vecchi was Rudy's boyhood friend. Thomas' father, who managed the winery for thirty-five years, would collect money from neighbors to send to Caesare Mondavi in California to buy wine grapes. The contributors trusted Mondavi, who had lived on the Range before moving to California, and whose family originally came from the same hamlet in Italy as Vecchi's family. Out on the West Coast, where the Mondavi family had established a winery and become a large exporter of California wines, Mondavi would pack the wine grapes in ice and ship them in box cars to Hibbing. People would come and pick up the grapes (usually Zinfandel) go home and make their wine. Italians favored red wines. Yugoslavs liked both red and white. John Fena also had tank cars of wine shipped from California and bottled wines himself under the labels of Aro and Sunny Hill.

If work was God, education was the "pearly gates" for the Perpiches.[16] The message that Anton and Mary Perpich pounded into their four sons was "Get a good education. Get out of the mines." Tony Perpich recalled that his mother, who was more educated than other mothers in town, would say, "See, so-and-so can't work in the mine because he can't pass the physical. My word, so-and-so might lose his job because of his bad back. How much better for him to have an education." So, Tony said, "We put our efforts into [going to] college, really and truly." At night they would spread their homework out on the living room floor and study for hours. If they got a bad mark at school, their father would punish them when they got home. They had no money to buy books, but they checked out books from the school library and from a bookmobile that brought a library on wheels to the mining communities. George Perpich recalled, "We had no clothes on our backs, but we had $15,000 in the bank—saving for college." Rudy Perpich would often say when he became governor that he always knew, "Education was my passport out of poverty."

Politics was a lively topic at the Perpich dinner table. As Joe put it, "From my father we got the political DNA, and from mother we got the academic DNA. My mother used to say that it would be better to be dead than not to be educated, and she meant it."[17] Anton Perpich was a die-hard Democrat, and the family idolized President Franklin Roosevelt. The Perpich brothers read the editorial page in the newspaper first, not the comics. On Election Day Anton, who had become a U.S. citizen, and Mary Perpich, along with their neighbors and throngs of others across the Range who rarely went anywhere, dressed in their best clothes and traveled to the polls to exercise their right to vote.

Anton told his sons about the political conflicts and discrimination he had experienced growing up in the Balkans; he would not permit any kind of social, religious, or ethnic prejudice under his roof. While he did not go to see his son Rudy play in basketball games, he went to see the Harlem Globetrotters when they came to Hibbing. He thought the African-American team would need somebody to cheer for them.

On the other hand, Anton did harbor a vehement hatred of the steel companies that ran the Iron Range. This attitude was reflected in the populist views which his sons' carried with them into public office. Rudy Perpich later described those Depression years as a time of "guerilla warfare" between miners and steel companies.[18] Anton was active in organizing the United Steelworkers Union, and Rudy would tell stories about friends carrying his father home after fights with company guards and dropping him in a bloody heap at the front door.

The Perpiches were Roman Catholic, but they were not regular churchgoers. Lack of transportation made it difficult to get to the nearest Catholic Church, particularly in the winter and when the children were small. Moreover, there were no Croatian priests nearby with whom they might have felt as comfortable as were the immigrant Irish Catholics with their Irish priests.

The family spoke Croatian at home, and they and other children of Carson Lake heard Slavic tongues and other foreign languages spoken by their immigrant parents more often than English. Rudy Perpich entered school not knowing English, nor did he know about indoor plumbing. When he first saw a toilet flushed, he was horrified and ran home, telling his mother that a water pipe had burst, telling her "I got out, but I'm not sure if the rest of the kids made it or not."[19]

In first grade at Leetonia Elementary School, Rudy met Frank Ongaro, who became his lifelong friend. Frank came from one of the two Italian families in the mostly Slavic and Finn Carson Lake. Of the ten boys and five girls in that first grade, Rudy and Frank were among the five boys and five girls who made it all the way through to receive a high school diploma. Rudy and Frank went into the Army together, came back to attend Hibbing Junior College together, and later went on together to Marquette University and graduate school in Milwaukee.

Despite hardships, the Perpich sons remembered their youth as a happy time. Rudy stood out as a youth (just as he would later in life) with his tall figure, dark, curly hair, and good looks. He was intense, serious, and studious, but he liked sports, too. His father thought sports were foolishness. The younger boys came straight home from school and didn't "monkey around," as their father ordered, but Rudy got around that somehow. Tall and thin, he played end in football, and center and forward in basketball at Hibbing, both in junior high school and high school. But even on game days, Rudy first had to help get home chores done—chopping and sawing wood, milking the family cow. Only then, after two or three hours of work, could he hitch a ride back into Hibbing along with his friend Frank (who had also come home to do the afternoon chores) or ride back on the bus if they happened to have coupons provided by the school. (A bus ticket to Hibbing cost ten or fifteen cents and was too expensive for them to buy.) Years later Perpich would praise Coach Mario Retica for being the first Hibbing coach willing to use players "from the other side of the tracks." Retica responded that if he hadn't put Perpich on the team, he'd have passed up his best rebounder. Playing basketball got Rudy Perpich to his first restaurant meals. Coach Retica, concerned about the diet of some of his players, got them free passes to restaurants once a week.

Swimming, often in an abandoned open pit mine, was a popular summer pastime, while during the school year the Perpich kids loved to dance the polka and schottische and also the Lindy and the Jitterbug. The young people from the "locations" prided themselves on being better dancers than the Hibbing young people. Years later, when Rudy Perpich was governor, he once entertained a group of businessmen who were touring the lumber camp museum in Grand Rapids by linking arms with the guide and performing a fast jig.

Along with the work ethic, there was also a paternalistic ethic: The father was the absolute boss. Anton was a good-looking man—five feet six inches tall, 150 pounds, not big but wiry, and brown-haired. He had a keen sense of humor, was sometimes cantankerous and a tyrant, but was well-meaning.[20] "I think he could be pretty tough on those kids," recalled Thomas Vecchi, a classmate of Rudy's going back to their junior high school years.

Mary was tall, dark-haired, quiet, and very nice looking. Despite their strictness, Anton and Mary would have made any sacrifice to enable their sons to get ahead in the world.

Chapter 2

Us Versus Them

As a result of his boyhood experiences, Rudy Perpich felt like an outsider throughout much of his life. Even as governor he was never quite able to cast off the suspicion that his political critics were motivated by bias against his Iron Range background. For Rudy, his brothers, and those of their friends who grew up in the mining locations, and whose parents came from Europe, relations with the third and fourth generation youths from Hibbing were a matter of Us versus Them. In fact, for many immigrant children throughout the Range these adversarial conditions were a source of motivation. Often, as Tony Perpich once remarked, "I think maybe we worked harder at getting an education, trying to make our mark in the world."[1]

Looking back, Rudy's boyhood friend Thomas Vecchi once observed that in the location communities, "We all grew up with the idea that the mining companies were not very fair." Many Iron Range workers lived on property owned by the mining companies, where dust from the nearby mines dirtied the wash that was hanging out to dry. They had to buy their groceries at a company store on the location, and even the houses themselves were often company-owned. In such an environment the mining companies naturally came to be viewed as "the enemy," and among the young that attitude carried over into the schools, where everyone knew who the children of the company people were.

Through the first six grades the Perpich boys walked to school at Leetonia Elementary School in Carson Lake; during the junior high years they took the bus to North Hibbing Junior High School with youngsters from other mining locations. The location schools were largely controlled by mining company officials, and mineworkers' children were segregated from the executives' children until they reached eleventh grade and could attend Hibbing High School.

"I don't say we were discriminated against," Tony later reminisced. "Still, we didn't get into the [South Hibbing High School] school system until eleventh grade. It was the biggest thing in your life when we got into Hibbing High School and got to meet all these other people."

But at that late date social ties were unlikely to bloom or evaporate overnight, and those who were bussed in from the mining locations of Carson Lake, Leetonia, and Brooklyn often remained close friends. "I suppose if there was an inside or an outside group, we were the outside group," Tony remarked. But such divisions were far from absolute. The Perpiches got along well with the local Hibbing students. Tony was elected Homecoming King—the "King of Basketball"—during his senior year and was a member of the student council.

Yet the families of mine workers almost invariably remained poor. Very few people on the locations had cars, and they had little money to buy clothes, although the mothers were often good seamstresses and kept their children clean and neatly dressed.

The schools themselves were first class, with excellent gyms, hockey rinks, and in Hibbing, even a pipe organ and good paintings on the walls. Vecchi said, "We always knew our schools were special. We were always told how lucky we were to be able to go to those schools because of the mining companies. I am sure the mining companies [helped pay for and] built those schools as a hedge [write-off] on their taxes." In school the students were a lively bunch, but they didn't dare fool around. "You never ever questioned the authority of the principal or the teacher."

The Perpich brothers started their working lives early. Tony and George had a newspaper route, delivering the *Hibbing Daily Tribune* and the *Minneapolis Sunday Tribune* for twenty-seven cents a week. Rudy's lifelong work ethic probably stemmed from those hard times and from the examples of his parents.

In the summer of 1942, when they were fourteen, Rudy, Frank Ongaro, and some of their friends lied about their ages so they could work in the Great Northern Railroad roundhouse. The bosses knew they weren't sixteen, the minimum legal work age, but the United States had gone to war and labor was scarce; they badly needed help, and so they simply looked the other way. Rudy and Frank would walk several miles to the station and then spend the day cleaning the engines of the trains coming from Duluth. The sight of Rudy wearily trudging home after 11 p.m. dressed in his bulky safety boots, reminded his father of the ragamuffin Charlie Chaplin. At 56 cents-an-hour, $4.48 for an eight-hour shift, the pay seemed like riches to the high school sophomores. When school started in the fall, they continued for a while on the evening shift—in the morning they'd have to be up by six o' clock to get ready to go to school—but after a couple of weeks the coach told them he needed them to play football, and they quit.

In those days Rudy also pumped gas and worked behind the counter at the Carson Lake grocery store. He got to know people; he watched customers bargain with the owner over prices, and slowly he discerned the various ways that people deal with one another. Many of his ideas in public office stemmed from those early years. For example, he traced his concern for women's rights back to the times when he would be out delivering groceries and come upon a depressed housewife weeping, or bruised at the hands of her husband.

Sometimes Rudy took his young brother Joseph along in the delivery truck. Occasionally he would leave him in the truck while he was making a delivery, and one day, with the vehicle parked on a hill, Joseph started playing with the stick shift, squeezing it and putting it in gear. The truck rolled down the hill with Rudy running after, unable to catch it before it crashed. Joseph was unhurt, but Rudy had to pay for the damage to the truck out of his delivery wages.

Tony worked in the mines during those wartime summers and made 80.5 cents an hour. His mother banked every cent of it for his college expenses.

The Perpich boys were too young to go into military service at the time, but many of the young men of their immigrant mining community did enlist. Every morning neighbors would crowd into the Perpich kitchen to listen to the news on the radio, and Mary Perpich would translate for those of her neighbors who didn't speak English but were anxiously awaiting word of their sons and relatives fighting in Europe, sometimes in their own homelands. About once a month, Mary packed a box with canned goods and clothes and took it to the post office—in the winter on a sled and in the summer on a wagon—to send to relatives in Croatia who were often on the verge of starvation. This was a common practice among Iron Range immigrant families with relatives back in the Old World. When Mary and Anton Perpich visited Croatia forty years later, dozens of people came up to thank their savior, "nasha draga Marica" (our beloved Mary.)

Rudy graduated from high school in 1946, the year he turned eighteen, and that summer he drove a truck for an independent mining contractor who was "scramming" open pit mines—cleaning up leftover ore—in areas where the mining companies had finished their operations. Meanwhile, his friend Ongaro worked as a sampler at Hanna Mining Company. Once an ore cart had been loaded, Ongaro would take a rope with dots marked on it at regular intervals and throw it diagonally across the cart. Wherever a dot fell he would take a sample, to be sent to a lab for analysis to determine the value of the ore in the carts.

Throughout that summer Rudy urged Ongaro to go into the service with him so they could both qualify for education benefits under the GI Bill of Rights. Near the end of July the two finally went into Hibbing to fill out the papers at the Wilson Street fire hall, where the Army recruiters were stationed. That afternoon they took the bus from Carson Lake down to Fort Snelling, where they each signed up for a year-and-a-half, the minimum required to qualify for four years of education benefits.

Ongaro ended up in Korea. Army recruiters discovered that Perpich had taken typing in high school, and he was assigned to a typist job at Fort Dix, New Jersey. (Eventually he became a staff sergeant.) At Fort Dix he could visit his cousin George, a professional player with the Baltimore Colts and also the Brooklyn Dodgers football teams. George (the son of Anton's brother Rudy) later returned to Minnesota to coach the Hibbing High School hockey team.

In the army Rudy wrote his mother every week and told her about his dreams for the future. "You could start to see the glimmers of this man," Joseph latter recalled thinking, as the family read the letters over and over again. "He was clearly going to live a different life, and he was going to do something." Perpich was so lonely, though, he once went AWOL, hitching rides to go back home and return; luckily, he didn't get caught.[2]

When Rudy returned from the Army he enrolled at Hibbing Junior College, where the tuition was so low that he didn't find it necessary to tap heavily into his GI Bill benefits. It was here that he gained his first political experience, when he was elected president of his sophomore class, "probably because I was taller and bigger than anyone else," as he later quipped. He was also elected Mr. HJC (Hibbing Junior College) in his freshman year and was a star basketball player in the Junior College conference. Tony was also a Hibbing Junior College student at the same time, and he was elected president of the freshman class. "Leadership runs in the Perpich family," said an article about the two in the *Hibbing Tribune*. When the dean closed the smoking lounge because some students were playing cards and gambling, it was Rudy Perpich who led a brief and successful students' strike. "We broke the back of the administration in two hours," he recalled years later, still chuckling over the event.

After the rigid constrictions of Army life and years of seeing absentee industrial tycoons control the lives of his parents and thousands of mineworkers, Rudy felt it imperative that he take up a profession where he could be his own boss—he decided upon dentistry. But the decision wasn't entirely his own. He once told his friend Ongaro he'd thought of becoming a lawyer, but his parents were opposed to the idea: they didn't hold lawyers in high regard. His mother didn't think much of politicians, either, and at first she wasn't thrilled when her three oldest boys went into politics. She wanted her sons to be medical doctors or dentists. And so, after two years at junior college, Perpich went to dental school at the Jesuit-run Marquette University in Milwaukee, Wisconsin. He supplemented his GI school aid with jobs in the breweries, and he earned his meals by working in a dormitory kitchen. In the summers he returned home to work in the iron mines.

Rudy Perpich received his DDS degree in 1954. He was now a professional. He would no longer have to work in the mines. He had achieved his parents' dream.

Rudy's younger brothers followed him on his career path, just as they would follow him later into politics. Tony also attended Hibbing Junior College and went on briefly to pharmacy school in North Dakota before following Rudy to Marquette Dental School, where the two became roommates. After receiving his dental degree, Tony became a captain in the U.S. Air Force and served at Iwo Jima and other bases.

George went to Hibbing Junior College for two years and then to the University of Minnesota in Duluth for a year and a half, where he got his undergraduate degree in zoology. He considered becoming a teacher, but decided that the regimen didn't really appeal to him. Instead he went into the Navy and took up dental research at Great Lakes Naval Base. After leaving the Navy, he went to the University of Minnesota Dental School and, like his brothers, became a dentist. Tony made his home in Eveleth, and George lived in Chisholm.

Rudy was twenty when he first saw Delores Helen (Lola) Simic (sometimes spelled Simich) of Keewatin working in a malt shop. Smitten with the tall young woman in a yellow dress, he visited the shop three times that day and told a friend, "That's the girl I'm going to marry."[3] Six years later, after his return from dental school, on September 4, 1954, Lola and Rudy were married in a church in Aurora by a priest who grew up in Croatia. Tony was best man.

To know Rudy Perpich was to know his wife, Lola, because the two were almost inseparable. Jack Fena recalled walking down the hall of the building in Hibbing where his law office was located and "here was this ravishingly beautiful, tall, dark-haired woman standing on a ladder painting. A tall man with a butch haircut was holding the ladder for her." That was his introduction to Rudy and Lola Perpich. They were fixing up Rudy's new dental office.

Lola was born in Keewatin, the daughter of John and Anna Simic, both of Croatian descent. John Simic was an oiler for the Great Northern Railroad. Lola was given her nickname by her brother Mike when she was very young. The family was close-knit. Even when Rudy became governor, Lola visited her elderly mother regularly and did her laundry.

Lola was a junior in high school when she first met Rudy. Their encounter in Chappel's Malt Shop, considered in retrospect, had all the trappings of a made-for-Hollywood romantic movie script. At that time her height (five feet, eleven inches) bothered her; she was the tallest girl in her class, and there were only two boys taller. When Rudy, 6 feet 3 inches tall and four years older, came into the malt shop that day, she took notice. Rudy was obviously smitten with this tall, beautiful girl, and later he asked her to dance. "All he could do was polka, so we asked the band to keep playing them," she recounted later. She felt good to be with a tall boy she didn't have to look down at.

Lola graduated from Keewatin's Robert L. Downing High School and from Hibbing Junior College. She had thought about becoming a primary teacher but instead went to work in the Hibbing office of a major mining firm. "If they could have foreseen the battles Rudy would have with the mining companies, they probably wouldn't have hired me," she said later.[4] They were married in 1954, after Rudy got out of dental school. They had no money for a big wedding, so they "kind of eloped" and were married in the Catholic church in Aurora.

One of the classic stories that Rudy would tell laughingly about his stern father, who ruled his family with an iron hand even after his sons were grown, was about his wedding day. Rudy was almost flat broke that day, and as he left his parent's home with one small suitcase containing only a few clothes, a razor, and a toothbrush, Anton brought him up short by ordering Rudy to leave the suitcase and its

Rudy and Lola's wedding picture

contents behind and also to take off his tie and leave it too. "Your mother and I have three more [sons] to educate," he growled. And then he told Rudy to leave the fountain pen he'd given him for graduation. Rudy, who always respected his father's authority and strict discipline, obeyed. The newlyweds, driving a car lent by one of Lola's relatives, celebrated their nuptials with lunch at a Dairy Queen, after which they drove to Duluth for a honeymoon. There Perpich, who had brought nothing with him but the clothes he was wearing, bought himself underwear, a toothbrush, and a razor to replace the ones he had left at home.[5]

After a few days, when their money was spent, the Perpiches returned to Hibbing, and soon afterward Rudy opened a dental practice on Howard Street in the main part of the city. His practice was an immediate success; immigrants and their children came to him.

"He was the type of dentist who talked a lot, and you couldn't answer," Ongaro joked. Ronald (Ron) Dicklich, a youngster then, later a state senator, sat in Perpich's dental chair and heard his dreams of building a great university on the Iron Range and an interpretative center to tell the world about its history. Dicklich also remembered people paying Rudy in potatoes and chickens for their dental work.

The couple first lived in a basement apartment in Hibbing and then moved to a modest home on First Avenue. A son, Rudolph (Rudy) Jr., was born in 1959; a daughter, Mary Sue, was born in 1960. They later moved to a modest, white frame house at 2123 Sixth Avenue East in Hibbing, which friends said was beautifully furnished and looked like a page out of *Better Homes and Gardens*. Lola enjoyed skiing, and she played golf, tennis, basketball, and bocce ball. The family often took long walks in the woods at their lake cottage at Lake Esquagama near Biwabik. But there were seasons of grief, too. Lola had a miscarriage, and a few years later, after nine months of pregnancy, gave birth to a stillborn child. Yet by and large it was a happy, comfortable life. They were living the American dream. Rudy's gift to Lola one Christmas was piano lessons and a piano which he paid for in installments.

Carson Lake had been leveled in 1951 to make way for a mine, and the elder Perpiches were forced to move their little home to a lot in Hibbing. It had been enlarged slightly and a bathroom added, but it was still very modest.

Soon after the move, Anton, who was out of work at the time, was diagnosed with tuberculosis. He was sent to the Nopeming Sanitarium on a hill outside Duluth, where he had surgery to remove most of one of his lungs. He remained at the sanitarium for a year and a half, and during that time, although he chafed at the confinement, he taught himself to read English by reading Zane Grey and Louis L'Amour novels. Following his recovery the mining company agreed to re-hire him, although it refused to compensate him for his illness, arguing that he had contracted tuberculosis during the period when he was laid off. Anton felt lucky simply to get re-hired, but he soon found that he was no longer physically able to handle even light work, and at the age of fifty-five he quit. He remained unemployed for the rest of his life.

While Anton was at the sanitarium Mary took a job at the Hibbing General Hospital, first mopping the floors and later working in the laundry. She would come home exhausted at 5 p.m. and immediately fall asleep. She began experiencing bouts of severe depression, and during her final years in a nursing home she suffered from dementia, so that she didn't recognize even her husband "Tona."

The Perpich family
standing left to right–Joseph, Rudy, George, and Tony
seated–Mary and Anton

The strong protective feelings Rudy felt for his family throughout his life were evident even in those early years. He especially kept an eye on Joseph, thirteen years younger, and taught his youngest brother, who adored Rudy, that he could surmount any obstacle in life. He gave Joseph, then a teenager, the job of cleaning his dental office.

Joseph had first met Lola when she and Rudy were dating, and Lola made Joseph extra-creamy malts at the malt shop in Keewatin. After Rudy and Lola were married, they became something like Joseph's surrogate parents. He was often invited to their home in Hibbing where he could watch *Perry Mason*—his favorite show—on their television set. Lola would fix spaghetti and serve fruit Jell-O for dessert. Joseph thought the dinners were wonderful. When Joseph graduated from high school, Rudy took him to the best clothing store in town and outfitted him for the commencement exercises—a big event in that small town—in a pin-striped suit, a shirt with collar studs and cuff links, a classy tie, ribbed socks, and smart leather shoes. Young Joseph was thrilled and excited: "Like Walt Whitman, I 'sang the body electric' on graduation night and felt like James Cagney 'struttin' my stuff' on stage." Another member of that 1959 Hibbing graduation class was Bob Zimmerman, a shy youth, who was born in Duluth, moved to Hibbing with his family at age six, and later became the nationally famed singer-composer Bob Dylan. (Rudy Perpich, a member of the Hibbing School Board then, recalled that Bob Zimmerman was ordered by the principal not to use the piano in school any more because of the way he was pounding on the keys.) [6]

After graduating from Hibbing High School and attending Hibbing Junior College, Joseph went to the University of Minnesota where he earned a bachelor's degree, and, in 1966, a doctor of medicine degree. The only brother to leave Minnesota, he completed his residency in psychiatry at Massachusetts General Hospital in Boston and the National Institute of Mental Health in Washington and then earned a law degree in 1974 from Georgetown University. He was awarded a congressional fellowship giving him a job on the staff of the health subcommittee of the U.S. Senate Labor Committee headed by Senator Ted Kennedy of Massachusetts. There he met Cathy Sulzberger, an aide to Senator Jacob Javits and a member of one of the most influential media families in the nation. Her father, Arthur Ochs Sulzberger Sr., was publisher of *The New York Times* and was succeeded later by her brother, Arthur, Jr. Joseph and Cathy were married in 1974, and Rudy was best man at the wedding in New York.

Joseph became a prominent leader in medical research in Washington, D.C. In 1987 he went to the Howard Hughes Medical Institute in Chevy Chase, Maryland, where he became vice president for grants and special programs, directing the nation's largest privately funded organization for biomedical research and education.

In 1955 Rudy Perpich ran for the Hibbing School Board, which at that time was unheard of for a Catholic and an "outsider" from the miner/immigrant community. Even his close friends were surprised. "You had to be a Mason" to be on the school board, recalled Thomas Vecchi. The "Cousin Jacks" who came from England and Canada ran the school board as they ran almost everything. Perpich's friends helped him campaign, but he failed in his first attempt to get on the board. "He lost because it was too much of a shock for the town," Vecchi said.[7]

A year later Perpich ran again, and this time he won. One of the issues was whether or not women teachers should be paid the same as men, and whether married women, with the exception of widows, should be hired as permanent, full-time teachers.[8] Women were typically hired only as substitute teachers, and they were paid a lower salary, even during wartime, when there was a teacher shortage. Perpich, (later to become a champion of pay equity as governor), said in a campaign speech that all teachers should be hired and paid on the basis of qualifications and experience. Once on the board, he helped make that happen.

He made other waves. When he found the board was purchasing gas and oil for the school and school buses without calling for competitive bids, he pushed to get that changed. The first Christmas Perpich was a school board member, he came home to find a pile of unexpected gifts from businesses who furnished the school supplies for the Hibbing School District. There was wine, a case of whiskey from insurance people, turkeys, and other largesse. Rudy returned it all. The gifts stopped when the board adopted a policy of buying from the lowest bidder. Jim Michie, the school superintendent at the time, later recalled that Perpich thought for himself. "He wouldn't rubber-stamp everything the superintendent did."

(In 1977, Governor Rudy Perpich issued an executive order establishing a strict code of ethics for state employees. It prohibited the acceptance of gifts valued at more than $5 and discouraged the acceptances of gifts costing less. "We are going to demand that our officials and employees pursue a course of conduct which will give the public not the slightest cause for suspicion concerning whatever it is they are doing," Perpich said.)

The citizens of Hibbing liked the young school board member's refreshing ideas and the changes he initiated. He was reelected in 1959 without opposition and became board chairman.

Perpich soon became active in politics outside of Hibbing and across the Iron Range. "People began to realize this young man had a lot to offer," said Veda Ponikvar, longtime Chisholm newspaper editor and the Iron Lady who chronicled half a century of Iron Range history. "There was a charisma about that man, absolutely fascinating. He captured the imagination of everybody he ever talked to. He motivated people. He was one of the most gifted persons I have ever known. He was very compassionate, soft-hearted, very, very honest. His mind went constantly like a wheel; it never stopped. He had these tremendous ideas. People began to listen to him."

Rudy Perpich was a dreamer, but he also knew how to get things done.

Chapter 3

1960s. The Perpich Party of the North.
Sandy Keith. The Blatnik Factor. The War Dissent.

Rudy Perpich once called a plea for party unity "only a poorly disguised plea for party discipline." The alternative he chose, he said, was to "place party discipline behind you and work for a political and economic program that is meaningful for all people."[1] This was the rationale guiding him when, in 1962, after Hibbing had failed to get special legislation allowing it to sell bonds to build a new community college, Perpich filed for the state senate against twenty-two-year veteran DFL Senator Elmer Peterson, a Hibbing electrician.[2] Peterson, 58, had the backing of both the DFL Party and U.S. Congressman John Blatnik. He was a veritable Rock of Gibraltar in Iron Range politics, where political loyalty was second only to family loyalty.[3] "We thought no way could he [Perpich] win. Bucking the party was no little undertaking," Vecchi later recalled. Perpich himself later described it as a bitter campaign: "They ran a 'Keep America Red, White and Blue' campaign and tried to paint us as radicals and whatever during that era. It was the first confrontation we really had... all because we were saying the mining companies should pay their fair share of taxes and that we should have more diversified industries up here."[4]

One day Ronald (Ron) Gornick, an oil distributor from Chisholm, came out of his uncle's hardware store in Hibbing and saw Rudy and his wife Lola down the street. Gornick hailed Perpich and said, "I've got to thank you for breaking the monopoly of the petroleum business in Hibbing [school district] because I got business in Chisholm as a result." (When the Hibbing School Board began opening its oil purchases up for competitive bids, the Chisholm School Board followed suit.) Gornick doubted that Perpich could unseat Peterson but wished Perpich luck in the senate election. When Perpich asked, "Can you help me?" Gornick said he didn't know anything about politics, but he did have a big family. Perpich replied, "Hey, that's what you need is big families. Get them all to vote for Rudy Perpich." Word-of-mouth was a powerful weapon on the Iron Range. Gornick not only spread the word, he became a staunch Perpich supporter for life, as did many other voters who liked what they saw of the Hibbing dentist, and believed that new blood was needed in the senate.

Jack Fena, a state representative and Hibbing lawyer with an office next door to Perpich's above a bank on Howard Street, was an early Perpich supporter. When the Republican Party endorsed Peterson, Fena helped get the word out. It was almost illegal to be a Republican on the Range, and many DFLers figured that if Republicans liked Peterson, there had to be something wrong with him. Perpich won the election by a bare 221 votes out of 17,757 cast, and it was widely thought that the Republican Party endorsement of Peterson had tipped the balance in Perpich's favor. Nicholas (Nick) Coleman and another St. Paul man, Wendell Anderson, whose political careers later became closely linked with Perpich's, were also elected to the Senate in that election.

Once he'd been elected, Perpich set to work immediately to get the community college bonding bill passed. Another initiative he introduced and got signed into law gave iron mining companies a special tax reduction enabling them to process low-grade natural ore (not taconite). Perpich argued that if the bill became law, a Hibbing mining firm, Rhude & Fryberger Inc., planned to build a special plant which would employ about 100 workers.[5] The bill passed, and the plant was built soon afterward. It was Perpich's first "jobs, jobs, jobs" initiative, and it marked a switch from his previously deep-rooted antipathy toward the mining industry.

While Perpich was running for his first senate term in 1962, A. M. (Sandy) Keith was also on the ballot as a candidate for lieutenant governor, and he asked Perpich to help him out up on the Range.[6] Perpich agreed readily, and during the campaign he took Keith to all the right places, including an old-timers' dance where musicians played accordions and Perpich, an excellent dancer, danced the schottische. Keith stayed at the Perpiches' lake home during the visit.

The two had long since become well-acquainted. In 1960 Keith, a young Rochester lawyer and already at that time one of the Young Turks in the Senate Liberal caucus, was vacationing with his family in northern Minnesota. Word of Rudy Perpich and his growing political strength in northeastern Minnesota had reached him at the state capitol in St. Paul, and Keith wanted to meet the man. One morning he drove to Hibbing, walked into Perpich's dental office on Howard Street and introduced himself.

They hit it off immediately. "Oh, God, he was a handsome dog," Keith later recalled. "Tall, very black hair, a beautiful wife. We each had two children, almost the same ages. We liked each other." Keith was also tall and handsome, but blonde, with a shock of hair over his forehead like John F. Kennedy's. Both Keith and Perpich were fiercely ambitious, charismatic, and energetic, and both had grown up in homes where liberal politics was gospel. In time they became close friends.

Perhaps part of the affection that developed between the two, however, was a result of the fact that although their politics were similar, their backgrounds were strikingly different. While Perpich was the son of a poor immigrant miner, Keith's father was a prominent doctor at the Mayo Clinic. Perpich's mother worked in a laundry; Keith's mother was a community activist. While Perpich attended Hibbing Junior College before studying dentistry at Marquette University, Keith went to prestigious Amherst College in Amherst, Massachusetts, where he graduated magna cum laude and Phi Beta Kappa.

Keith earned his law degree at Yale and then served in the U.S. Marine Corps for two years in Korea. He started his law career by clerking for Republican Harry Blackmun, legal counsel for the Mayo Clinic in Rochester. Blackmun was later appointed by President Richard Nixon an associate justice (1970-94) of the U.S. Supreme Court.

Unlike Keith, who was a compelling speaker, Perpich was notorious then and later for his less than eloquent public speaking ability. He tended to rush through his prepared texts and often mutilated syntax; he didn't stop for applause, but he sometimes stopped awkwardly in mid-sentence. After he became governor, he confessed that he still broke into a sweat when he was put in the spotlight and expected to perform.[7] But no one was better with people one-on-one, or in small, informal gatherings. *Star Tribune* columnist Jim Klobuchar wrote that Perpich's problem was a lack of patience with the English language: "He would rather talk with his shoulders and eyebrows."[8] On the campaign trail Keith soon discovered another Perpich trait: "He was full of ideas, even in those days. He sort of loved to try them out on people, even if they were crazy. He had a wonderful mind, always looking for new ideas."

When Keith went to bed on election night in 1962, he was 40,000 votes behind. Then the northern Minnesota votes started coming in. Perpich had helped deliver a big chunk of the Iron Range to him, and Keith woke up to find that he had been elected lieutenant governor, defeating Republican C. Donald Peterson, a state legislator and lawyer from Edina.[9] Keith said Rudy was very helpful in his election as lieutenant governor: "I owed him a great debt of gratitude."

Two years later, when Keith ran for governor, challenging Governor Karl Rolvaag from his own party, he again sought Perpich's help in northeastern Minnesota, and once again Perpich delivered, both in winning DFL convention delegates for Keith and in the primary election campaign. Keith won DFL Party endorsement for governor in a historic, hard-fought twenty-ballot convention marathon, but Rolvaag, rejecting the party endorsement and campaigning on a "Let the People Decide" theme, defeated Keith by better than two-to-one in the September primary. In the subsequent general election Rolvaag lost to Republican Harold LeVander by a vote of 680,593 to 607,943, and before long Keith, once the popular, fair-haired boy of the DFL Party, was widely viewed as a back-stabbing Judas by many DFLers and depicted as a "smiling barracuda" by Republicans. But Perpich stuck with him, as Keith in turn would stick with Perpich after his crushing 1978 defeat. (At the time Republican-oriented members called themselves Conservatives, and DFLers Liberals.)

Following the election defeat Keith returned to Rochester to practice law. He went into partnership with former state senator Robert Dunlap, a Conservative, and together they built the largest law firm in southern Minnesota. It didn't make Keith rich. He often represented poor and middle-class clients who couldn't pay the fees in divorces, child custody, domestic abuse, and other family-related cases.[10]

Meanwhile, in 1966, Rudy Perpich was re-elected to the Senate, winning 56 percent of the vote over Elmer Peterson, who was trying for a comeback. Rudy's brother Tony, then thirty-four, also ran for the Senate that year, mainly to help Keith, whom he greatly admired, and just as his brother Rudy had done earlier, Tony unseated a long-standing DFL incumbent, Senator Thomas Vukelich of Gilbert.

Two years later three other DFL legislative incumbents on the Range were unseated, and some observers suspected that the Perpich brothers had given behind-the-scenes support.[11] The Perpiches denied the allegations, although Rudy did work to unseat Representative Jack Fena of Hibbing and supported his opponent, John Spanish, a former Hibbing city council member. Fena, House Minority Leader Fred Cina of Aurora (considered the most influential DFLer in the Legislature), and Representative Loren Rutter of Kinney, all lost their seats after being accused of maintaining unusually close ties with the mining companies. St. Louis County Commissioner William Ojala and other members of the so-called Perpich faction attacked Cina, in particular, for his support of the 1964 Taconite Amendment to the state Constitution, which guaranteed mining companies equitable tax treatment. Perpich himself criticized Fena for accompanying other legislators on a South American mining tour. Fena's "fun in the sun" participation in the trip, he said, "at the expense of the Minnesota taxpayer will not benefit this area one iota."[12]

Fena and Perpich later patched up their differences, and Fena downplayed the falling-out the two had experienced during those years, while acknowledging that they did have their disagreements.[13] In any case, the defeat of the three veteran DFL legislators fueled the perception that the Perpiches had become the political power hammer of the Range.

In the Senate, Rudy and Tony Perpich were in the minority which called itself Liberals rather than DFLers, until a 1974 law made party designation mandatory for legislators. They had little real power, however. The Perpich brothers introduced many progressive bills which didn't pass, though the ideas they contained drew attention and sometimes heated debate. They pushed for changes in everything from taxes to the size of the legislature, and they fought tirelessly for greater benefits to be allocated to the Iron Range, which they said had been too long ignored by politicians. They suggested that elderly homeowners be given a property-tax break and proposed to pay for that partly with a one-cent tax increase on cigarettes. They cosponsored a bill for a proposed constitutional amendment to reduce the voting age in Minnesota from twenty-one to eighteen. (Voters in 1970 approved a constitutional amendment reducing it to nineteen, and a 1971 amendment to the U.S. constitution made it eighteen.)

Rudy Perpich unsuccessfully sought a four-year college for the Range, and cosponsored legislation with St. Paul Senator Nicholas Coleman that would have prohibited actors from appearing in cigarette advertisements. He called for a 2 percent gross-receipts tax on businesses, services and corporations to replace Minnesota's real-estate and personal-property taxes, but opponents pointed out that no other state had tried such a tax and called it an unworkable idea.

In 1967 Rudy Perpich opposed a state gasoline-tax increase and suggested that the payroll be cut instead. He made headlines by touring the Minnesota Transportation Building and singling out employees whom he said were not working.[14] Both Tony and Rudy voted against the sales tax approved by the Conservative-controlled legislature that year and voted no on the re-passage of the bill after Republican Governor Harold LeVander had vetoed it.

Back home George was handling Rudy's Hibbing dental practice as well as his own in Chisholm. Tony traveled home to take care of his patients on Saturdays and Sundays.

The Blatnik Factor

Iron Range politics, always acrimonious, was further enlivened in those days by the political feud that arose between the Perpich brothers and Congressman John Blatnik. Though he had been political kingpin on the Range for a long time, Blatnik could not ignore the fact that the Perpiches were rapidly building a new political dynasty which might one day threaten his congressional seat.

A former teacher and school superintendent from Chisholm, Blatnik began his political career in the state senate (1941-1946) with the Farmer Labor Party. During World War II, he served in the Air Corps Intelligence and the OSS and was hailed as a hero by working closely with Josip Tito's Communist partisans behind enemy lines in Yugoslavia. In 1946, two years after the birth of the DFL Party and two years before Hubert Humphrey and Eugene McCarthy went to

Washington, Blatnik was elected to Congress. In his first campaign he defeated fourteen-year Republican incumbent William Pittenger, and he was re-elected fourteen times with huge majorities before finally retiring in 1974.

Blatnik eventually became a powerful force in the U.S. House, heading the important Public Works Committee, which enabled him to do a lot of good things for his district. He was a key player in the establishment of the St. Lawrence Seaway and the Interstate Highway System. He helped establish the 110,000-acre Voyageurs National Park and was a sponsor of almost every piece of water-pollution legislation enacted between 1956 and 1972, including the Clean Water Act, the chief federal remedy for polluted waters.[15] The working people of the Iron Range, who had fought for education and economic security, saw Blatnik as one of their own and saw their long-sought political power realized in him.

While serving in the state legislature, Blatnik had sponsored legislation in 1941 to levy taxes on taconite on the basis of production, five cents per ton, in lieu of *ad valorem* or property taxes. This system was favorable to mining companies, and Blatnik's labor union supporters also embraced the program as a way to create new jobs by promoting the expansion of the taconite industry. Decades later, Blatnik championed the passage of the 1964 Taconite Amendment, which was also intended to encourage mining companies to invest in taconite mining and processing. But it required a delicate balancing act for the Eighth District congressman to continue promoting the taconite industry while preserving his national reputation as "Mr. Pollution Control." The Perpiches accused him of being the protector of the mining industry.

Blatnik's father, like Perpich's, was an immigrant miner. Although the Perpiches were Croatian and Blatnik was Slovenian, both camps staunchly denied that ethnic differences had anything to do with their political battles. The Perpiches regarded Blatnik and his political allies as tools of the mining, banking, and lumbering interests in northeastern Minnesota, while portraying themselves as populist champions of the working people who were exploited by those interests. Tony once remarked that when Blatnik was first elected to Congress, he was a liberal, "but the longer he served, the more conservative he became, and it was widely believed he was 'in with' the mining companies."[16] Blatnik denied that he was the stooge of the steel industry, and said, "I was first elected to Congress [1948] fighting the steel industry."[17] Vecchi thought it was probably true that Blatnik was close to the steel companies. "I think John had worked out his own way to deal with the mining companies. To get support, he had to do this and that."

Blatnik, with his twenty years' congressional seniority, was understandably angry when, in 1965, Governor Rolvaag bypassed him to appoint Walter Mondale to the U.S. Senate seat when Hubert Humphrey became President Lyndon Johnson's vice president. A year later Blatnik lent his support to Keith for governor against Rolvaag, putting him and Rudy Perpich on the same side for once.

Northeastern Minnesotans joke about "Iron Range Alzheimer's disease," suggesting an Iron Ranger may forget everything else but never forgets an enemy. But in 1983, at a reception in Washington where both retired Congressman John Blatnik and Governor Rudy Perpich were present, Blatnik approached the governor, shook his hand, and the two made peace.[18]

The careers of Blatnik and Perpich were both inextricably linked with the fortunes of the mining interests, and both faced the same question, "Does legislative support for the mining companies really benefit the working people, or is it just one more case of hand-outs going to those who need it least?" To shed some light on this issue, it might be well for us to take a closer look at how conditions changed in the industry over time, and what challenges these changes presented to mining interests, workers, and legislators alike.

In 1951 Minnesota produced 82 percent of the nation's total iron ore output and set a new annual mining record of 79 million tons. But the huge demands of World War II and the Korean War eventually depleted the rich seams of high-grade ore in northeastern Minnesota, and production began to dwindle. Ore from Liberia, Labrador, and other places was finding its way to U.S. blast furnaces with increasing frequency, and the future of the Range looked bleak.

In anticipation of precisely these distressed conditions, Edward Davis and his colleagues at the University of Minnesota's Mines Experiment Station had been working for several decades to develop a commercially feasible method for mining taconite—a low-grade iron ore containing magnetite that was more difficult to extract than the high-grade ore containing hematite. These low-grade deposits were extensive on the Range, but getting them out of the ground required new drilling methods and the use of liquid fuel. Once the ore had been mined, the problem remained of separating the iron oxide from the surrounding waste particles.

Eventually the mining companies became convinced that Davis's prospects of success were good, but they were concerned about how this new taconite industry would be taxed. They pointed out that they would have to invest hundreds of millions of dollars to build plants, install machinery, and construct railroad lines from the mines to processing plants. In response, in 1941 the legislature passed the John Blatnik bill, which Governor Harold Stassen signed into law. It exempted the taconite companies from the traditional *ad valorem* (value) tax and imposed instead a fixed tax-per-ton on pellets actually shipped; the taconite industry was also allowed to pay occupation and royalty taxes at a lower rate than that generally required of the ore industry.

It was hailed as the salvation of the Iron Range when Davis, working in concert with several iron-ore mining and steel-manufacturing companies, came up with an economical "beneficiation" process, which consisted of removing impurities by magnetic separation and then converting the iron concentrate into marble-sized, 65 percent pure iron pellets. Using this method, in 1955 the E. W. Davis Work of the Reserve Mining Company at Silver Bay was opened, launching large-scale production of taconite in Minnesota. Reserve produced its first commercial taconite pellets on October 21, 1955. Its first shipment was made on April 6, 1956.

Before long, the mining companies were pushing for a state constitutional guarantee that state taxes on the taconite industry would go no higher than taxes on other industries in the state, and the subject once again became a hot political issue. Supporters of the amendment said the guarantee was crucial to protect mining jobs in northeastern Minnesota and to ensure that companies would invest the hundreds of millions of dollars necessary to build the huge taconite processing plants. Republican Governor Elmer L. Andersen, who spearheaded the drive for the amendment, said it would create more jobs on the Range.

Opponents called it a sellout to the mining companies and a desecration of the Constitution. Liberal Senator Jack Davies of Minneapolis, one of a handful of legislators who fought the amendment until the end, said, "I think that outside the treatment of Indians, it's the most disgraceful thing that has happened in Minnesota politics." St. Paul Liberal Senator Karl Grittner described it as "a giant conspiracy on the part of the Republican Party and big business in Minnesota." Republicans in general favored the amendment. Many DFLers opposed any kind of concession to big business. The DFL Party platform endorsed "fair and equitable" tax treatment for iron mining, without a constitutional amendment.

The turning point came when Senators Humphrey and McCarthy and Congressman Blatnik met with Roger Blough, chairman of U.S. Steel. Blough promised that U.S. Steel would build additional facilities on the Range if the amendment passed, and in return the DFL leaders promised their support. Much of the opposition died out, and even the Steelworkers' unions, which were initially opposed, became supporters of the amendment.

The proposed amendment became a major issue in the 1962 election. State Senator Vladimir Shipka, representing Itasca and Koochiching counties, opposed the amendment. He lost his bid for reelection, and seeing Shipka's defeat, others switched to support it. Rudy Perpich was a thirty-six-year-old freshman senator when the 1963 legislature approved putting the proposed amendment on the ballot in 1964. Perpich reluctantly supported the legislation because of its promise of relief for the Range, but said it shouldn't be in the Constitution. The measure to put the amendment on the ballot sailed through both Conservative-controlled houses of the legislature and was signed by Governor Elmer L. Andersen, its leading champion, on the eve of his cliff-hanger election defeat by Karl Rolvaag. Rolvaag had opposed the amendment in his 1962 campaign for governor, supporting instead a "fair taconite tax" statute. When a 1989 expiration date was later added to the proposed amendment, he too became a supporter.

The Minnesota AFL-CIO voted in 1963 to support the amendment, subject to the condition that steel companies prove "good faith" by initiating construction projects. When the companies reported in 1964 they had done so, the AFL-CIO voted overwhelmingly to continue supporting the amendment, despite opposition from the Minneapolis Central Labor Union Council.[19] Rolvaag and Attorney General Walter Mondale traveled to Rochester and persuaded Dr. Charles Mayo to head the Citizens' Committee for the Taconite Amendment which conducted a mammoth, bipartisan, statewide promotional drive. Rolvaag was honorary chairman of the committee which distributed 700,000 bumper stickers and plastered Vote-Yes messages on billboards in every corner of the state. It also ran pro-amendment commercials on radio stations narrated by sports personalities including Vikings quarterback Fran Tarkenton and Twins catcher Earl Battey and handed out hundreds of thousands of sample pellets.

On November 3, 1964, eighty percent of those voting in the election supported the amendment. It was more than enough to ratify it and thus limit taxes on the taconite industry for twenty-five years to no more than the equivalent taxes on other businesses.

Whether the amendment, with its assurance of long-term tax stability, had indeed been crucial to the development of the taconite industry remains a matter of dispute.

The War Dissent

The same year that the Taconite Amendment was up for approval, the Perpich brothers became involved with presidential politics. Tony was chairman of the Lyndon Johnson for President committee in the Eighth District, with Humphrey on the ticket as the vice presidential candidate. The Perpiches worked to defeat Republican Barry Goldwater, who they thought was "trigger happy."[20] Tony Perpich said later, "In retrospect we were duped, for Johnson made a greater mess than Goldwater might have." Tony told Alpha Smaby, author of *Political Upheaval*, "What happened during the Johnson administration was the greatest disappointment of my political life—watching politicians going mad, literally becoming willing partners to untold savagery [Vietnam War], and convincing themselves they were doing the right thing."

By 1968 Minnesota, like the rest of the country, was deeply divided over the war in southeast Asia. Tony Perpich and his wife Irene, a medical doctor, spent most of their time organizing the antiwar movement led by Senator McCarthy and turning out protesters at DFL precinct caucuses on the Iron Range. Irene's brother, Dr. William Kosiak, organized the antiwar movement in Lake and Cook Counties. Rudy Perpich also supported Eugene McCarthy's presidential challenge to President Johnson, even though Minnesota's own native son Hubert Humphrey was Johnson's vice president. The Perpich camp turned out an unprecedented number of voters at the March 5 DFL caucuses on the Range.

At the hard-fought 1968 state DFL convention, the McCarthy supporters put up a slate of candidates for party offices, but they were outnumbered and outmaneuvered by the Humphrey forces. Rudy Perpich was the McCarthy candidate for national committeeman against John Blatnik. Unfortunately, by the time Perpich was nominated and called to the podium, he had left the convention.

In other business, the DFL convention delegates approved a little-noticed platform plank opposing the disposal of taconite tailings into Lake Superior. The plank was put before the delegates by a platform committee headed by Grant Merritt, a descendant of the Merritt family who had first discovered the rich ores of the Mesabi Range. Merritt, a Minneapolis lawyer, was a spokesman for environmentalists who were concerned about patches of greenish water that had appeared in the lake where Reserve Mining Company dumped its tailings.

In the March 12 New Hampshire primary McCarthy won a surprising 42 percent of the vote, and although President Johnson won 49 percent, the press interpreted the event as a major victory for the Minnesota senator and a repudiation of Johnson. A few weeks later the President announced that he would not run for reelection. Hubert Humphrey then became a candidate for president. At a tumultuous national Democratic convention in Chicago marked by violence and clashes between McCarthy and Humphrey forces, Humphrey became the first Minnesotan nominated by a major party to be president of the United States. But despite his long championship of liberal programs and crusades on behalf of poor and working people as a U.S. senator and vice president, Humphrey's loyalty to President Johnson and the U.S. involvement in Vietnam proved an insurmountable handicap. He was narrowly defeated by Richard Nixon in the November election, crushing his longtime dream of being president.

Douglas (Doug) Johnson, mayor of the small city of Cook, was awestruck when he first met then-state Senator Rudy Perpich in the late 1960s. "He was so warm, bubbly. He was always very optimistic, very positive all the time," Johnson said of Perpich. "He had dark, naturally curly hair; he was good looking, lot of charisma. He was extremely popular in my community. People really liked him."[21]

Johnson, a truck driver's son and high school counselor, was well-liked himself. Short, stocky, with a cherubic grin, he wore a leg brace and walked with a limp from a bout with polio when he was fourteen months old. When Johnson, a political greenhorn, decided to run for an open seat in the Minnesota House of Representatives in 1970, it was critical for him to get Perpich's support. He and two friends from Cook met in the Perpich basement in Hibbing with Rudy and Lola and the two Perpich children, and Perpich agreed to help him. "I was a young mayor from a small town, not living where the major population was. I would not have gotten elected without Rudy's support, and he had a very, very powerful political organization in the Chisholm area where I had to pick up my votes," said Johnson. Cook was not actually part of the Iron Range, but its people and their interests were almost a political extension of the Range. The House and Senate districts at that time included a piece of the Range, and Johnson had supported Perpich for the Senate. Johnson thought Perpich might have gone out of his way to help him because "I think he just wanted to change the Good Old Boys elected there for years." Perpich forces, particularly in the more populous Chisholm area where Johnson had to pick up most of his votes, jumped in to prepare his literature, manage his campaign and canvas door-to-door on his behalf. Johnson, twenty-eight years old, won election and was re-elected in 1972 and 1974. He was elected to the Senate in 1976, succeeding Tony Perpich when he stepped down, and later became chairman of the powerful Senate Tax Committee. As Johnson gained seniority and power in the legislature, his disarming boyish smile continued to mask a growing political savvy and negotiating skill; he became another important Perpich ally and longtime friend.

Meanwhile, the Perpich/Keith friendship continued to bind the northern and southern Minnesota DFL political forces. In fact, their alliance with state Senator Nicholas (Nick) Coleman, a charismatic young Irishman from St. Paul, and other rising stars in the DFL Party of the late 1960s and 1970s launched a new era in Minnesota politics and the DFL Party. First the battle between Keith and Governor Karl Rolvaag for the governorship in 1966, mentioned above, and later the crisis of conscience caused by the Vietnam War crystallized the group's emerging independence from the Old Guard of Hubert Humphrey, Orville Freeman, and Walter Mondale. And as the decade advanced, America's growing involvement in military activities in Vietnam drew the attention and the criticism of more and more bright young middle-class professionals, lawyers, students, and teachers. These were the activists that had packed the 1968 DFL precinct caucuses, sending a strong message to the Democratic leadership in Washington that it would be prudent to disengage immediately from further involvement in Southeast Asia. After the nation had finally extricated itself from the conflict, these young activist leaders (Perpich and Keith prominent among them), who felt no great allegiance to DFL party elders, continued to pursue their own brand of "new politics," bringing together former Vietnam War protesters, women's rights and gay rights advocates, environmentalists, and advocates for the poor and disadvantaged into effective political coalitions.

Rudy, George, and Tony Perpich

Chapter 4

Lieutenant Governor Rudy Perpich
and Senators Tony Perpich and George Perpich

Times were tough on the Iron Range in the late '60s, and the tax burden was a big part of the problem—or so the Perpich brothers declared. The taxes on homes had risen sharply in northeastern Minnesota, while for many years the taconite mining companies had paid no property taxes at all. The five-cents-a-ton production tax that they did pay to local governments in lieu of property taxes had been established in 1941, in the infant years of the taconite industry, but times had changed. Over the long haul it was far less, critics said, than what the mining companies would have paid under regular property-tax rates.

Rudy Perpich called the system "a gross injustice." Taking land away for national parks, together with lower tax yields because of the switch from natural iron ore to taconite, had placed an unusually heavy burden on the home owner. In 1969 Rudy introduced legislation to junk the production tax and require all taconite mining companies to pay property taxes at the same rate as other industries. Opponents of the bill said homeowners had been getting by for years with greatly undervalued property, while mining companies had been picking up much of the tab for schools, sewers, fire, police and other municipal services. Perpich and St. Louis County Commissioner William Ojala said they would not pay their real-estate taxes due May 31, and called for "a massive tax strike" on Minnesota's Iron Range.[1]

The Perpiches organized rallies on the Capitol steps to publicize the issue, and many Iron Range residents came to St. Paul in cars and chartered buses to protest. It was the first trip to the Capitol for many Iron Range residents, and the Perpiches provided them with detailed instructions how to get there, including right and left turns. Tony and Irene Perpich's daughter, Julia, 7, and her cousin, Rod Robinson, 9, took part in the demonstrations, carrying homemade signs reading "Even the Tooth Fairy pays more than 5 cents." At an April 19 demonstration Tony called the Conservative-controlled Legislature "big business oriented" and warned that "the Northeastern Minnesota tax rebellion will sweep the entire state."[2] Rudy told the protesters that the mining industry was bleeding them white.

The rallies were effective. Republican Governor Harold LeVander came out of his office to speak to the crowd that afternoon and was applauded when he said, "I see no reason why there should not be some increase in the production tax."[3] Senator Stanley Holmquist of Grove City, the Senate Conservative leader, assured the Iron Range crowd, "I think further study will indicate that the production tax on taconite could very well be increased." After Iron Range taxpayers demonstrated twice at the Capitol for an increase in the taconite tax, and despite opposition by mining companies, the 1969 Legislature increased the taconite production tax for the first time in twenty-eight years, more than doubling it to 11½ cents-per-ton. LeVander signed the bill into law.[4]

Elated East Iron Range residents held a "tribute dinner" at the Eveleth Armory to honor Rudy and Tony Perpich, other area leaders, and a parade of liberal legislators from the Twin Cities, for persuading the Legislature to increase taconite production taxes.

As a result of this and other issues, Rudy Perpich was attracting attention throughout the state. Midway through his second term in the senate, in mid-1969, he said he was "just about positive" he would give up his state senate seat because of opposition from the mining industry, which had sponsored a series of meetings aimed at undermining his re-election campaign.[5] "I'm better off with a wider base," he remarked. Perpich planned instead to seek DFL endorsement for lieutenant governor if former Vice President Hubert Humphrey ran for the Senate seat to be vacated by Senator Eugene McCarthy the following year. If Humphrey didn't run, and Blatnik decided to seek McCarthy's seat, Perpich said he would run for Blatnik's seat in Congress.[6] Humphrey went for the U.S. Senate, and that fall Perpich began campaigning for DFL Party endorsement for lieutenant governor. He had his eye on the governor's office and believed that the only way a "hunky" from the Iron Range could get there was through the back door.[7] Rudy took out a $20,000 mortgage on his home to finance his campaign, and he and his wife Lola set out on a grueling schedule. After Perpich worked in his Hibbing dental office until five p.m. every day, the Perpiches would drive somewhere to campaign, usually to the Twin Cities or southern Minnesota. Rudy shook hands and made speeches, and when the event was finally over he and Lola would return to Hibbing, Lola driving and Rudy sleeping in the car. They would often arrive home as late as 2 a.m. for a few hours sleep. The next day they did it all over again.

Congressman Blatnik remained publicly neutral with regard to Perpich's efforts to win the nomination for lieutenant governor. With the rising strength of the Perpich faction, advisers counseled Blatnik, who was also running for re-election, not to risk an open encounter. While Iron Range voters still supported Blatnik, they also supported Perpich because of his battle against the iron mining companies and the politicians who supported the companies. One unidentified source on the Iron Range told a reporter, "They'll still vote for John, but they won't stand up and clap."[8]

Delegates to the 1970 state DFL convention in Duluth, held the last weekend in June, became embroiled in an intensely competitive race for the gubernatorial endorsement. The field included a smorgasbord of attractive candidates: two politically talented and promising state senators from St. Paul, Wendell (Wendy) Anderson and Nicholas (Nick) Coleman; Hennepin County Attorney George Scott, a party stalwart; David Graven, a University of Minnesota law professor who was cutting a swath as a forceful young party leader; and former state Agriculture Commissioner Russell Schwandt, who had a strong following in rural areas. Warren Spannaus, a former state DFL chairman (1967-69), had also been a candidate, but he dropped out before the convention and sought party endorsement for the attorney general spot instead. Robert Short, millionaire owner of the Leamington Hotel in Minneapolis and a trucking business, Admiral Merchants, was threatening to run in the primary against whoever was endorsed for governor, and State Representative D. D. (Don) Wozniak of St. Paul said he might run in the primary if political maverick Short did not.

Late Saturday afternoon, on the sixth ballot, Wendell Anderson, an ex-Olympic hockey player and lawyer who had headed Vice President Hubert Humphrey's 1968 presidential campaign in Minnesota, won the 60 percent of the votes necessary for endorsement.

While the delegates were struggling through the day-long gubernatorial contest at the Duluth Arena-Auditorium, Rudy Perpich was busily seeking delegate support for the lieutenant governor endorsement. (It would be the last election where lieutenant governor candidates ran independently from governor candidates, although the gubernatorial endorsee's wishes carried weight with delegates. In 1972 voters approved a constitutional amendment pairing the two on the same ticket, which took effect in the 1974 election.)

A small group of party leaders met privately early Sunday morning in David Graven's suite at the Radisson Hotel, among them U.S. Senator Walter Mondale and Hubert Humphrey, the endorsed candidate for the Senate seat being vacated by Eugene McCarthy. Humphrey, apprehensive about his Senate race and his Republican opponent, Third District Congressman Clark MacGregor, felt he needed a strong DFL ticket to shore up his campaign. At that point attorney general candidate Spannaus seemed virtually assured of endorsement to run against Republican candidate Robert Forsythe of Edina.[9] Spannaus had been given credit as party chairman for bringing party factions together after the Vietnam War split, but his call for gun-control legislation had drawn considerable opposition. And although he was well liked by party members for his personal warmth and hard work, his speaking style was less than riveting. Humphrey asked Spannaus to drop out. Spannaus, who had been tipped off by his close friend Mondale about what was going on, refused, so the party leaders, not wanting an eleventh-hour conflict, set their sights on finding the strongest possible candidate for the lieutenant governor race. Anderson asked Graven to be his running mate, and Humphrey, Mondale, and Congressman Donald M. Fraser of Minneapolis urged him to do so, but Graven said no. Some Anderson supporters also unsuccessfully approached Nick Coleman.[10]

By the time weary delegates got around to the lieutenant governor endorsement that Sunday, the enterprising Perpich had built up substantial support. He had placed on delegates' seats an attention-getting gimmick, a handy form for tallying the roll-call votes with two aspirins attached. Doug Johnson was a state convention delegate and voted for Coleman for governor. He supported his fellow northeastern Minnesota legislator, Perpich, for lieutenant governor, although he later remarked, "We were pretty uneasy when Wendell Anderson was endorsed, because we knew many of the old-time power brokers in the party didn't like Rudy Perpich." Perpich was not one of the Good Old Boys. He had made political enemies as well as friends by supporting Sandy Keith for governor in 1966 over Karl Rolvaag. Memories were still fresh of his joining anti-Vietnam War protesters who embarrassed Humphrey when he was vice-president under President Lyndon Johnson. But seeing the support Perpich had mustered, Anderson decided to gamble and go along with this Iron Range dark horse. Even if any of the defeated contenders for governor, Graven, Coleman, or Scott, had agreed to go for the lieutenant governor endorsement, it was apparent that pushing someone other than the already-announced candidates could set off an unwanted floor fight. As the DFL leaders began planning for the coming campaign against a formidable Republican slate, party unity became all important.

Perpich and Nick Coleman, assistant senate minority leader and an owner of an advertising/public relations agency, had found they had much in common while sitting next to each other in the senate, and they'd become close friends. Both had supported Eugene McCarthy for president in 1968, both were Roman Catholics, and both desired to advance bold, new, innovative government initiatives. Perpich backed Coleman for the endorsement for governor. In turn, Coleman nominated Perpich for the lieutenant governor spot on the party ticket and was given a lot of the credit for cinching the endorsement for him. According to Doug Johnson, after Coleman dropped out of the gubernatorial contest he demanded that in exchange for his support, Anderson must accept Perpich as the lieutenant governor candidate. Coleman had expected Graven's backing for governor when he dropped out and felt that Graven had betrayed him when it was not given.[11] Sandy Keith, who was not at the convention but was privy to the inside wheelings and dealings, said Perpich was not Anderson's first choice, and added, "I am sure Nick got him the endorsement."[12]

In the voting for a lieutenant governor candidate, Thomas Byrne, a former St. Paul mayor, dropped out after trailing on the first ballot, and with Coleman's help, most of his votes went to Perpich. Perpich, pulling heavily from the Twin Cities and St. Louis County (Duluth, Iron Range) delegations, won the endorsement on the second ballot, defeating Jon Wefald who was endorsed later for the state auditor's race. (Wefald, a Gustavus Adolphus College instructor, was the 1968 DFL candidate for Congress in the Second District and a grandson of Knud Wefald, the Farmer-Labor Party's first congressman.)

After the 1970 convention, Anderson's party-loyal rivals abided by the endorsement, paving the way for the DFL Party to close ranks behind the Anderson-Perpich ticket. It wasn't all one big happy family, however. Tony Perpich and some other DFL liberals supported Earl Craig Jr., a Minneapolis African-American running against Hubert Humphrey for the U. S. Senate. Craig was executive director of a New Democratic Coalition trying to move the Democratic Party toward more progressive politics. It was a hopeless campaign, but Craig, a passionate advocate for peace and justice for the poor and minorities, became a respected spokesman for the left wing. (He was later elected to the Democratic National Committee, became director of The Urban Coalition in Minneapolis, and headed the Minneapolis Neighborhood Revitalization Program.)

On the Republican side, Attorney General Douglas Head, backed by the Hennepin County "Young Turks" of the Republican Party, won endorsement for governor after a five-ballot battle at the state GOP convention. Lieutenant Governor James Goetz had the votes of many in the conservative wing of the party, and the split may well have led to Head's defeat in November.

The Pizza King Jeno Paulucci, a native of Aurora, Minnesota who became a millionaire industrialist selling frozen foods, had an on-again off-again relationship with Rudy Perpich over the years, and in 1970 it was off. Paulucci, known for his colorful style and unpredictable behavior, bought billboard space urging citizens to vote for DFLer Wendell Anderson for governor and Republican Ben Boo for lieutenant governor. He paid for a half-hour election-eve TV special on which Humphrey and Anderson, DFL candidates for senator and governor, appeared, the one condition being that Perpich, the DFL candidate for lieutenant governor, would not appear on the show.[13] The conventional wisdom was that Anderson would win, but that Perpich would lose.[14]

On November 5 the jubilant DFL Party celebrated the election of Anderson as the state's third DFL governor, the return of Hubert Humphrey to the U.S. Senate, and the election of DFLers to three other state offices, including Rudy Perpich as lieutenant governor, Warren Spannaus as attorney general, and Ron Anderson as Public Service Commissioner. Anderson easily defeated Head, 737,921 votes to 621,780, but Perpich, not well known across the state, was elected by only a 17,254 vote-margin, with a total 671,749 votes to Boo's 654,486. Still, it was a giant leap forward for Perpich, and one of many times when he would end-run the party establishment. The Iron Range, where citizens believed going to the polls was a sacred obligation, went all out for its favorite son. DFL Party leaders praised Perpich for rounding up a hefty share of the votes for the ticket, and DFL State Chairman Richard Moe called the election the end of "our long drought."[15]

In fact, it was a good year for the Perpich brothers all the way around. Tony was unopposed and re-elected to the Senate that fall; George was elected to Rudy's vacant senate seat, winning 57 percent of the vote in the general election after defeating two DFL House members, Bernard Bischoff and John Spanish, in the primary election. In January all three brothers took leave from their dental practices and went to St. Paul. George quipped, "The Iron Range is going to be a lot quieter now that we're down here."[15]

John Denver sang at the inaugural of Governor Wendell Anderson, the youngest governor in the nation at age thirty-seven. But it was Lieutenant Governor Rudy Perpich who captured the spotlight when the legislative session began. The political fireworks started right away, and the Perpich brothers were in the thick of it. At that time the lieutenant governor was the presiding officer of the Minnesota senate. When the Senate convened January 5, there were thirty-four Conservatives, as Republican-oriented members called themselves, and thirty-three Liberals or DFLers including Tony and George Perpich. But the Liberals, led by Senator Nick Coleman, who coached Perpich from the floor on parliamentary procedures, challenged the seating of Conservative Richard Palmer of Duluth, saying he could not take office until charges of unfair campaign practices filed against him by DFLers were resolved. Palmer had campaigned as an independent, but after the November 3 election decided to caucus as a Conservative.

Perpich, as presiding officer, ruled that Palmer could not be seated. Perpich also ruled that as lieutenant governor he could break the resulting 33-33 tie vote on procedural matters, and the DFL senators seized control. Supreme Court Chief Justice Oscar Knutsen, who was there to swear in the senators, angrily walked out of the chamber with Conservative senators. Conservatives appealed to the state Supreme Court, but the DFL senators argued that the Senate had the power to exercise its own authority in this situation, and that the court had no right to interfere. At stake was the control of the Senate, the appointment of committees, and the passage of legislation in the body.

The next day the two hostile sides sat glowering at each other for four hours, and when Palmer tried to vote he was not recognized by Lieutenant Governor Perpich. At one point Conservative leader Stanley Holmquist sarcastically addressed Perpich as "Your Highness," but later apologized. On January thirteenth, after arguments in which Chief Justice Knutsen took issue with the Senate DFL position, the Minnesota Supreme Court ruled in favor of the Conservatives, saying that Perpich had no authority to block the seating of Palmer and that the lieutenant governor did not have the right to vote on Senate matters. Coleman ridiculed the opinion, saying, "Parts of it look like they were written by Lewis Carroll." The next day Conservatives regained control of the Senate with a 34-33 margin, and saw to it that Rudy Perpich's brothers, Tony and George, were banned from choice committee seats.

When he first took office in 1971, Rudy Perpich vowed, "I'm not going to be a sit-back lieutenant governor." But the new lieutenant governor's only constitutional charge was to wait for the governor to resign or die. His office was a small space located on the steps outside the main doors, at the opposite end of the Capitol building from the busy suite of offices of Governor Wendell Anderson and his staff. There wasn't even a sign on the plain, frosted-glass door. ·

After the Supreme Court ruled that he did not have constitutional authority to vote on Senate matters, Perpich angrily declared that the lieutenant governor should be given year-round duties or the office should be abandoned. He threatened to quit and astounded the House Appropriations Committee by asking for a reduction in his budget for the next two years. Assuring the lieutenant governor that he was valued, Governor Anderson and his wife Mary hosted a dinner at the governor's mansion honoring Perpich and his wife Lola to boost the lieutenant governor's morale and to acknowledge the crucial role Perpich had played in the 1970 DFL election campaign. Anderson told Perpich he wanted him on the ticket with him in 1974 and favored an expansion of powers for the lieutenant governor.[16]

The Perpich Brothers at the Capitol

The three Perpich brothers were all well-liked in St. Paul, though they differed a good deal in temperament. Tony, shorter and stockier than Rudy, was less mercurial than his brothers. "I like living a structured life," he said. George, dark-haired, husky and muscular, was both a lover of country music and the most liberal of the three. He could sometimes be gruff, and he was well known for his colorful, sledgehammer rhetoric and booming baritone voice. "I'm not going to stop a train by sitting on a mule with a crowbar," he once remarked, "I want some dynamite." One of his best-known epithets for political adversaries was "those lousy bastards." In 1976 he turned back a tough primary challenge from Ed Matonich of Hibbing by running newspaper advertisements with pictures of his beat-up 1959 Chevrolet pickup alongside the new Lincoln Continental driven by his opponent, and the caption "My opponent, the downtown Hibbing lawyer—who does he really represent?"

One day George was walking down a Capitol hallway, when he saw an elderly man approaching. The man eyed the length of Perpich's hair and his extra-long sideburns and said, "You look like one of those hippies. Why don't you get a haircut so you'll look like a person?" George replied, "I just got a haircut."

If the Perpich brothers were viewed as a little different, well, that was something expected of Iron Rangers. The Range was a place apart, and those who came from there were proud of their heritage. *Minneapolis Star* columnist Jim Klobuchar, a native of the Iron Range himself, affectionately embellished the Perpich lore. Klobuchar's background was similar to the Perpich's. He was from Ely; his Slovenian father was an iron miner. As a youngster, Klobuchar played hide-and-seek behind sheets of potica pastry hung on chairs, and like the Perpiches he worked in the iron mines while going to school. Klobuchar first met Rudy when Perpich was lieutenant governor. While political opponents referred to the Perpich brothers as The Dynasty, Klobuchar wrote that there was no such thing as a Perpich dynasty on the Range. "There are only warring enclaves where occasionally an unnatural armistice prevails. The successful politicians up there are the ones who can hold the warfare down to sporadic brawling, avoiding actual bloodshed and secession. The Perpich brothers, Rudy, Tony, and George, managed this tricky piece of mine-field diplomacy better than most. At the same time they happily contributed to the overall strife, without which politics just won't work on the Range."[17]

Indeed, it was far more than a family dynasty. The Perpich brothers were trailblazers in a great working-class push for political and economic power on the Range and beyond. Their compassion for people, ideals and goals, even their rough-and-tumble style of politics, were rooted in the ethics and values of the Iron Range and the life that Anton and Mary Perpich had made for their four sons in the mining community of Carson Lake. They were often accused of off-the-wall ideas and vindictive treatment of political enemies, but in time they met and joined others with a similar vision of political and economic empowerment for the powerless and the poor. Humble folk throughout the state took pride in the rise of the immigrant iron miner's sons. The success of the Perpiches gave Range people in particular the confidence that they were as good as anybody else.[18]

Rudy Perpich often regaled his colleagues with funny stories about his family and the Iron Range. He would relate, imitating his father's immigrant dialect, about a time when the assessor came to appraise the value of Anton's little house. Anton didn't understand the man was there to re-value his home for tax purposes and hospitably offered his visitor the customary glass of wine. When the young assessor said, "It's not much of a place," speaking of the house which was Anton's pride and joy and its ownership quite an achievement for a poor miner, Anton was infuriated. He took away the wine, saying, "What are you talking about? This is my place. I bought it." The assessor explained, "No, you don't understand. I work for the assessor. I'm here to value your place for taxes." Anton finally got it. He set the wine back for the man and quickly agreed, "You are right. It's nothing but scrap."

Then there was the time Rudy bought his father a $1 tie for his birthday. Anton knocked him flat on the floor for spending money on something so foolish. Another Anton quote which Rudy used on appropriate occasions: "Talk is cheap, and whiskey costs money." Rudy told about the down-to-earth Perpich brothers and their father attending the posh New York wedding of their youngest brother, Joseph, and Cathy Sulzberger. Anton bought the only tuxedo of his life for the festivities, which included the wedding, the reception, and a banquet afterward in the Park Lane Hotel. At the banquet there were place settings with a confusing array of silverware and plates. The Perpiches were nervous because they didn't know which utensils and dishes to use, but the irrepressible George grabbed a piece of silver in each hand and sweeping the other pieces away, declared, "We're from the Iron Range. Up there, people eat with a fork in one hand, a knife in the other hand, and everybody has a good time." Everyone laughed, and the Perpiches relaxed and enjoyed themselves.[19]

It was hard for the Perpich brothers to maintain their dental practices on the Range and at the same time legislate in St. Paul, even though the Legislature then met only every other year. More and more of their time was spent on politics. George was a top strategist in Rudy's successful election campaigns. Tony stayed out of the political front lines, particularly after the fight he had with James Oberstar in 1974 over the Eighth District Congress seat. And as Rudy climbed the political ladder, Tony and George found to their chagrin that everything they said or did was scrutinized in light of their older brother, the governor-to-be and governor. Tony insisted they weren't as close as some people thought. "Rudy and George and I are three totally different individuals, and rarely during the years that we served in the Senate did we consult with one another or seek one another's opinions about what each of us was planning to do politically." A case in point is when Rudy came out against abortion. George and Tony were staunch supporters of abortion rights. Friends said the brothers would have vehement arguments and not speak to each other for weeks.[20]

Yet individually or together, the bold and visionary Perpich brothers led the charge for changes and created an atmosphere for new ideas, though their legislative initiatives often failed. In 1971 Tony and George introduced an unsuccessful bill supported by Lieutenant Governor Rudy Perpich to lower the minimum age from 21 to 18 for a wide range of things from buying a drink to becoming eligible for a pharmacist's license. The Perpiches sought an environmental and redevelopment fund for northeastern Minnesota. (Such a fund, called the Year 2002 fund because of its long-range planning, was eventually established in 1977.) They called for limiting the "manipulative power" of lobbyists in pushing through special interest legislation "to the detriment of Minnesota taxpayers."

Governor Anderson and the Conservative-controlled Legislature were deadlocked over the omnibus tax bill in the 1971 regular session, and Anderson called the lawmakers back for a special session which dragged on throughout the summer. The Perpiches and other DFLers attacked the omnibus tax bill sponsored in the regular session by the Conservatives, calling it a "sellout" to the iron-mining industry. Under it, they said, the taconite companies would receive a reduction in state taxes at the same time that other industries would have their taxes raised. House Conservative Majority Leader Ernest Lindstrom of Richfield denied that Conservatives had sold out to mining interests and called the DFL charges "a complete lie." George Perpich angrily introduced a bill that would require taconite companies to pay for the maintenance of the state capitol. "They might as well," he said. "They own it anyway."

Although George said, "There's going to be a lot of little kids back home with holes in their teeth," the Perpich brothers took leave from their dental practices to barnstorm the state that summer, campaigning for higher taxes on taconite production. Joined by now-friendly Jeno Paulucci, they hit hard in the hometowns of Conservative legislators who opposed an increase.[21] In the special session the Legislature did raise taconite production taxes by fourteen cents per ton, phased in over the next eight years. The longest special session in legislative history extended into the fall before Anderson succeeded in pushing through his "Minnesota Miracle." The nationally acclaimed program greatly increased state funding for schools, shifting a greater portion of education costs from local property taxes to the state income tax. It made major strides in equalizing spending per pupil among school districts and equalizing property taxes among taxing districts. The Legislature approved a substantial increase in state taxes, including a sales tax hike to finance the reform measure, and finally adjourned October 30.

Meanwhile, Rudy Perpich was still restless. After being elected lieutenant governor in 1970, he had wanted to put down his dental drill and close the door on his Hibbing dental office—he liked government better. He'd hoped to become the governor's strong legislative liaison, but that didn't happen. Perpich, who was brimful of ideas for reforms and innovations, was regarded as a "loose cannon" by some in Anderson's inner circle. Naturally enough, his penchant for going around the state and making off-the-cuff and controversial statements unsanctioned by the governor made Anderson's office nervous. For example, Perpich said four of the state's mental hospitals should be closed and patients moved to small community-based homes, a de-institutionalization idea he got from his psychiatrist brother, Joe. He proposed sending a team of specialists into every state institution for the retarded or mentally ill to see whether the patients should be there, or in some other setting, or released outright.[22]

Rudy called for decentralization of state government, suggesting that Marshall would be a good location for the Agriculture Department, and an area north of the Twin cities suburbs would be a good location for the DNR. The Minnesota Lands, Minerals, and Waters Division might better be headquartered in Hibbing instead of St. Paul, he argued, and he planned to move his own office to Hibbing when the Minnesota Legislature, which then met every other year in regular session, was not in session. Perpich scolded Charles Hill, President of Rochester State Junior College, for refusing to permit attorney William Kunstler, the defense attorney in the trial of the Chicago Seven, Vietnam War protesters, to speak on campus. His support of a plan to exempt Brainerd from the 1967 law which he cosponsored, requiring cities to fluoridate their water as a tooth-decay preventive, drew fire from fellow dentists and the Minnesota Dental Association.

Perpich was concerned that much of the Iron Range history was disappearing, not only the buildings but the very people who remembered the Range as it was originally. He called, therefore, for interpretative centers around the state, one about iron mining in Chisholm and others about lumbering, farming and other important parts of Minnesota development. His dream of an Iron Range Interpretative Center was realized in 1976. It was a memorial that honored Perpich's parents and all immigrants and preserved their history for future generations. The Pillsbury family of Minneapolis donated land for the center on the edge of the spectacular Glenn open-pit mine at Chisholm. Building funds were provided by the state and federal government and the City of Chisholm.

Perpich pushed aggressively for the cleanup of abandoned mines, and called for the iron mining industry to replace jobs lost by a Duluth steel plant shutdown. That angered steel companies, whom Perpich accused of instructing the Hibbing City Council not to allow him to ride in the Bicentennial parade in his home town. Perpich insisted he wasn't against the mining companies, though there can be little doubt that the memory of the treatment he and his parents had received at the hands of the mining company and railroad, when they'd been forced to move out of Carson Lake, continued to rankle him. Anton Perpich had built a fence around his garden on the land he rented for years from the railroad company, where his little house was located. When mining companies told Carson Lake residents to leave the location in 1951, "they came with the bulldozers and just tore that fence down, like it wasn't there." Rudy went to see a mining company executive about it and was made to wait. After a long time, the clerk went in to remind the executive that the young man was still there, and Perpich heard the company boss say, "Let the hunky wait." Twenty years later Rudy Perpich, the lieutenant governor, was still seething at that slight, and lashed out at the mining industry: "The son of a bitch. The dirty son of a bitch. And now they won't clean up all the mess they made so people could live there again."

Perpich railed at skyrocketing health care costs, which he said were driving American families under. He called for a national health care program that included national health insurance, a crash program to train medical personnel, a quasi-mandatory domestic peace corps that would send newly trained medical personnel to areas where there were extreme shortages, and a massive commitment to fund research dealing with cancer, heart disease, the common cold, tooth decay and other illnesses.[23]

Rudy clashed with legislative leaders, including his good friend Senate Minority Leader Nicholas Coleman, when he drafted a controversial legislative reapportionment plan after the 1970 U.S. census. Under the plan, the size of the Minnesota Senate would have been reduced from 67 members to 33, and the size of the House from 135 to 99. Opponents, including House DFL Majority Leader Irvin Anderson of International Falls, argued that reducing the size would shift decision-making away from elected legislators to staff aides. Coleman worked with Senate Majority Leader Stanley Holmquist to put together a bi-partisan compromise reapportionment plan keeping the current 202-member, two-House Legislature intact. They expected their plan would meet the Supreme Court's 1964 landmark "one-man, one-vote" rule.

Perpich's unsanctioned plan to cut the size of the Legislature threatened to throw the 1972 election machinery into chaos. State Representative Jack Fena represented himself and Perpich in a court suit over the reapportionment plans before a three-judge Eighth Circuit Court of Appeals panel. The panel was headed by Judge Gerald Heaney of Duluth, a close friend of former Governor Orville Freeman, and an Eighth District DFL leader and labor lawyer before his appointment to the bench. Fena told the court that all recent Minnesota governors had favored a reduction in the size of the Legislature, then the eighth largest in the nation. When Heaney asked Fena how he had voted on the bill, the Hibbing legislator confessed, "I voted 'No' your Honor. As a sitting legislator, I'd rather pluck out my own eye than reduce the size of the Legislature." But, he explained, he was not running for re-election and was on the other side now. Heaney and the court ruled in favor of the legislative reduction plan. When the Minnesota Senate filed an appeal of the lower court order, the U.S. Supreme Court refused to hear arguments on the case, but the high court reversed the lower court and threw out the reduction proposal. Fena and Andrew Kozak, a Perpich aide, said Perpich believed Coleman and Holmquist flew to Washington and talked with Justices Warren Burger and Harry Blackmun, former Minnesotans, and convinced them to do so. Rudy Perpich was furious at Coleman.[24]

Chapter 5

The 1970s. Vietnam. The New Titans.

Rudy Perpich, speaking at peace rallies, called for swift withdrawal of U.S. troops from Vietnam. In the Senate he and Nick Coleman cosponsored a bill declaring the war unconstitutional—sending a message to Washington, if nothing else. In 1971, when he was lieutenant governor, Perpich took part in an antiwar march in Washington, and labeled President Nixon's decision to keep troops in Vietnam for an unspecified amount of time "nothing short of barbaric." He urged audiences "to make a pledge not to vote for a person who will vote to support continuation of the war." In 1972 he began a partial fast, saying he would cut out breakfasts, desserts, and all liquids except water until the United States ended its military involvement in Vietnam. He urged students to follow his lead in applying pressure on the Nixon administration to end the war by boycotting products geared to the youth market such as soft drinks and candy.[1] Allan Spear, an associate professor of history at the University of Minnesota, who was elected to the state senate in 1972, also opposed the U.S. action in Vietnam. He soon became a big fan and lifelong supporter of Perpich. "I saw him as a gutsy guy. In 1968 he was one of the few elected officials who supported [Eugene] McCarthy. He was a populist liberal."[2]

Hubert Humphrey was gearing up for another run at the presidency, and Perpich reluctantly endorsed the Minnesota senator for the Democratic nomination for president. He said he preferred Senator Edward Kennedy of Massachusetts but didn't think Kennedy would seek or accept the nomination.[3] But the Minnesota DFL Party, at a raucous state convention in Rochester, endorsed Senator George McGovern of South Dakota. McGovern and Humphrey supporters battled throughout the convention. The liberals pushed through platform planks supporting same-sex marriages, legalization of marijuana and amnesty for draft dodgers, a platform which prominent DFL leaders, including Governor Wendell Anderson, disavowed.[4] McGovern won the Democratic nomination but was soundly defeated by President Nixon in the November 7 election. Nixon and Vice President Spiro Agnew even carried historically Democratic Minnesota, tallying 898,269 votes, well ahead of the McGovern-Shriver ticket's 802,346.

At the local level, however, with new redistricting lines reflecting population changes and growth, particularly in the Twin Cities metropolitan area, jubilant DFLers won control of both the Minnesota Senate and House. It was the first time in state history that Democrats had a majority in both Houses. After ten years of control by Republican-oriented Conservatives, DFL-allied Liberals now held a whopping 78-56 majority. The political pendulum had swung the other way.

There were emerging giants among the new Liberal majority members and also among a wave of bright young Conservative minority legislators, who captured some of the new suburban seats created by redistricting. Like the titans they succeeded, these eager legislators saw service in public office as a high honor, and the giving up of a part of their lives as a privilege and opportunity to shape policy for the good of the state.

In the House, Martin Olav Sabo of Minneapolis, the former Liberal minority leader, was elected Speaker, considered the second most powerful office in state government after the governor. Sabo, the son of Norwegian immigrants and a cum laude graduate of Augsburg College, had first come to the House in 1961 at the age of 22. Shrewd, partisan, a strong ally of organized labor, he was a firm leader who kept his caucus members in line. Closemouthed with the press, he never displayed his emotions, but friends and adversaries alike knew to tread carefully with the stoic speaker.

DFL Young Turks took over in the Senate. Coleman was elected majority leader by Senate Liberals. Both Tony and George Perpich won reelection to the Senate. Tony, the bane of the iron mining companies, became chairman of the tax committee. Gifted with charm, a sharp wit, and keen political acumen, Coleman was a master of legislative gamesmanship and a powerful and effective majority leader. Republicans called the silver-haired Coleman the "Grinning Shark," a sobriquet he seized upon with glee. He and his idealistic band of DFL state senators were impatient to go ahead with many initiatives they had long dreamed of passing. The flood gates opened, and under the aggressive leadership of Governor

Wendell Anderson, Coleman, and Sabo, the eager new majorities passed reams of pent-up consumer, environmental, labor, and campaign-finance-reform legislation, which the Conservatives had long bottled up.

One of the first actions by the new Liberal majority was to repeal the sixty-year-old law providing for the nonpartisan election of legislators, restoring party designations which had been abandoned in 1913. During the 1973-74 session the Liberals passed an ethics and campaign financing law that included an income tax check-off for public financing of campaigns and tax credits for political contributions. They established a state energy agency and a major new housing financing program, implemented no-fault automobile insurance, initiated statewide utility regulation reform, and repealed laws that had given railroads and mining firms tax breaks. The 1973 Legislature ratified the proposed Equal Rights Amendment to the U.S. Constitution, voted Vietnam-era veterans a cash bonus, enacted the first state minimum-wage law, and repealed the "Little Hatch Act," thereby allowing public employees to become involved in politics.

Coleman himself authored a number of new laws: gun control, state income-tax reduction for low-income people, liquor reform aimed at breaking up monopolies, laws protecting tenant rights and human rights, and legislation making it illegal to discriminate against homosexuals. The Senate majority leader called it a landmark session. "This is the sort of leadership a legislature ought to take," Coleman said when the Legislature adjourned in March, 1974. "It shows that the Legislature is again able to respond to the needs and demands of the people."[5] In order to make such a record, Coleman said, the Sixty-eighth Legislature became the first to work full-time. The 1973 session met for five months and the 1974 session for ten weeks, often six days of ten or more hours a day. Lawmakers increased the salary of legislators from $8,400 to $12,000 annually.

If their zeal for legislating sometimes put the feisty young DFL senators at odds with governors and House leaders of their own party, that added to the zest of the battle. Yet Coleman, with all his persuasive skills, was not always able to maintain peace and harmony within his independent-minded caucus. At the end of the 1976 session he lost control of the Senate in a last-night brouhaha, and some members of his caucus, determined to get pet bills passed, refused to honor his request for adjournment.[6] After the Legislature finally did adjourn, Coleman was so frustrated that when he went to leave the Capitol at 2 a.m. and found a front door locked, he kicked the glass out. The Senate Majority Leader at first denied rumors that he had broken the glass, but later he confessed that he had stuck his foot through the door. "That was the only thing I got through all night," he quipped.[7]

In 1973 Governor Anderson, still trying to pacify his restless, energetic lieutenant-governor, gave Perpich several assignments, including a program to improve the state's aesthetic environment. Perpich was charged with coordinating the work of state agencies that were planting trees and removing junked cars, billboards, and dilapidated buildings. Anderson also named Perpich to represent the Governor on several less visible boards and commissions.

In addition, Anderson appointed the lieutenant governor honorary chairman of the Bicentennial Commission, a thirty-five-member state group created in 1972 by executive order of the governor in conjunction with the federal American Revolution Bicentennial Administration, planning for the nation's two-hundredth birthday. The Minnesota commission had $400,000 to support its own and local projects. Many cities were forming their own bicentennial commissions, spurred by the opportunity to secure state and federal grants for local projects. Minneapolis was given money to rejuvenate Nicollet Island in the Mississippi River, for example.

The honorary chairmanship of the state commission was considered a ceremonial job, however, and at first Perpich didn't want it. It soon became clear to him, however, that the post was a door to opportunity. The lieutenant governor stepped up his travels, becoming a leading promoter of the Bicentennial celebration. He drove 170,000 miles, bringing citations to local officials and handing out bicentennial flags in every part of the state. "I can't tell you how many communities he visited in my district alone," said Senator Roger Moe of Ada in the Red River Valley. "It was all good, soft, fluffy stuff that people felt good about." These visits set the stage for Perpich's eventual bid for governor. He got to know the state, made important friends and contacts such as Moe, and began to think about things he'd do if he ever did become governor.

Robert Aronson, the lieutenant governor's aide, whose charge was to make his boss more visible, conceived the idea of Perpich doing short, historical "minutes" for radio use. The eight-member staff in the lieutenant governor's office researched historical tidbits such as Joe Rolette, who ran away with the bill to move the capitol, and Jane Grey Swissholm, who was the first woman newspaper publisher in Minnesota. Aronson borrowed audio equipment from the Senate, fixed up a recording room in a walk-in safe in the Capitol basement, and wrote scripts for Perpich. He contacted all of the radio stations in the state, asking them if they would run the "Minnesota Minutes" gratis, as a public service feature, and more than a hundred agreed to run them daily. The lieutenant governor's office provided thirty tapes a month to each station which ran them several times a day. That went on for two years. It had a tremendous impact. Perpich told Aronson, "You made me a household name." If Anderson's office was aware of what Perpich was up to, no one said anything. "It was 'Rudy is down the hall. Keep him down there and keep him busy. Get him out of our hair,'" Aronson said. "That is what governors do to lieutenant governors. It's what presidents do to vice presidents."

The Perpiches' feud with John Blatnik continued, extending to the congressman's longtime staff aide, James Oberstar of Chisholm. When Blatnik announced he was retiring in 1974, Oberstar immediately declared himself a candidate for the seat with Blatnik's blessing. Friends of Rudy Perpich, not wanting the seat to go to a Blatnik man, urged the lieutenant governor to run, but Perpich's wife and children were not for it, and with regret, he said "no" to the idea, not knowing if he would ever have another opportunity to move up. "I believe I have a job to finish here in Minnesota," said Perpich. "In addition, I do not, at this time, wish to commit myself, and my family, to a career and life in Washington."[8] Perpich sent Blatnik a telegram trying to persuade him to run one more term, but Blatnik would not. So it was Tony Perpich who stepped up to vie with Oberstar for the DFL Party endorsement for the Eighth District Congress seat.[9]

Tony won the endorsement at the district convention in Grand Rapids in May, after a fierce thirty-ballot battle that had all three of the older Perpich brothers and their wives working the convention.[10] Oberstar then announced that he would run in the September 10 DFL primary anyway. With the Perpich camp accusing him of foul play, he attacked Tony Perpich in an advertising blitz with the theme, "Who's kidding who, Tony?" and questioned his opponent's positions on a number of issues, including a Tony Perpich-proposed $30,000 study of dividing St. Louis County in two to separate the Iron Range from off Duluth. The Eveleth senator had said the county was too large to be manageable, and said Range residents felt left out of the county political process, which set off a furor in Duluth.[11]

Blatnik campaigned actively for Oberstar. The 1974 election was the first since the legalization of abortion by the U. S. Supreme Court, and Tony Perpich, who supported the ruling, became one of the first Minnesota politicians to be targeted by the heavy guns of the antiabortion movement. In the primary election Oberstar trounced Perpich, who lost all eight counties in the Eighth District. Oberstar won heavily in Duluth where Republicans encouraged party voters to cross over and vote for Blatnik's protégé.[12] Oberstar went on to win the congressional seat in the general election.

Lieutenant Governor Rudy Perpich refused to endorse Oberstar after the primary, saying, "Jim Oberstar took a chapter out of the Watergate book and used it."[13] That battle left deep scars. Tony and Rudy ended up on a sour note, too. Friends said the brothers did not speak to each other for several years after that 1974 convention, but did not know why. Tony would say only that both were busy with their dental practices and young families.[14] In 1980 George made an unsuccessful attempt to challenge Oberstar for the DFL endorsement. George also was "pro-choice" and had blocked several antiabortion bills as chairman of the Health, Welfare, and Corrections Committee in the senate. He, too, was targeted by the powerful Minnesota Citizens Concerned for Life (MCCL) antiabortion organization.

State Senator Doug Johnson later became an admirer and close personal friend of Oberstar, but he was in the Perpich camp in those early years and said, "Those days you had to pick sides in the Perpich—Blatnik/Oberstar War. You had to be on one side or the other. You had to come through some pretty tough fights."

That fall Anderson and Perpich were re-elected overwhelmingly. This time the lieutenant governor was re-elected as Anderson's running mate, rather than independently, under a new constitutional amendment which also made the office a full-time position. The salary was increased from $9,600 to $30,000. Perpich quit his neglected dental practice.

In 1975 Senator George Perpich took on the mighty Minnesota AFL-CIO and its powerful president, David Roe, by sponsoring a bill banning the use of union dues in political campaigns, a recommendation of the State Ethics Commission. During Senate floor debate George Perpich, lashing out at the short-statured, cigar-smoking Roe, a close ally of Governor Anderson, referred to Roe as "Governor Roe" and urged his colleagues to vote for the bill "to show all the people of Minnesota that today, at least, he is not yet King David." Late one night George was speaking for a bill in the Senate and saw Roe, who opposed it, sitting up in the gallery. George stopped, pointed to the labor leader, and thundered, "And David Roe would sell the Virgin Mary into prostitution for another dime an hour."[15]

Roe said George Perpich was seeking revenge against several Duluth and Iron Range locals of United Steelworkers of America who supported James Oberstar in the recent Congressional race against Perpich's brother Tony. Tony Perpich had accused Roe of arranging to have the Eighth District AFL-CIO organization withhold its endorsement from him before the primary, which Roe denied.[16] Tony said he had won the backing of nearly all the local unions but that their representatives failed to vote for his endorsement as promised at the district level. With the almost solid support of Republican members, the bill banning political campaign use of union dues passed in the Senate. It stalled in the House, however. Speaker Sabo was a staunch friend of Roe and the AFL-CIO, and the union had been a dependable contributor to DFL campaign coffers.

Rudy Perpich pushed legislation to ban mining and timber cutting in a 260,000-acre area of the Boundary Waters Canoe Area (BWCA). During the debates he took a swipe at his longtime antagonists, the iron mining companies on the Range. He told a Minnesota House committee, "The mining companies have played the role of overlords in this state for the past seventy years, depleting the mineral wealth of the state and not paying their fair share in taxes, destroying the natural beauty of the land, polluting streams and lakes, and now mining interests want to exploit the BWCA. The Boundary Waters Canoe Area belongs to all of the people of this nation, and we must preserve it."

On the other hand, in 1976, when the U.S. Forest Service proposed to ban snowmobiles in the BWCA, he joined Congressman Oberstar in favoring a compromise which allowed snowmobiling until there was evidence of environmental damage. "We just have to have a reasonable approach," he said. "For the feds to take it all over doesn't make sense."

Chapter 6

The Back Door Opens.
Governor Rudy Perpich

Lieutenant Governor Rudy Perpich was ecstatic as he strode down a New York City street on the morning of July 15, 1976, confident that his political destiny was assured. He had just seen on television Democratic presidential nominee Jimmy Carter put his arm around Walter Mondale and declare that the Minnesota senator was his choice as a running mate. This event set the stage for a reshuffling of the state's top offices and opened a new political era. The door was now open, albeit the back door, for the Iron Ranger to become governor.[1]

Wendell Anderson, forty-two, ruggedly handsome and proud of his Swedish heritage, was a rising star on the national scene. He had attracted media attention with the "Minnesota Miracle" tax and education reform, which was aimed at equalizing per-pupil spending among schools by having the state take over a large share of the school-financing burden from local districts. In 1973 he hit the jackpot when his picture appeared on the August 13 cover of *Time*, flashing a big smile and holding up a six-pound Northern pike. The picture and 11-page cover story lauding "The Good Life in Minnesota" conveyed an image of Minnesota as a high "quality of life" state. Though rooted in fact, the entire feature had been a publicity coup planted and cultivated with *Time* by David Lebedoff, a Minneapolis lawyer and senior adviser to the politically ambitious Anderson.[2] At about the same time, in his *Book of America: Inside 50 States*, Neil Peirce wrote: "Search America from sea to sea and you will not find as close a model to the ideal of the successful society as Minnesota."

When the Minnesota DFL delegates and Governor Anderson, the high-profile chairman of the platform committee, traveled to the Democratic national convention in New York City for what turned out to be Mondale's triumphant anointment for vice president, Perpich was forgotten. He went on his own, uninvited, once again an outsider with no official status and with no role to play in the events going on at Madison Square Garden.

But Mondale's run for vice president was the political bolt of lightning that could change it all. A Carter-Mondale victory would clear the way for Anderson to leave the governor's office to take Mondale's vacant U.S. Senate seat, at which point Perpich would become governor. There would be no more snubs. He envisioned himself sitting behind the big mahogany desk where governors had sat since 1905 in the corner office of the Capitol. He vowed he would be a governor the likes of whom the State of Minnesota had never seen before. His mind raced ahead, brimming over with ideas he wanted to carry out as Governor. He wanted to make Minnesota "the brainpower state" with education reforms, and position the state on the cutting edge of new technology. He wanted to make the state the health-research center of the world. He wanted to reorganize state government and create a one-step Human Services Center with an ombudsman for the mentally retarded. He would have welfare-to-work programs with recipients working on environmental projects. He wanted to abolish real-estate and personal-property taxes and replace them with a two-percent gross-earnings tax. And he wanted to restore economic prosperity to his beloved, depressed Iron Range.

That November Jimmy Carter was elected President and Walter Mondale was elected Vice President, defeating Republicans Gerald Ford and Robert Dole. The Carter-Mondale ticket carried Minnesota by 56 percent. Minnesota led the nation in the percentage of eligible voters who voted in the 1976 general election, with 75.4 percent or 1,978,590 Minnesotans going to the polls. Senator Hubert Humphrey received 1,290,736 votes, at that time the most ever received by any candidate for public office in Minnesota.

Mondale, the second Minnesotan to be elected to the nation's second highest office, prepared to resign his Senate seat. Wendell Anderson, the Golden Boy of Minnesota politics, was expected to arrange for his own appointment to the U.S. Senate although he made no immediate statement. Minnesotans became aware there might be a new governor, and many began to wonder who this tall, salt-and-pepper-haired dentist, Dr. Rudy Perpich, really was. A self-described "Hunky from the Iron Range," Perpich had a reputation around the Capitol of being an unpredictable "shoot-from-the-hip" figure. Capitol wags joked about whether Perpich would present his budget in Croatian.

Rudy Perpich (left), Nick Coleman, Wendell Anderson (2nd from right), and two unidentified men

Suddenly there was a steady stream of long-lost friends and would-be new friends with wish lists. There were jobseekers and reporters, even the national press, finding their way to Rudy's door. The presumed-next governor was deluged with invitations for appearances. Perpich later told reporters that during this time neither Anderson nor anyone in his office ever talked with him about the governor's plans or the mechanics to carry them out. Perpich said in an interview that he considered Anderson to be the best qualified to become Minnesotans new senator and would appoint him without question.[3] He was convinced that Anderson would serve the state in the tradition of Humphrey, McCarthy, and Mondale, and felt that adverse public reaction to a self-appointment was unlikely, although similar maneuvers had been poorly received in other states. Perpich pointed to Anderson's landslide reelection vote in 1974 and his high ratings in opinion polls.

However, the Minnesota Poll published by the *Minneapolis Tribune* that fall found 55 percent of respondents opposed such maneuvering by Anderson, while only 23 percent favored it, with 22 percent undecided.[4] Anderson's chief of staff, Tom Kelm, advised the governor to appoint a caretaker to finish out Mondale's term if the seat opened up, then run in the 1978 election for the position, but the governor was confident that the people of Minnesota would support him if he took the shortcut, self-appointment route.[5]

Over the summer Perpich became increasingly uneasy waiting for a sign from Anderson. He asked to meet with the governor in New York City after the announcement of Mondale's selection to be Carter's vice presidential running mate, and the two talked for about an hour in Anderson's hotel room. But the governor did not take Perpich into his confidence as to his future plans, saying he had made no decision and was concerned about the impact on his family of a possible move to Washington. Even after the election, when Perpich again asked to meet with Anderson, and was invited to breakfast at the governor's mansion on Friday, November 6, the governor did not disclose his decision.[6] Nor did he ask if Perpich would appoint him to the Senate if Perpich became governor. There was no agreement, "honest to God," Perpich said, that if Anderson resigned, Perpich would appoint him to the Senate.

Perpich was disappointed that Anderson did not invite him to sit in on the preparation of the 1977-79 budget, already underway, which Perpich would have to take over if he became governor. Their meeting ended, Perpich said, with Anderson telling him he was doing a good job as lieutenant governor, and that he should continue working hard. Perpich told his brothers, Tony and George, he really didn't know what Anderson was going to do. With the days passing by and no word from the governor, Perpich's hopes dimmed. On Tuesday, November 9, a week after the election, a disconsolate Perpich had still heard nothing, and at lunch that day he told his wife and children, "I don't think it's going to happen."

But it did happen. At 1:42 p.m. that afternoon, Tom Kelm, Anderson's chief of staff, called Perpich and asked him to meet with the governor at 9 a.m. the next day. Though nothing specific had been revealed, Perpich anticipated that Anderson was going to resign. "I was on Cloud Nine," he said.

That night he didn't sleep. When he arrived at the capitol at 7:30 a.m. the next morning, an hour-and-a-half early, he was handed a press release with a brief statement by Anderson. It said, "I would like to announce that I intend to represent the people of Minnesota in the United States Senate for the next two years. It is my hope and prayer that my work there will earn their support, and justify my election to a full term in 1978." Anderson did not mention that he was resigning as governor, saying only, "I will leave the office of governor in good and experienced hands. Rudy Perpich has twenty solid years of service as a school-board member, state senator, and lieutenant governor. He is bright and honest and dedicated to the people of this state. I have great confidence that Governor Perpich and the DFL Legislature will continue and enhance the Minnesota record of solid accomplishment."

Minneapolis Star **headline, November 10, 1976**

That morning Perpich and Anderson called a joint press conference. Perpich, elated and looking "gubernatorial," wore a conservative, dark, pin-striped suit, white shirt, and black-and-white polka-dot tie. He was accompanied by his wife, Lola, son, Rudy Jr., seventeen, and daughter, Mary Sue, sixteen. He said, "At this moment, I'm the happiest person on earth. By this time next week, both my feet will be back on the ground." Nobody got word to Alec Olson, the President of the Senate, who would now become the new lieutenant governor, in time for him to get to the Capitol. He was plowing on his Spicer farm that day.

If Perpich thought this was cavalier treatment on the part of the governor's office, he never complained publicly, but he was never to express any great loyalty to DFL Party leaders closely allied with Wendell Anderson either. Always a loner and a political maverick, he had almost dropped out of politics. He had not attended his Eighth District Congressional Convention or the state DFL Convention that year, arguing that he had been giving full time to his Bicentennial Commission job and didn't want to politicize it. Close friends who felt the DFL establishment and Anderson's office had treated Perpich poorly, speculated that if he did, indeed, become governor, there would be a major shakeup at the Capitol.

When it appeared Perpich would become governor, Senate Minority Leader Robert Ashbach, a moderate Republican who had watched and worked with Perpich on legislative initiatives, predicted that his former Senate colleague would do better than most expected. "If I had car trouble on the highway, I'd rather have him come along than Wendy [Anderson]," Ashbach said. Perpich would be more open, was more inclined to do things himself than to turn it over to staff as Anderson did, and was not as political and "devious" in making appointments, Ashbach observed. The Senate minority leader's prophecy for Perpich was to prove perceptive.

Friends said Perpich was a decent and honorable man who didn't smoke and rarely drank, a populist who cared deeply about society's underdogs, the poor, handicapped, elderly and working men and women, and a leader with refreshing ideas about what state government should do. He was "absolutely clean—there's no way you could buy him," said longtime friend Frank Adams. Adams and others described Rudy Perpich as a man who was devoted to his family and looked to his wife, Lola, as his closest adviser.

Perpich was arguably one of the best-prepared men ever to take the oath of office as Governor of Minnesota. He had served six years on the Hibbing school board, 1956-1962; eight years as a state senator, 1963-1971; and five years as lieutenant governor, 1971-1976. As lieutenant governor, he had crisscrossed the state, talking to more than 400,000 people, speaking in schools, making the most of his Bicentennial Commission job and encouraging cities to establish history centers and other history-related projects. In his role as state aesthetics coordinator, he had prodded citizens, local officials, and mining companies to plant trees, get rid of unused railroad ties, clean up ravaged mining sites, re-sod hills, and stock abandoned mining pits with fish.

Perpich plunged into the job of governor-designate, but it was a difficult period, with Anderson and his staff still keeping tight rein on the actual governing. "This is a tough time… You are not governor yet. You have to walk a fine line," Perpich said. On a typical day during his "transition" period, Perpich, driving his own car en route to an appearance in Mankato, gave a reporter who had asked to accompany him a glimpse of what he would do as governor. Jumping from topic to topic, not finishing sentences, his thoughts always getting ahead of his words, he said he would hit the road after he became governor, and get out and talk with people. "I never did like desk work… [It would] kind of kill me if I had to sit behind that desk all the time… I think Alec [Olson, the lieutenant-governor-designate] should really be involved. I'm just going to say, 'Alec, what do you want to do?'"

He denied claims by critics that he was anti-business. "It's part of that mining companies [thing.] All I have ever asked is that mining companies pay their fair share, pay the same rate of taxes others do in the state." Perpich said he was listening to all sides in the debate over a new metropolitan area sports stadium. "George and I discussed it for about an hour. He is out there making contacts and discussing it. He's got some ideas. I don't want that thing to drag out forever and ever. We should come up with some type of plan and not play games." He planned to meet with the Twins and the Vikings officials and others, Perpich said. He had called Twins' owner Cal Griffith to get more information. "She [a woman in Griffith office] said, 'How do you spell that [Perpich] name? Well, I don't know if he's back in town or not. I'll have him return your call,'" but Griffith never called back.

Rudy chose his brother George to be his right-hand operative, concentrating on health and welfare issues. "He's going to get me in trouble every week, but I love him," Perpich said of his outspoken younger brother. "You have got to have somebody like George around. He tells you off twice a week. He'll give you the shirt off his back." George had been unopposed for another four-year senate term in 1976. The hero of feminists with their abortion-rights agenda, and the arch-enemy of Minnesota Citizens Concerned for Life, the state's leading "pro life" organization, in 1977 he became chairman of the Senate Health, Welfare, and Corrections Committee.

Already the governor-designate's days were crowded. While Perpich was driving to Mankato, his secretary, Lynn Anderson, sorted through a pile of mail and read the speaking invitations. An invitation to a cocktail party at the Minikahda Club? "My days of socializing are over," Perpich said. Wayne Thompson and James Heltzer, emissaries from the Twin Cities business community, wrote asking for a dinner meeting. Okay, he would meet with them at his favorite haunt, Farrell's Ice Cream Parlour in Roseville. He declined an invitation to the DFL Party's Victory Dinner on Dec. 13; he had a cousin's wedding to attend. "Your family pays a price [for public office], very obviously, like mine does. You can't totally disregard your family life."

"I'm having fun," he told a reporter. "I'm very excited. How often do you get this opportunity? I'm going to work hard at it." He was afraid, however, that people would think that he'd have no time for them, now that he was a big shot.

At Mankato State University, he received a warm welcome. Before his speech he discussed an upcoming appointment with a regional health official, who said he'd have a tough time finding a qualified minority person to fill the job, as Perpich had hoped to do. Perpich replied, "Well, find me the best unqualified then. That's the only way you are going to get them into the process." Inside he told a faculty group that he'd listen and learn, that he would shoot for at least fifty percent women and minorities in his appointments, and would name a committee, a mix of professional and private citizens from outside his office, to help him with appointments. He rushed off without lunch, saying, "That's really kind of a waste of time." During his years as governor he prided himself on being at the Capitol or on the road by 7:30 a.m. or earlier and working until 10 o'clock or later at night.

On December 29, the dream finally became a reality. Rudy Perpich, forty-eight, was sworn in as the thirty-fourth governor of Minnesota by St. Louis County Court Judge Gail Murray, a friend from Hibbing.[7] He was Minnesota's first governor from the Iron Range and the state's first chief executive of Eastern European ancestry. It was a triumph for the many Range people who had come from countries across the ocean to work in the mines, who had endured hardship and made sacrifices to build a new life and find opportunities for themselves and their families.

There was naturally a good deal of doubt and conjecture about how the new governor would actually perform. He was a stranger to many of the state's four million citizens. Stepping in at mid-term, he had the disadvantage of working with a readymade cabinet and staff inherited from Anderson that hadn't been too friendly to him in the past, and had limited opportunity to pick his own people. He had less than a month to prepare a 1977-79 budget to recommend to the Legislature at a time when money was very tight, and less than two years to prove himself before the 1978 election. Along with Anderson's Palace Guard, much of the political establishment was cool or unenthusiastic about welcoming the new governor who was coming into office by the back door.

Minneapolis Star columnist Jim Klobuchar wrote that when Perpich told his father he was going to be governor, Anton Perpich, still not keen on his son being in politics, said, "Rudy, I better get another bottle of wine."

In an inaugural speech that lasted less than two minutes, given at a simple noon ceremony in the Capitol rotunda, Perpich recalled his boyhood in a poor mining family on the Iron Range. Noting that he could not speak English when he entered kindergarten, he said he was grateful for the opportunities provided him by his hard-working parents and by the state's education system, which had allowed him to rise to be governor. "This could not happen in many parts of the world," he said. "I pledge to work hard so that present and future generations will have the same opportunities I had and will be able to enjoy the highest quality of life and live a little bit better than ever before."

Perpich told reporters he would continue to carry out Anderson's programs and proposals for the 1977 legislative session, including the governor's pledge not to ask for a tax increase. He promised that his administration would not be "status quo" and that "a lot of changes are forthcoming." He said he hoped to build a track record good enough to get himself re-elected to a full four-year term in 1978, and said, "If they'll give me six years, there's no doubt in my mind that other states will be looking at Minnesota [accomplishments] and so will Washington."[8]

It was Minnesotans' first glimpse of the Iron Range governor's style, and most of them loved it, laughing affectionately as they got to know Perpich better. There was no traditional inaugural ball with the governor's Grand March and no fancy parties. He declined offers by scores from individuals and organizations who wanted to sponsor inauguration parties. Perpich said he did not want to waste time and needed to get to work on critical matters before the state.

He set the tone for being a "people's governor" and running an "open, down-to-earth administration," his stated goals, by starting the day attending a polka mass at the Church of the Assumption in St. Paul with his family. He issued a blanket public invitation to the mass, and the one thousand-seat church was overflowing with well-wishers, with many more standing outside. R. Frank Perkovich, pastor of the Church of the Resurrection in Eveleth, who celebrated the mass, referred to the governor as "Rudy" throughout and asked him to be a peacemaker, a community builder, and the "father of the family of Minnesota." Perkovich told Perpich, the first Roman Catholic to be governor since statehood, that his task was to give hope and love to the state. The Joe Cvek polka band, the "Mass-ters," from Eveleth—an accordionist, a guitarist, a bass player, and a drummer—played Yugoslavian ballads and church music, and the congregation joined in singing, "God is love and God is mighty." Perpich invited all citizens of the state to the inaugural ceremony and to an open house in the governor's office to shake hands. Thousands accepted his invitation, including hundreds from the Iron Range, many of whom rose early that morning in -20° F temperatures to drive to St. Paul. With music by the Hibbing High School band, the new governor and First Lady Lola greeted well-wishers until after midnight.

Perpich stepped out of the reception line briefly to sign a certificate of appointment naming Wendell R. Anderson to fill the Senate position vacated by Vice President-elect Walter F. Mondale at 12:01 that day. At 4 p.m. new Governor Perpich signed his first two executive orders. One created a task force on drought aid, and the other established an assistance program providing job security for state employees with chemical-dependency problems.

The next day Perpich issued his first press release as governor. His first order of business, he announced, would be to do what he could to resolve the dispute over Reserve Mining Company's discharge of tailings into Lake Superior, pending the outcome of a court battle over alternative on-land dumping sites. Although he had said the previous day that he would be tough on environmental issues such as Reserve Mining tailing-disposal problems, Perpich's statement was couched in more conciliatory words than Reserve officials might have expected from the man who threw rocks at a steel plant as a youth. "It is extremely important that we not only stop the pollution of Lake Superior, but see to it that the 3,000 people that are dependent on Reserve for their livelihood continue to have jobs," Perpich declared.

His first day in office he put state employees on notice that those not doing their jobs would get their walking papers. "There's not going to be any screwing off as long as I'm governor," he said.[9] As governor, he said, he intended to come to work before most people and stay five, six or seven hours after they were gone, and indeed, he did.

While many DFLers were uneasy about this new, unknown governor, Independent-Republicans were jubilant. They saw Perpich as weak and vulnerable, and eagerly started planning for the 1978 election. State Independent-Republican Chair Charles "Chuck" Slocum felt that while Perpich would not be a pushover, he had little following outside of northern Minnesota and would be far easier for the Republicans to replace as governor than Anderson would have been.

Rudy's passionate love for the state and its people was unquestioned even by those who found fault with the substance behind his spirited style, and laughed at what they considered his foibles. It was the statewide political debut of a man who would become, in time, one of the most colorful, creative, and energetic governors in Minnesota history.

Chapter 7

Coffee Pots. Reserve Mining Company.
Powerlines and Polka. The Stadium. Rosalie Wahl.

Upon assuming office, Perpich was faced with an array of challenges. Reserve Mining was being accused of polluting Lake Superior by dumping taconite tailings into the lake at its Silver Bay plant, a bitter protest was brewing in central Minnesota, led by farmers opposed to the high-voltage power lines that were crossing their land, and various proposals were being floated as to where to locate and how to finance a controversial new sports stadium.

But in the beginning, Minnesotans were fascinated with the unconventional, enthusiastic, energetic new governor, and he wasted little time before starting to shake up the state bureaucracy. He ordered the Minnesota Patrol to begin strict enforcement of the state's 55-miles-an-hour speed limit, which he said would save gasoline. He disconnected coffee pots in state offices and urged citizens to turn down thermostats to save energy during a critical heating-oil shortage. He made good on his promise to crack down on government spending and "show the door" to employees who weren't doing their jobs.

One evening early in his administration, Perpich summoned state department heads to a meeting at the governor's mansion and ordered them to get rid of employees who weren't doing their jobs, make drastic cuts in paper work, and determine whether all the space available in the 2,600 state facilities was genuinely needed. He said he would back them if they decided a facility should be closed or an employee dismissed. He called for a reduction in the Department of Welfare's medical assistance program. "That's going to break us if it continues," he warned Commissioner Vera Likins. "We'll just have to get tough with all those vendors, doctors, pharmacists and others who provide medical services. Tell people it's not open-ended. We can't afford it."

He halted the buying of file cabinets, to reduce paper proliferation. He ordered a moratorium on buying new state cars and a check to determine whether all the cars in use were really needed.

Perpich, who did almost no traveling outside of Minnesota in his first term, asked all state officials to cut out-of-state travel by one-third, which he said would save an estimated $750,000 in the next year. He named Robert Goff, an advertising partner of senate majority leader Nicholas Coleman, to head a new task force charged with eliminating waste in state government. He created a "citizens' advocate" post in the governor's office to help people cut through government red tape and assist those who had problems with state agencies.[1]

On January 5 Perpich delivered his first State of the State message, the most formal ceremony of the session, to a joint assemblage of the Minnesota Legislature, constitutional officers, and Supreme Court justices in robes, who were each announced individually by the Sergeant-at-Arms and then escorted into the House chamber by members of the National Guard in full-dress uniforms. The new governor raced through his speech in typical Rudy-Perpich-style, without pausing for applause. He asked lawmakers to approve what he termed the farthest-reaching and most comprehensive energy-saving program ever considered by any state, cutting energy use by 10 percent and providing alternative energy sources in government buildings. The governor called for making Minnesota a "model of excellence" in health research in the U.S. through substantial state aid to facilities at the University of Minnesota, the Mayo Clinic in Rochester, and state agencies. He said he would put a major emphasis on both providing jobs and environmental protection in his 1977 legislative program, declaring the two goals compatible.

Perhaps the most important measure of a governor's performance is how well he does with his legislative agenda, however, and the 1977 legislative session was a major test for Perpich. While legislators were wary about how to treat the popular new governor, they were, as always, independent and jealous when it came to opening the state purse. They praised Perpich for proposing in his two-year, $6.35 billion state budget to return an expected $183-million surplus to taxpayers, though there were questions as to exactly how such a thing might be brought about. His top tax priority was to simplify the individual income-tax form to give what he said would be a permanent $100-million tax reduction, but he never submitted a specific plan to that effect, and the Legislature scrapped the idea.

He asked for $20 million for stepped-up health research at the University of Minnesota and elsewhere; after the governor reduced his request several times, the Legislature approved a token appropriation of $1.5 million. He supported successful legislation initiated by others for $18 million in bonds to finance trails for cross-country skiers, hikers, and bicycle riders. He called for increasing the bonding authority of the Housing Finance Agency from $600 million to $900 million to provide more low-income housing; the Legislature authorized $300 million. His proposals for a big boost in the summer youth-employment program, and for a new Department of Economic Security, with responsibility for financial assistance programs, work training, rehabilitation and job placement, were approved by the Legislature.

"Perpich appears to be riding a great wave of popularity as a result of his unorthodox and unpretentious style," Steven Dornfeld wrote in the *Minneapolis Tribune*. But overall, Perpich's 1977 legislative record was spotty. While he was engaged in such activities as ordering the removal of coffee pots from his office as a protest to rising energy prices, donating his pay raise for the purchase of bocce balls for Minnesota communities, and meeting with just about any individual or group who asked to see him, he was losing major portions of his legislative program in the heavily DFL-Senate and House. Unlike his predecessor, Wendell Anderson, Perpich played almost no role in the formulation of the massive tax bill passed by the Legislature that year.

One of the most unusual traits of the new governor was his openness. Governors before and after Perpich went about their business in their private offices, and often the press and public didn't know the nature of the meetings or who was there. But Perpich's staff issued detailed daily schedules of his office meetings, and reporters and the public were free to walk into almost any of them. He believed so strongly in openness he threatened to take the doors off of his office. That irked many who wanted to speak with the governor privately, as well as some advisers, who thought there were things the governor ought to do without reporters listening.

Rudy also dismayed his staff by disappearing from his office for days at a time without telling them where he was going, to personally investigate issues such as the dispute over a 400-kilovolt power line in west central Minnesota.

One night the governor was billed as the main speaker at a $50-a-person Minnesota House DFL fundraising dinner at the Leamington Hotel in Minneapolis. Representative Carl Johnson, master of ceremonies, introduced Perpich, joking, "You know, Rudy, you can do the polka a hell of a lot better than you can speak." When the audience laughed, Perpich said, "I think they agree with you, Carl," and asked whether the crowd of about 600 people wanted to hear him speak or do the polka. Shouts of "Polka, polka," drowned out the few who called "Speech." So the governor stepped down from the head table, grabbed a surprised but delighted waitress and whirled her around the dance floor to the rousing polka music of the Vic Tedesco band. The audience loved it. House and Senate leaders, top state officials in the audience, and legislators and their spouses stood and clapped in time to the music as Perpich and the waitress in her apron hopped, skipped, and jumped around the ballroom.

"I love this job. I'm just like a teenager in love," the governor said. His schedule was jam-packed, and it would remain so throughout his political career. If people wanted to meet with him, and he was booked during normal working hours, he would have them come at 5:30 in the morning or at night, frequently late, to the governor's mansion. "There are some people who don't require more than four or five hours of sleep," he said. "I've been like that all my life. If I went to bed at 10, I'd be up at 2:30 in the morning."[2]

Perpich would point out to reporters and others the vacant spots at the top of the walls in the reception room of the governor's office. Those, he said, were purposely left empty by Capitol architect Cass Gilbert for future portraits of the greatest governors, and that was where he wanted his picture to be some day.

When he took office Perpich kept many holdovers from the Anderson administration in his cabinet and staff, but he nevertheless had more than 100 appointments to make, mostly to state boards and commissions. A longtime advocate of involving more women and minorities in government, Perpich reiterated that his goal would be to give them half of the openings. He established an Open Appointments Commission to help him find qualified people for those appointments and announced that any eligible citizen could apply for a position. He appointed Gloria Griffin, a feisty feminist from Tonka Bay who had recently lost a congressional campaign, to chair the commission. She had approached Perpich after the election, asking for jobs for five women on her campaign staff—a common practice among losing candidates—but Perpich told her, "I don't do 'plums.'" He liked the gutsy Griffin, however, and before taking office as governor he put her in charge of a committee to find a new Pollution Control Agency (PCA) commissioner and promised he'd appoint a woman. The committee submitted the names of several women, including Sandra Gardebring, a 30-year-old PCA staff lawyer, and one man, John Herman, a lawyer and leading environmentalist. At a dinner held for the candidates to meet the governor, Perpich asked Griffin if they should tell Herman he didn't have a chance since the job was going to a woman, but Griffin said no. On his first day in office, Perpich named Gardebring the executive director of the Pollution Control Agency, his first Cabinet appointment. In time she became one of his favorite troubleshooters, and he later named her to a succession of high positions—chair of the Metropolitan Council, commissioner of the Department of Human Services, justice of the Minnesota Court of Appeals, and justice of the Minnesota Supreme Court.

In filling vacancies Perpich relied heavily upon the recommendations of the Open Appointents Commission; in many cases he was not acquainted with those whose names were submitted by the commission before his initial interviews with them. During the Commission's first year, half of the appointments were women or minorities.

One of Perpich's most difficult tasks upon assuming office was to find a chief of staff to replace Tom Kelm, who had been credited for much of Anderson's success as governor. Kelm was headed to Washington with the newly-appointed U.S. senator. The governor first approached Commissioner of Finance Gerald Christenson, who, not wanting to leave his commissioner post, turned him down. His second choice was DFL State Representative Harry (Tex) Sieben III of Hastings. Sieben was a successful trial lawyer and a politically savvy, veteran legislator, whose family had been politically powerful in Dakota County going back to the early 1900s. But Tex, who liked being in the Legislature and had just been re-elected, felt an obligation to stay there.[3] (Sieben became Speaker in 1980, and he and Perpich were close allies.)

Perpich eventually turned to Tom Kelm and others on former Governor Anderson's staff for suggestions for a chief of staff. One evening the group was brainstorming in Kelm's office when Anderson walked in and said, "I have another suggestion, Terry Montgomery."[4] When Perpich called Montgomery, a 38-year-old Sauk Rapids DFL activist and moderate, and asked if he might be interested in "that Kelm job," Terry said he was, and the governor invited him to Hibbing to talk about it. Montgomery discussed it with Rudy and Lola in their kitchen over hot fudge sundaes, and he was hired. Montgomery took a two-year leave from his job as vice-president for university relations at St. Cloud State College. He had worked as a reporter for the *Minneapolis Tribune* and for WCCO-TV, and had run unsuccessfully for Congress in 1970 against Sixth District Congressman John Zwach, a Republican. Slim and with immaculately coiffed blonde hair, Montgomery was a dapper dresser given to wearing cowboy boots. He drove a Corvette and owned radio stations in Princeton and Little Falls.

The legendary Kelm had not only been Anderson's executive secretary and chief staff aide, but also his political strategist and legislative lobbyist and a tough fighter. Representative Ernest Lindstrom, Richfield Republican and a House majority leader when Conservatives were in control, described Kelm as "the Boss Tweed of the governor's office." Montgomery, on the other hand, was a facilitator, friendly with the press, skillful in promoting his boss, and adept at putting a positive spin on the governor's ideas and actions.

Early in Perpich's first term a dispute arouse when two power companies, the United Power Association of Elk River and the Cooperative Power Association of Edina, announced plans jointly to build a 430-mile power transmission line from North Dakota to just west of the Twin Cities. Farmers and anti-powerline protesters, concerned about the health and safety hazards of the high voltage line, called legislative hearings "charades" and asked the governor and Legislature to impose a moratorium on the construction. But even sympathetic legislators feared a moratorium would be ruled unconstitutional, and that the state would incur a heavy financial liability for such an action.

On the Monday immediately following his State of the State address, Perpich turned words into action, by driving out to listen to and talk with the farm people and local officials of Pope County regarding their views on the power-line controversy. Unaccompanied by staff aides, reporters, security men, or a driver, and without letting his staff know where he was going, Perpich simply showed up for a surprise visit on the doorsteps of west-central Minnesota farmers, intent on finding out for himself what was happening.[5]

Upon his return to St. Paul, Perpich expressed the belief that he had succeeded in getting people to "cool off for a time" and let the legislative process work instead of going to court. He also criticized the power companies for not talking with the people themselves. But when angry farmers later chased utility surveyors and construction crews from their fields with tractors and other farm machines, and toppled completed power-towers at night, drawing the attention of national media, Perpich responded to the request of the Pope County sheriff for assistance by dispatching State Patrol officers to keep the peace. Finally, a year later, on January 6, 1978, after a gathering of protesters confronted the patrol and other law enforcement officers who were guarding utility property, Perpich ordered more than two hundred additional patrol officers to the scene to maintain order in what had become a potentially violent situation. Perpich later said that he and his administration had spent more time on the power-line dispute than anything else and had "gone the extra mile to act with justice and humane concern for the rights of all parties" in trying to resolve the controversy. He even called for a scientific study of the issues involved by a science court, although the suggestion came to naught when no agreement could be reached on how it would operate. (The science court was actually suggested by Joseph [Joe] Perpich, Rudy's brother, whom the governor frequently consulted when he was struggling with tough problems, especially on medical and science matters.)

The Legislature eventually passed, and the governor signed into law, a bill that substantially increased the compensation paid to owners of land crossed by power lines.[6]

Another hot issue landed on the governor's desk when the Minnesota Vikings football team demanded a new covered stadium and threatened to leave Minnesota unless they got it. Minneapolis business people who wanted to tear down the old outdoor Metropolitan Stadium in Bloomington and build a new one downtown pledged financial backing for part of the cost. Harvey MacKay, Vikings booster and former president of the Minneapolis Chamber of Commerce, warned that if the Vikings and Twins were to leave Minnesota "We'd be well on our way to being a frozen Omaha." Polls showed that the majority of voters were adamantly against public financing for a new stadium.[7] Bloomington and St. Paul community and business leaders opposed a downtown Minneapolis site. House Speaker Martin Sabo of Minneapolis wanted the stadium in his city and used his powerful influence to that end. Perpich backed a "no site" bill for a new "Hubert H. Humphrey Metrodome" sports stadium. Representative Al Patton, a DFLer from Sartell and a capable legislator, was picked to carry the bill because he was from outside the Twin Cities area and presumably neutral on the stadium location. Perpich invited about 20 lukewarm legislators, including Iron Rangers, to his office in groups of threes and fours to lobby them, with marked success. The legislation was passed and signed by the governor. It provided for a two-percent hotel-motel liquor tax in the seven-county metropolitan area to finance a new stadium, but the location and design were left up to a seven-member citizens stadium commission to be appointed by the governor. Perpich set up an advisory committee to help him find appointees and specified only that the commissioners be broadly representative. He said he never asked prospective commission members what site they would vote for.[8]

Perpich called his friend Ron Gornick about 10:30 one night, and Gornick asked, "Rudy, what the heck are you doing up working this late?" The governor told Gornick, "You know us god-darned Iron Rangers work hard. We work steady." He said the Legislature had passed the stadium bill, and he wanted his first appointment to the new stadium commission to be Gornick. The Chisholm gas station/motel owner was just stepping down from former Governor Anderson's Small Business Task Force and had doubts about taking on a new government job but reluctantly agreed. Perpich named Dan

Brutger, owner of a St. Cloud construction company which eventually included the 11-state Thrifty Scott Motel chain, to be the chairman. Brutger, whom Perpich didn't know and who had never been active in politics, was recommended by Perpich's chief of staff Montgomery who came from St. Cloud. With this project as with everything, the governor was a demanding taskmaster who wanted things done in a hurry. Gornick said, "With Rudy Perpich it was, 'Here's your job. Do it, and let's do it quick,' and sometimes that's how you get into trouble because you go faster than the wheels of government can move. When he got angry, he'd chew people out. I was in his company when he did that to a few," Gornick said.[9]

As it turned out, Gornick cast the deciding vote in favor of a Minneapolis site when the other commission members were split 3-3 between Minneapolis and Bloomington. (When Al Quie defeated Perpich in 1978, Gornick asked the new Republican governor to reappoint him and other members to the commission, so they could finish getting the new $72 million stadium built and paid for, and Quie did.) However, the stadium law was ruled unconstitutional because it wasn't passed by 60 percent of both legislative bodies, the vote required for bonding bills. The two-percent liquor tax in the bill also was ruled unconstitutional. In 1979, after more political wrangling, Governor Quie signed new legislation for a $55-million domed stadium in Minneapolis, financed by local business donations and a limited hotel-motel and liquor tax within a special tax district in the area of the stadium.)

Perpich delegated problems to his staff and commissioners less often than Wendell Anderson and other governors had, more frequently checking them out himself. Nothing seemed too trivial to get his attention. He asked state government agencies and employees and their families to stop using non-returnable beverage containers. He arrived unannounced in the tiny town of Milan, in western Minnesota, to talk with residents who were complaining about their telephone service and rates. He backed a bill to legalize Laetrile, a purported anti-cancer substance that medical and national cancer experts said was worthless; the bill never became law. (His medical-doctor brother, Joe, was at odds with Rudy on the merits of Laetrile.) He ordered that a permanent Christmas tree be planted in front of the Capitol, rather than hauling one in every year. He went out to meet with community groups on Hiawatha Avenue in Minneapolis who wanted Hiawatha to be a boulevard with a light-rail transit system, rather than a freeway.

Speaking on Minnesota Public Radio one morning, Rudy revealed that after the legislative session ended, he planned to hit the road and drop in at shopping centers for three or four hours at a time to talk with people. "I think a lot of things are being solved because we're listening to people," he said. When a northeastern Minnesota woman called to tell him about a problem, he asked for her phone number and promised to visit her that weekend. He promised to travel to every community in Minnesota in the next year—and he did show up in many, if not all of them.

Perpich was a fan of bocce ball, an Italian game similar to lawn bowling that was popular on the Iron Range, and said he'd like to set up a bocce ball court in every community in the state. One afternoon Rudy Boschwitz, the owner of a chain of retail building supplies stores and later a Republican U.S. senator from Minnesota, happened to be in the governor's office for the signing of a proclamation. Perpich challenged Boschwitz to a game of bocce ball to start the program. Boschwitz told reporters after the cordial visit of the two Rudys that Perpich was going to be hard for Republicans to beat in 1978 and said, "He's very personable, very nice. The last time I was here, Wendy Anderson was just like a stick by comparison."[10] Perpich succeeded in bringing the annual National Bocce Tournament to Minnesota in 1986, the first to be held away from the West Coast.

Perpich rejected the advice of friends who suggested he take lessons to improve his image on television. "I'm not a fancy Dan," he said. His unpredictability, openness, and plain-folks manner continued to push his poll ratings upward. The Minnesota Poll published April 10, 1977, by the *Minneapolis Tribune* reported that the electorate was giving Perpich high marks for job performance. Perpich scored higher in the poll than any chief executive in recent history during the early months of the term, far exceeding expectations.

But the problem of Reserve Mining Company's alleged pollution of Lake Superior was threatening to extinguish the glow.

Reserve Mining

It had been argued from the beginning by interested parties that there was no need to worry about Reserve Mining Company's discharge of taconite tailings into Lake Superior at its Silver Bay plant.[11] Dr. E. W. Davis, the University of Minnesota professor who had directed the original taconite research and was widely known as Mr. Taconite, had urged at public hearings that Reserve be allowed to discharge its waste into the lake freely, rather than being required to put the tailings on land, which would be an expensive operation. "You will never see the slightest tinge of red" in the lake from the tailings, he said. "Chemically they will have no effect whatever on the lake." Opponents argued that Reserve would be making a dumping ground out of one of the most beautiful lakes in the world. In the end the company got its permits, built the Silver Bay plant, and named it the E. W. Davis Works.

In the ensuing years there were worrisome claims of pollution. In 1969 Charles Stoddard, a top regional official of the U. S. Interior Department, released without the approval of Interior Secretary Stewart Udall a report of a major study showing the dumping of taconite waste was polluting Lake Superior.[12] Stoddard was denounced by Reserve, which said the study was riddled with errors, and Udall distanced himself from it. Among those attacking the report, saying it did not prove there was pollution, was Congressman John Blatnik. A May, 1969, *New York Times* article reported that Blatnik had tried to suppress the release of the controversial Stoddard report, which the Minnesota congressman denied. Subsequent editorials in the *Times* and the *Washington Post* questioned Blatnik's standing as "Mr. Water Pollution Control."

In 1972, William Ruckelshaus, Environmental Protection Agency (EPA) administrator, got the go-ahead for court action, although some aides to President Nixon, including Minnesotan Maurice Stans, his secretary of commerce, were not keen on suing a powerful business such as Reserve. The U.S. Department of Justice, with the assistance of the EPA, filed a lawsuit, *United States v. Reserve Mining Company*, with environmental groups joining in. The plaintiffs' claims of pollution from the taconite tailings were bolstered by mid-1973 announcements by the EPA and the Minnesota Pollution Control Agency (PCA), now headed by Grant Merritt, that effluent from Reserve's Silver Bay plant and the drinking water of North Shore residents contained a high concentration of asbestos-like fibers, a known human carcinogen. With the colorful and outspoken federal Judge Miles Lord sitting on the bench, it became a nationally-publicized landmark case for the emerging environmental movement versus big business.

Judge Lord ordered a halt to the dumping into Lake Superior. Reserve appealed, and the Eighth Circuit Court of Appeals found that Reserve was polluting Lake Superior with a potentially injurious asbestos-type fiber. They ordered Reserve to find an on-land disposal site and then remanded the case back to the federal district court in Minnesota.

U.S. District Judge Edward Devitt fined Reserve a total penalty of $837,500 for violations of its discharge permits prohibiting clouding or discoloration or adverse effects on public water supplies, and ordered the company to halt its discharge into Lake Superior by midnight, July 7, 1977. If the company did not have an approved on-land disposal site by then, it would be forced to shut down its open-pit mining operation at Babbitt, Minnesota, which employed about 3,000 workers.[13]

Stoddard was vindicated by the federal courts, which ruled that Reserve was polluting Lake Superior with potentially injurious asbestos-type fibers.[14]

Reserve then proposed to switch the dumping to the so-called Milepost 7 site. The State of Minnesota rejected that site; state officials and environmentalists favored a more costly Milepost 20 site, which they believed to be safer because it was farther from populated areas. Spokesmen for the Department of Natural Resources (DNR) and environmentalists expressed concerns about the safety of dams which would have to be higher at Milepost 7, and said dam failure there would result in the tailings waste flowing back into Lake Superior. Reserve appealed in state court, saying it couldn't operate profitably at the Milepost 20 location, and would close the Silver Bay plant rather than use it. On January 31, 1978, a panel of three state district judges overruled the PCA and DNR and ordered them to issue the permits Reserve needed to use Milepost 7. The PCA and DNR appealed to the Supreme Court, asking it to uphold their administrative rejections of Milepost 7 on environmental and public-health grounds.

While the court deliberated, many, including leaders of organized labor, were waiting nervously to see what Perpich would do about Reserve, recalling that he had wrangled with the company for years over a host of issues. There were fears that the new governor would seek tough sanctions against Reserve, triggering the closing of the taconite plant, although Perpich pledged in his State of the State message that a way would be found to stop Reserve from discharging taconite tailings into Lake Superior and at the same time preserve the jobs of workers.

Lieutenant Governor Perpich had accused Reserve of engineering the removal of U.S. District Judge Miles Lord from the pollution case after Lord, in April, 1974, ordered a halt to the dumping in the lake. The U.S. Eighth Circuit Court of Appeals in St. Louis had removed Lord from the case, saying he had become an advocate for the plaintiffs and had exhibited a "gross bias" against the Silver Bay taconite processing company. "Reserve Mining Company polluted Lake Superior, endangered the health of North Shore residents, and had an effective judge removed from the case," Perpich had said at the time.[15]

Governor Wendell Anderson had proposed giving Reserve up to $70 million in state tax credits to build an acceptable disposal system at the Milepost 20 site, but Perpich did not immediately endorse that idea. After he took office as governor, Perpich, with Reserve threatening to shut its Silver Bay plant, said he was preparing a bill to put Reserve property on property-tax rolls; the company then was paying production taxes in lieu of property taxes. He also proposed an increase in the taconite production tax to be used to give income protection to the Reserve employees who would lose their jobs if the mining company closed the plant.

The Reserve dispute widened the split between Perpich and Attorney General Warren Spannaus. Perpich flew to Cleveland on March 1, against Spannaus's advice, to meet with officials of Reserve Mining Company. He had ducked out of sight the previous two days, missing a National Governors Association meeting he was scheduled to attend and once again did not inform his top aides where he was going. He said on his return he had been preparing for the Cleveland meetings and had talked with people who were knowledgeable about the issue, including former Governor Elmer L. Andersen, who had led the fight for the Taconite Amendment, and whom Perpich respected and consulted frequently. The mining officials, in what Perpich called an "eyeball to eyeball" meeting, agreed to a plan pushed by Perpich, under which neither side would appeal the forthcoming Minnesota Supreme Court ruling on Reserve's disposal site. But Spannaus, whose lawyers had been battling for years to get the company to stop dumping into Lake Superior, at first refused to go along, much to Perpich's chagrin. Spannaus said it was up to the attorney general to make the final decision whether to appeal and said he didn't want to have his hands tied. Perpich argued that it was up to the plaintiffs, the heads of the Pollution Control Agency and Department of Natural Resources. Perpich denied there was any serious rift between him and Spannaus. "We differ on this taconite thing, but my brother, George, and I also differ on issues," he said.

The controversy was also dividing the DFL Party in other ways. Miles Lord threatened to resign his judicial office and run against U.S. Senator Wendell Anderson, who reportedly favored the Milepost 7 site if it were found environmentally acceptable.[16]

The Minnesota Supreme Court on April 9, 1977, unanimously ruled in favor of the Milepost 7 site preferred by Reserve. The court ordered two state environmental agencies to issue permits allowing the company to dispose of taconite waste at the site, subject to stringent conditions designed to protect the environment and alleviate the potential health threat from the asbestos-type fibers. The opinion written by Associate Justice James Otis said the "undisputed evidence" showed that safe dams could be built at Milepost 7 to contain the taconite waste.

The ruling dismayed state attorneys and environmentalists who opposed Milepost 7. It was also a blow for Spannaus, who said he was disappointed but saw no grounds to further appeal the case. On April 22, State Auditor Robert Mattson, in a major turnabout, withdrew his opposition to the use of Milepost 7. Mattson, a vocal critic of that site, revealed his decision in a letter to fellow members of the state Executive Council and the Land Exchange Review Board, two panels whose approval was required to transfer certain state-owned lands needed by Reserve for the disposal site. Saying he shared the disappointment of the other constitutional officers who were members of those boards, Mattson wrote, "However, the Supreme Court has made its decision, and I accept it." Other state officials also came around, including Spannaus and State Treasurer Jim Lord, the son of Miles Lord, the federal judge.

Judge Devitt lifted his order requiring Reserve to halt its discharge into Lake Superior by midnight July 7, on condition that the company begin work at the Milepost 7 on-land disposal site immediately and make every "reasonable effort" to halt completely the lake discharge by April 15, 1980. Reserve had suggested that date, saying it could make the switch by then, provided it received the go-ahead from the state.

On July 7, 1978, the long dispute finally came to an end when Perpich announced an agreement under which Reserve Mining Company would remain in Minnesota and construct an in-land taconite tailing disposal facility at Milepost 7. He was joined at a press conference to make the announcement by Reserve Mining president Merlyn Woodle and William Verity and William De Lancey, chairmen respectively of Reserve's parent companies, Armco and Republic Steel of Ohio. The new $370 million Milepost 7 disposal basin would be the largest pollution-abatement program ever undertaken in Minnesota, and the plant would be operational by April 15, 1980, they said. "The new facility will satisfy all of the conditions necessary to protect and enhance our environment," the governor promised. Perpich praised Reserve for its perseverance in becoming the first large-scale taconite mining and processing company in the world and hailed the company as "a cornerstone of the economy of northeastern Minnesota."

Perpich had steadfastly refused to state his position on the merits of Milepost 7, saying that the site question would be settled in the courts and that his opinion was unimportant. The next year, in his 1978 State of the State speech, Perpich said Milepost 7 was not his first choice, but added, "In our democracy there is a system of law to resolve disputes. If democracy is to endure, our respect for the law must also endure."

Perpich and Spannaus, whose offices were across the hall from each other on the first floor of the Capitol, were increasingly at odds over other issues. The attorney general was angry when the governor publicly embarrassed Spannaus's good friend, Wes Lane, director of the Division of Emergency Services, by ordering Lane home from the presidential inaugural in Washington because of the energy crisis. And when Perpich directed state officials to take out their car phones in an economy move, Spannaus, who had a phone in his privately-owned car, refused to do so, saying he needed to be available for emergencies. Perpich, who took the radio telephone out of his own car, said he hadn't meant to include Spannaus in the order.

Spannaus's office felt the governor was over-zealous and meddling in the attorney general's domain on other matters. Both were members of the Land Exchange Board and at odds over the sale of wetlands by private owners to the federal government. Some county boards had refused to endorse the sales to the U.S. Fish and Wildlife Service, believing that Perpich and Natural Resources Commissioner William Nye had told them that the Land Exchange Board had given counties the right to veto the federal sales. But Spannaus told the counties that the board had no right to delegate that authority and said he had never taken that position as a member of the board. Conservationists accused Perpich of jeopardizing the wetlands program.

Again, when Perpich said he would ask Spannaus for an opinion on the constitutionality of an expense-payment increase legislators gave themselves, Spannaus reportedly thought Perpich was passing the buck on a sticky political issue and balked. Perpich dropped the request.

When Minnesota Supreme Court Justice Harry McLaughlin went to the federal bench, there was a vacancy on the state court to be filled by the governor. Perpich called Sandy Keith, informing him that he planned to fulfill a promise he had made to the DFL Feminist Caucus earlier that year by appointing a woman. He was considering several women in a well-publicized search: Hennepin Municipal Judge Diana Murphy, (who later became the first woman appointed to the federal bench from Minnesota and the first woman appointee to the U. S. Eighth Circuit Court of Appeals); Roberta Levy, a University of Minnesota law professor (who later became the first female Hennepin County District chief judge); Delores Orey, a St. Paul lawyer who taught at William Mitchell College of Law, and Rosalie Wahl, a William Mitchell College of Law associate professor and director of the school's criminal justice clinical program, who had worked as a public defender.[17]

Wahl, 52, had strong support from DFL feminists as well as the Minnesota Women's Political Caucus and Minnesota Women

Lawyers. A divorced, single parent, she had a soft-spoken manner and compassion for those less fortunate than herself which reflected her Quaker faith and belied her toughness. Determined and plucky, she decided to attend law school at age 38, because "I was tired of sitting outside doors waiting for the men inside to make the decisions."[18] She earned her law degree in 1967, attending William Mitchell while raising five children, the youngest born during her second year in law school. Perpich called her in for an interview and asked what her positions were on abortion and capital punishment. She told the governor she was a "pro choice" supporter of abortion rights and opposed capital punishment.[19] He took her into an adjoining office to talk with several advisers: Nicholas Coleman, the senate majority leader; Hy Berman, University of Minnesota history professor; Montgomery, the governor's chief of staff, and William (Bill) Kennedy, Hennepin County chief public defender. After she left, Perpich called for written votes. Later he sent her the five pieces of paper which were 4-1 for Wahl's appointment including the governor's "yes" vote. Perpich told Keith he liked Wahl, and he intended to appoint her. "He picked the most perfect one," said Keith.

Just before Perpich announced his decision, DFL feminist leaders Koryne Horbal and Jeri Rasmussen visited with the governor at the mansion late at night, securing a final, firm commitment from him to appoint Wahl. They knew critics would say that Wahl lacked judicial experience, but, Horbal said, "She had life experience. That's why we supported her."[20] On June 3, when Secretary of State Joan Growe announced at the Minnesota Women's Meeting in St. Cloud, as the governor asked her to do, that Wahl would be the first woman appointed to the state Supreme Court, three thousand ecstatic women rose to their feet cheering. Many jumped into their cars and formed an impromptu cavalcade through the city, ringing bells and shouting. The governor also announced the appointment of Wahl that night in Hibbing, speaking at the high school graduation of his son, Rudy Jr.

The history-making appointment was the pay-off for years of campaigning by the women's rights movement. Wahl, speaking at the St. Cloud meeting, called it a high-water mark for women of Minnesota. She remembered generations of women who had gone before them, advocates for those whose rights had been denied or infringed, women who had to obey laws they had no part in making and could not vote for those who did, and for those who could not speak in public. "Every person—poor or rich, black or red or brown or white, male or female—has the right to equal justice under law. I will endeavor, with the other members of the Court, to make this dream a reality," she promised.

Wahl was sworn in on October 3, taking her seat along with the eight men on the Court. She said of her personal feelings when she became the first woman to don the robe of the high court, "It felt great. It was the job I had always wanted and never knew existed." She had never dreamed of that kind of a vocation because women just had never aspired to such a high position.[21] Addressing the court, she said she was awed and humbled, and that she would endeavor, with the other members of the Court, to make equal justice under law a reality for all.

But many in the legal establishment considered Perpich's choice outrageous, charging that

Governor Perpich congratulating newly sworn in associate judge Rosalie Wahl

Wahl was lacking in trial court experience and credentials, while overlooking the fact that she brought a new dimension to the high court with her criminal defense background.

Nor was such criticism merely talk. In 1978 Wahl had to run for election. Supreme Court justices rarely faced serious challenges in those days, but a bevy of candidates lined up to dispute Wahl's seat on the bench. Keith, who supported Wahl, said, "All the Democrats ran against her: Mattson [former Attorney General Robert Mattson], Foley [Olmsted County District Judge Daniel Foley], Plunkett [St. Paul Municipal Judge J. Jerome Plunkett]. We had to beat them all, and we did."

Wahl campaigned hard, eliminating Foley and Plunkett in the September primary and soundly defeating Mattson, after a heated contest, in the November general election. She became a respected member of the Court, albeit too liberal for some. She was re-elected in 1984 and in 1990 and reached the mandatory retirement age of 70 in 1994. During her 17 years on the court, she built a national reputation for defending the rights of the poor and people of color.[22]

In 1989, 12 years after Perpich had appointed her to the court, he wrote to her, praising her work. "I hear that Rosalie Wahl is not only an unusually astute justice but also that she has mentored many an upcoming [sic] young attorney," he wrote. "There cannot be too many caring people in this world. Thank you for confirming my trust in both your ability and what you have done and continue to do for the women and the judicial system of Minnesota."

Perpich appointed Harriet Lansing, 33, the first woman judge on the Ramsey County Municipal Court (as it was called then, before municipal and district courts were merged.) She had been the first female St. Paul city attorney. About six months after she had been appointed, Perpich heard of disparaging remarks being made about Justice Wahl by other members of the court. Concerned that Lansing also was finding a not-so-supportive atmosphere, he showed up one day with a red rose to boost her morale. In 1983, Perpich appointed Judge Lansing and another woman, Judge Susanne Sedgwick of the Hennepin County District Court, to the new Court of Appeals. Sedgwick had become the only female judge in the state when, in 1970, she ran and was elected, with the support of Young Turk lawyers, against a sitting judge for Hennepin County Municipal Court. She later become the first woman judge on the Hennepin County District Court.

While Perpich enjoyed having the power to help women crack the glass ceiling and to right other wrongs, there were other parts of his job he didn't like. Once a National Guard officer came in to tell the governor they had to end the search for a hunter who had disappeared in the north woods. The Guard had gone all out, but could not sacrifice men and helicopters to continue the search. The hunter had been lost for too many days for there to be any hope left. Perpich was dismayed and asked, "Do I really have to call the widow and tell her we're giving up?" The officer said, "Yes," he had to do that, and by now, there were three or four troopers in the room. Tears welled up in the governor's eyes, and he took off his glasses to wipe them away. "God, this is awful. Just a few more hours [search] tonight?" Perpich pleaded. The officer said regretfully they really could not get a plane in the air because of bad weather, and they had to call it off. Gloria Griffin, who was present, said she'd never seen Perpich so sad. The governor asked everyone to leave him alone and said, "I'll do it as soon as I collect myself." Griffin recalled, "He looked so forlorn sitting alone at his desk as we all trooped out. It was not fun."[23]

He hated being on the Board of Pardons and called it a "primitive, Neanderthal" system. (The Board of Pardons consists of the governor, the attorney general, and the chief justice of the Supreme Court. It has the authority to grant pardons and commutations.) He told Griffin, "Gloria, having a man's life in your hands–that's terrible—isn't it? There's got to be a better way."

In August, following an operation, doctors announced that U.S. Senator Hubert Humphrey had widespread and inoperable pelvic cancer. The news fell like a political bombshell. It didn't seem likely he could serve out his term, which would end in 1982. Perpich quietly started meeting with a few close friends and advisers about the possibility of Humphrey not completing his term.

Perpich's popularity continued high. A Minnesota Poll published by the *Minneapolis Tribune* in October found that 56 percent of those surveyed thought he was doing an excellent or good job. In a test race for governor, conducted by the poll, Perpich outpolled Independent-Republican Congressman Albert Quie, a potential opponent unfamiliar to many outside his First District in southeastern Minnesota, by a margin of 25 percentage points. Fifty-three percent of those interviewed said they would vote for Perpich, 28 percent said Quie, and 19 percent were undecided. The Minnesota Poll also found that most respondents in the survey—57 percent—thought state government operated efficiently, compared with 42 percent who held that opinion in 1973 when Wendell Anderson was governor. While Perpich's activist image as governor was probably a factor, the state budget was now solidly in the black and that also contributed to his popularity with voters.

Chapter 8

The Minnesota Massacre

Senator Hubert Humphrey lost his long battle with cancer and died January 13, 1978. Minnesota mourned, and President Carter and other U.S. leaders attended his nationally televised funeral in St. Paul. The death of the "Happy Warrior" marked the end of a political era, and Republican Party leaders had high hopes of regaining a U.S. Senate seat as the winds of political change began to blow.

State law required that the governor appoint a successor to serve until November, when a special election would be held to fill out the remaining four years of Humphrey's term. Cars streamed in and out of the iron gates at the governor's residence, as Perpich conferred with advisers, interviewed potential appointees, and weighed his momentous decision. His good friend Nick Coleman wanted the job. Fifth District Congressman Don Fraser announced his candidacy for the fall election. Robert Short was also planning to run. Humphrey's widow, Muriel, was an obvious candidate, possibly as a caretaker until the fall election, if she were willing. In the coming general election the future of the DFL Party which Humphrey had fathered three decades earlier would be at stake, with two U.S. Senate seats, seats in the Minnesota House, the governorship and other constitutional offices up for grabs.

It was a tough decision, and Perpich played it safe by picking Muriel Humphrey, thinking that few would criticize the appointment of the widow of the beloved Hubert Humphrey. It wasn't clear that she wanted it or would accept it, however, and the governor conferred at great length with Bruce Solomonson, her son-in-law, about how to proceed.[1] On the afternoon of January 24, Governor Perpich's office sent word to the Capitol press room that the governor was flying to Fort Lauderdale, Florida, to ask Muriel Humphrey to take the Senate seat for the next nine months. A dozen reporters and photographers scrambled to get tickets for the evening flight, some of whom did not have time to run home to pack a suitcase. The flight made several stops along the way, and it was 2 a.m. when the weary entourage checked in at The Barefoot Mailman Hotel in Hillsboro Beach.

At 11 a.m. the next morning Perpich held a press conference in the lobby of the ocean-front apartment building where Humphrey was visiting her daughter, Nancy Solomonson, and Nancy's husband Bruce. The white-haired, 65-year-old Muriel, dressed in a yellow pants suit, came down to the lobby, and Perpich began to read from a hastily edited, handwritten statement: "I am proud to announce that Muriel Humphrey has accepted the appointment to the U. S. Senate. In the course of arriving at this decision I sought the counsel of many people, and Muriel Humphrey has the overwhelming support and love of Minnesota. The advice offered by Minnesota Senate Majority leader Nick Coleman best represented the sentiment I have heard. That Muriel Humphrey should be appointed to fill the senate [seat]…mainly because she better than anyone else could continue the programs and philosophy of Hubert Humphrey, the greatest public servant Minnesota has ever produced."

Muriel Humphrey, appearing nervous, was accompanied by her son, state Senator Hubert H. "Skip" Humphrey III, who planned to run for Congress that year. She said in her soft-spoken manner, "I hope Hubert is guiding me today," adding that she wanted to complete some of the legislation on which her late husband had been working. She would not say whether she would run in the fall election to fill out the remaining four years of his term, and Perpich said he did not ask her.[2] She was sworn in on February 6 by Vice President Walter Mondale and became the first woman from Minnesota ever to serve in the U.S. Senate. At the time she was the only woman in the Senate and the twelfth to serve.

The uncertainty as to whether she would run put both DFLers and Independent-Republicans in a dilemma. Some who wanted to run for the Senate were reluctant to oppose her and hesitated to jump into the race. But in April, the gentle, shy woman who had been at her late husband's side through twelve hectic campaigns and thirty-three years of marriage, told more than 4,000 DFLers at the party's annual dinner (newly renamed the Hubert H. Humphrey Dinner) that she would not run that fall. Her health was questionable. She had had major gall bladder surgery the previous year and was hospitalized for exhaustion shortly before her husband's death. She had had enough politics for a lifetime. She wanted to resume life as a private person and spend time with family and friends.

Nick Coleman was deeply disappointed when Perpich passed over him for the U.S. Senate appointment.[3] He felt that the governor had promised it to him and was indebted to him because Coleman had helped Perpich secure the lieutenant-governor spot on the DFL ticket in 1970.[4] Soon after Muriel Humphrey said she would not run in the fall, Coleman announced he would be a candidate for the seat, but Donald Fraser had already been campaigning quietly for a year, and Coleman, soon realizing that he would never catch up to him, dropped out of the race.

Although Perpich had agreed to endorse Coleman for the Senate if Muriel Humphrey decided not run, a chill had crept into their relationship, and there were long periods when they didn't speak to one another. Coleman and his first wife, Bridget Finnegan Coleman, had socialized a good deal with Rudy and Lola, but Coleman had initiated a painful, expensive, and highly publicized divorce from his wife of twenty-five years, with whom he had six children, in order to marry Deborah Howell, a thirty-four year old *Minneapolis Star* reporter who covered the Capitol, and this grated against the Perpiches' sense of values.[5]

For his part, Coleman was irritated at Perpich's repeated failure to forewarn legislators of decisions such as his creation of a budget-surplus watchdog panel. The two also disagreed sharply on issues such as reducing the size of the Legislature and abortion rights.

In February, 1978, Seventh District Congressman Bob Bergland resigned to become President Carter's secretary of agriculture. Bergland, a Roseau farmer and DFLer, had held the Congress seat in the big, sprawling northwestern Minnesota district since 1970 and had won re-election the previous November with 73 percent of the vote. A special election February 22 to fill the vacant seat drew national attention because it was the first congressional election since Carter had become president and was considered a bellwether.

In the brief campaign candidates braved icy roads and gusts of blinding snow to campaign in the bitter subzero weather. Independent-

Republican Arlan Stangeland, a Barnesville farmer and former state representative, wore a snowmobile suit as he campaigned. DFLer Coya Knutson often wore two pair of slacks and at times was so cold she put on all the clothes she had in her suitcase.

Knutson, 64, of Oklee, was making a gallant comeback try with a shoestring campaign. The only woman in Minnesota ever elected to the U. S. House, she had served two terms in Washington (1955-59) before an infamous "Coya Come Home" letter, written by her alcoholic husband Andy, undermined her re-election bid. Despite a parade of top Democrats into the district to campaign on behalf of DFL candidate Michael Sullivan, including Vice President Walter Mondale, Stangeland was elected with 57 percent of the vote. Independent-Republicans hailed his election as a harbinger of a fall victory for their party.

Meanwhile, controversy surrounding Boundary Waters Canoe Area (BWCA) was tearing the DFL Party apart. As early as 1902 the federal government had begun setting aside forested public land for conservation and recreation in Cook and Lake counties in northeastern Minnesota. Over the years more land was added bit by bit, and restrictions were placed on road building, logging and shoreline development. In 1964 Congress passed the Wilderness Act, designating the BWCA as one of the nation's wilderness areas. It also contained a key provision put there by the late Senator Hubert Humphrey, which applied only to Minnesota. The provision instructed the U.S. secretary of agriculture to manage the BWCA "without unnecessary restrictions on other uses," specifically timber. Other language inserted by Humphrey allowed motorboats to operate in certain parts of the BWCA, a provision that pleased northeastern Minnesotans, many of whom earned their living as resort-owners, outfitters, and guides.

On the other hand, environmentalists wanted to remove the special provisions and give stronger wilderness protection to the region. Congressman Phillip Burton of California sponsored a bill that would have halted logging and greatly limited the use of motorboats and snowmobiles in the BWCA, while also imposing strong federal controls on the corridors leading into the area. The bill was co-sponsored by Minnesota's Bruce Vento, Fourth District congressman, and supported by Don Fraser, Fifth District congressman, and many environmentalists and Twin Cities residents, but it set off an uproar in northeastern Minnesota, where it was opposed by many residents and businesses.

Other Minnesota representatives in Washington were divided over the issue. Congressman James Oberstar sponsored a conflicting bill that would have opened about one-third of the BWCA to snowmobiles and motorboats. Oberstar also wanted to permit logging in that area. Fraser introduced a competing measure that would have excluded logging, snowmobiles and motorboats from the entire BWCA. The battle lines were drawn.[6]

Perpich was opposed to the Burton bill. He objected that it would give the federal government control over private as well as government lands in the new area—lands that included many resorts, businesses, homes, and harvestable forestlands. "I'm not for letting the feds take over the waterways," he said. Perpich also felt that snowmobiles should be allowed in the area, because "there aren't that many up there." And motorboats should have access to peripheral areas. He suggested that the California Democrat didn't realize how vast an area was affected. "I don't think he knows what the hell is going on," he said of Burton, not mentioning Fraser and Vento.[7]

Later that year, Perpich testified before a congressional subcommittee, siding with Fraser in calling for a ban on mining and logging in the wilderness area but aligning himself closely with Oberstar in favoring multiple uses in a portion of the BWCA. Senator Wendell Anderson supported Oberstar's less restrictive measure and argued that motorboats and snowmobiles should be allowed in the BWCA. Environmentalists, backing the Burton-Vento-Fraser proposals, accused Anderson of switching his stand after earlier statements about the need for wilderness preservation, to salvage his crumbling political campaign.

At the state Independent-Republican convention in June of 1978, Albert (Al) Quie, a twenty-year Second District congressman and the owner of a 240-acre dairy farm near Dennison in southern Minnesota, was endorsed for governor. A deeply religious, evangelical Christian, Quie was a leader in prayer groups and made headlines when he led former Nixon aide Charles Colson to become a born-again Christian. A graduate of St. Olaf College and former U.S. Navy pilot, he had served a term (1954-1958) in the Minnesota Senate before going to Washington. Lou Wangberg, Bemidji school superintendent, was endorsed for lieutenant governor over State Senator Nancy Brataas of Rochester.

Had it not been for her stand in favor of abortion rights, Brataas might have been a more suitable choice. When first elected in 1975, she was the only woman in the Minnesota Senate. She was popular with party moderates and became an expert on workers-compensation reform. A former state Republican chairwoman, she ran her own political-consulting business and had developed an effective, computerized, voter-turnout operation that became a national model. She managed get-out-the vote efforts for Nixon, Ford and Reagan, as well as for numerous U.S. Senate and U.S. House races. After her defeat in the lieutenant-governor endorsement contest, she worked for the Quie-Wangberg ticket and organized a masterful get-out-the-vote phone blitz that was key in the ticket's November victory. Yet despite her years of carrying water for the Republican elephant, in 1984 Brataas was again rejected by antiabortionists, who dominated the party, in a bid for endorsement for the First District congressional race.

At the state DFL convention in St. Paul later that summer Wendy Anderson and Don Fraser were endorsed for the U. S. Senate, and Rudy Perpich for governor. Fraser's endorsement did not come easily. About 1,000 residents of northeastern Minnesota arrived by bus to picket, sit in the gallery, carry signs and noisemakers, and disrupt the convention whenever Fraser's name came up. Their candidate was favorite son Senator Doug Johnson of Cook, who had announced his Senate candidacy the previous week in an attempt to block Fraser's endorsement. The northeastern Minnesota delegation objected to Fraser's support for legislation restricting the use of motorboats and snowmobiles in the BWCA, and also his support of handgun control and abortion rights. When Fraser went to the platform to make his formal acceptance speech, there was an uproar, and John French, convention chair, was unable to restore order. The protesters ceased their demonstrations and noisemaking only when James Oberstar, the Eighth District congressman, went to the podium and urged that the

Minneapolis congressman be allowed to speak. Oberstar, who opposed abortion and tough handgun-control laws and favored less restrictive BWCA regulations, was leaning toward Robert Short, who had by-passed the endorsement system and filed as a candidate in the DFL primary.

U.S. Senator Wendell Anderson had also lost some of his popularity with the party's liberal wing, and they gave him a chilly reception. Vice President Mondale worked to bring the bitterly divided party together in support of the ticket, and pleaded for unity in his convention speech.

Throughout the summer Perpich slipped in the opinion polls, and DFL leaders were naturally worried about the governor's slide. Although he remained a likeable, folksy governor, he was a reluctant campaigner, and his unorthodox style frustrated many in the party. As his campaign brochure read, "Rudy Perpich is not a typical governor."

Forrest Harris, Perpich's campaign chairman, acknowledged that the campaign was slow in getting started—there was no campaign plan, no schedule of events.[8] DFL legislators grumbled about a lack of communication with the governor's office. They complained that Perpich wasn't coordinating his campaign with DFL legislative candidates and others on the ticket, nor was the governor getting out a focused message on their behalf. Representative Robert Vanasek of New Prague said there was a feeling among House DFL steering committee members that "if we don't get together, it's going to hurt him and the House."

Quie had started the previous fall organizing a campaign and raising money, and early in 1978 began advertising heavily on radio, television, billboards, newspapers, and even in national magazines. His ads questioned Perpich's competence as governor, while projecting his own twenty-year congressional career as one of stability and capability.

Perpich and Quie easily won lopsided victories in their respective primary elections and headed for a showdown in the November general election. Quie and his running mate, Lou Wangberg, defeated Robert W. Johnson, a St. Paul attorney and former legislator, and his lieutenant-governor candidate, Roger Hanson of Vergas. Perpich and Johnson turned back a challenge from power-line protester Alice Tripp, a retired high school English teacher and Stearns County farmer/activist in the power-line dispute. Her running mate was Barry Casper, chairman of the physics department at Carleton College.

The DFL primary for the bitterly contested U.S. Senate race between party- and labor-endorsed Fraser and millionaire-businessman Short was a cliffhanger. On the morning following the September 12 election both the Minneapolis and St. Paul newspapers had Fraser winning. The *Pioneer Press* banner headline on page one trumpeted "Fraser beats out Short." Fraser had taken an early, and seemingly insurmountable lead, winning nearly three-to-one in Minneapolis and also clobbering Short in the rest of the Twin Cities area. The *Minneapolis Tribune* headline across the top of page one similarly proclaimed, "Fraser apparently beats Short."

But they had reckoned without the massive Eighth District vote, which poured in after newspaper deadlines late Tuesday night. Here Short, the party outsider, held a commanding lead. The Wednesday afternoon edition of *Minneapolis Star* declared, "Short rallies, takes 3,438 lead." Thursday's *Pioneer Press* backpedaled and reported "Short victory took all night." It pictured the gleeful Short looking at a picture of the late President Harry Truman who was prematurely reported as the loser by the *Chicago Tribune* when he defeated Thomas Dewey in 1948. The final vote had Short with 257,269 votes to Fraser's 253,818. Fraser supporters said there had been a substantial Republican crossover vote, which Republicans denied.

The DFL-voting Iron Range showed its conservative colors in voting for Short, a vigorous campaigner who painted Fraser as a big-spending liberal, and made the most of the strong sentiment in the North against the eight-term, Fifth District congressman. Antiabortionists and anti-gun control forces plastered "Dump Fraser" bumper stickers on autos across the Range. Fraser countered that Short "sounded more like a Republican in the campaign than a Democrat." The Fraser campaign accused Short of trying to buy himself a Senate seat by spending $1 million, mostly out of his own pocket, in his primary challenge, and of misstating Fraser's voting record in last-minute ads. (The Short campaign denied the charge.) Short, the son of a North Minneapolis fireman, who said his family had pinched and scraped to get by, defended his spending, "I didn't steal it. I didn't marry it, and I didn't inherit it. I earned it myself with hard work."[9] Short, who had also run on a DFL primary ticket in 1966 with Governor Karl Rolvaag when Rolvaag defeated DFL-endorsed Sandy Keith, called party endorsement "a thing of the past" and said it "ought to be consigned to the Dark Ages."

Fraser, a quiet, reflective man, went to bed Tuesday night thinking he had won and woke up Wednesday morning to learn he'd lost.(A year later he was elected mayor of Minneapolis, where he remained for fourteen years, the city's longest-serving mayor.)

Now the DFL Party's nominee, Short got ready for the November 7 general election, where he would face Republican David Durenberger, legal counsel to the H. B. Fuller Company, headed by former Governor Elmer L. Andersen. Durenberger, who had been executive secretary to Governor Harold LeVander, easily won the party nomination over three opponents including former University of Minnesota President Malcolm Moos.

Quie plastered his campaign slogan in big black letters on hundreds of billboards across Minnesota: "If this man can't improve state government and cut taxes at the same time, he won't make excuses—he simply won't run again." It was a slogan that would come back to haunt him four years later after he was forced to raise taxes, borrow, and cut the state budget time and again during an extended recession. He did not identify himself as a Republican on his billboards or campaign literature, a practice he had followed in his congressional campaigns, where he drew votes from independents and DFLers as well as Republicans.

Picking up on a nationwide tax revolt and a Minnesota Poll published in the *Minneapolis Tribune* which found that eight of ten Minnesotans thought taxes were too high, both Perpich and Quie called for tax cuts. Quie proposed a 10 percent across-the-board income tax reduction, a plan DFLers said would benefit wealthy taxpayers more than poor and middle-income people. Perpich, on the other hand, proposed a major income-tax rate reduction, focusing on middle-income residents. He also made government cost-cutting a major issue in his campaign, arguing that an array of penny-pinching initiatives by state employees, ranging from keeping lower inventories of supplies to cutting travel, would result in a $50-million saving in the current two-year budget period. The DFL governor was endorsed by the Minnesota AFL-CIO and the Minnesota Education Association, the state's largest teachers' organization, even though Quie, a member of the U.S. House Education and Labor Committee, was regarded as a leader on education issues in Congress.

On October 1, the *Minneapolis Tribune* published a Minnesota Poll showing Perpich leading Quie, 51 percent to 42 percent, in a sampling of likely voters; Short had 46 percent to David Durenberger's 39 percent, and Rudy Boschwitz's 48 percent to Anderson's 44 percent. There was growing uneasiness within the DFL camp, however. Sandy Keith, who was helping Perpich campaign in southern Minnesota in October, said, "All of a sudden I realized we were getting creamed. We could lose the whole thing. It was falling apart."[10] Southern Minnesota was pretty much Republican territory anyhow, and Quie was popular in that area. Radio stations there reported that Quie was doing well in polls. Perpich thought the campaign was going well. "He was really quite happy," Keith said. Keith worried that Perpich wasn't talking with Harris, who headed his campaign, or with anybody else. "I went up [to St. Paul] to talk to him, told him 'We've got to get going, get someone in every precinct.' It didn't happen."

Meanwhile a U.S. Justice Department and federal grand jury investigation of irregularities in the handling of funds of the Upper Great Lakes Regional Commission, a little-known federal-state agency with offices in Duluth, was casting a shadow on the DFL ticket. The investigation involved the apparent disappearance and possible misuse of up to $1 million in federal funds provided for two Duluth economic-development projects. Appointees of Governor Wendell Anderson, working for the commission, allegedly had used thousands of dollars in public funds for DFL political purposes. Ultimately (after the election) two aides in the Duluth office, Michael and Barbara Pintar, were convicted in federal court of misusing federal money and violating the Hatch Act by using the commission office to benefit DFL politicians. The alleged beneficiaries included Congressman Oberstar who said he did not realize that his campaign workers illegally used the office for political purposes.[11] Independent-Republicans attacked DFLers for "skullduggery" and mismanagement of commission funds. Shortly before the election, Senate majority leader Nick Coleman and

Senator William McCutcheon of St. Paul, chairman of the Legislative Audit Commission, held a press conference at which they refused to release the working papers of the audit commission's investigation of the Upper Great Lakes Regional Commission and its DFL-appointed staff. The papers reportedly listed dubious financial practices involving the funds by the governor's office, and named the individuals involved.[12] A few days later, in a televised debate with Perpich, Quie demanded that the papers be made public. In an election post mortem, Quie said he could sense that voters, with Watergate still fresh in their memory, were growing suspicious of the DFLers, thinking that they had something to hide. That was the turning point in the campaign.

Perpich, like Quie, opposed abortion except when necessary to save the life of the woman and in cases of rape and incest. But on the Sunday before the election, Quie's supporters slipped 250,000 "pro life" leaflets under the windshield wipers of cars parked at Roman Catholic and conservative Protestant churches. The leaflets called Quie a dependable supporter of the abortion opposition movement and said DFL Governor Rudy Perpich was not. Quie was described as a congressional sponsor of the Human Life Amendment to make abortions illegal, while Perpich, the leaflets said, had refused to answer a questionnaire by the Minnesota Citizens Concerned for Life, the chief Minnesota antiabortion lobbying organization. Thousands of Minnesotans identified as antiabortion received phone calls reminding them to vote.

On Election Day, November 7, 1978, almost the entire DFL state ticket went down to defeat, and Perpich was swept out of office along with the rest. Quie and Wangberg won decisively with 830,019 votes, 52.3 percent, to Perpich and Olson's 718,244 votes, 45.7 percent. Independent-Republicans won both U.S. Senate seats. Millionaire-businessman Rudy Boschwitz defeated Anderson, ending his 20-year political career, and Anderson joined the ranks of seven other governors who had themselves appointed to the Senate in the twentieth century and then failed to win election. Durenberger defeated Short, who was never able to overcome the hostility of liberal DFLers. The election of Boschwitz, who was Jewish and had been born in Germany, and Durenberger, who was German-Catholic, was a notable ethnic leap for the Republican Party, which had traditionally run Scandinavian-

Lutherans for statewide office. Fundamentalist Christians and New Right conservatives from diverse backgrounds—many of them former DFLers—were key in the Republican victories.[13]

DFLers suffered another blow on Wednesday, when a final vote tally showed they had lost control of the Minnesota House which was tied 67-67 between DFLers and Independent-Republicans. It was the first legislative tie in state history and set the stage for a rancorous and deadlocked 1979 session. The Senate DFL majority was thankful it hadn't been up for election. Independent-Republican Arlen Erdahl, former public-service commissioner and former secretary of state, was elected to the First District Congress seat vacated by Quie, defeating state Senator Gerry Sikorski of Stillwater. Martin Sabo, after nine terms in the Minnesota House, the last six years as Speaker, was elected to the Fifth District Congress seat which Fraser was giving up. Independent-Republicans jubilantly hailed the 1978 election as the Minnesota Massacre and a historic turnaround in the once DFL-dominated state.

Quie, who refused to take public financing, thus avoiding the campaign spending limit, spent $1 million in his campaign, almost double the amount spent by Perpich, who did accept public financing. A factor in Perpich's loss was the widespread defection to Quie of state employees, many of whom felt Perpich was disparaging them for political gain by ordering them to unplug their coffee pots and limit their office purchases. Perpich himself blamed his crushing defeat mainly on the DFL Party split that arose in the bitter Short-Fraser fight over Humphrey's U.S. Senate seat. He also thought his role in the power-line dispute might have figured in his election loss.

Pundits pondered the question: If the highly-esteemed Muriel Humphrey had headed the party ticket in the fall, would that have prevented the "Minnesota Massacre" election that brought down Wendell Anderson, Rudy Perpich and other DFL candidates? President Carter wanted her to run. Others had also urged her to consider it, including leaders of organized labor and feminist groups, who believed that much of the affection and popularity enjoyed by her late husband had been transferred to her and thought she would be a formidable candidate. Perpich said if Muriel Humphrey had run for a full term, the Short-Fraser split would have been averted, and he and much of the rest of the DFL ticket, with the possible exception of U.S. Senator Anderson, would have been re-elected. "I think I would have made it," he said. Defeat, he said years later, is "like falling off a cliff…physically and emotionally."[14]

Lola Perpich, a serious, quiet woman who rarely spoke to reporters, sent a letter to newspaper editors on November 24 lashing out at Governor-Elect Quie, accusing him of interjecting religion into the campaign and carrying a "Bible in one hand and a bucket of mud in the other." Quie campaign officials denied the accusations and added that some of the activities Mrs. Perpich was complaining about were undertaken by independent groups promoting Quie's candidacy. She attacked Quie volunteers who put the "pro life" leaflets on cars in church parking lots the Sunday before the November 7 election, too late for a response by Perpich. Quie's campaign manager, Robert Andringa, replied that the leaflets had been placed by an organization known as "Minnesotans for a Pro-Life Governor," headed by Marsie Leier, who also happened to be a member of the Quie campaign committee.[15]

In her letter Lola Perpich also objected that Quie had implied throughout the campaign that he "is a Christian and that Rudy is not." She cited newspaper advertisements by the Quie campaign calling the congressman "a great Christian for our next governor," the mailing of thousands of letters in the final days of the campaign which she said had "obvious religious overtones," and name-calling by the Quie campaign which she said called her husband "Crazy Rudy" and "Rubberstamp Rudy." Perpich said that her husband had been an active Christian since childhood but didn't believe in using religion as a political ploy.

At a formal farewell to the press on December 29, Perpich said, "I think we did a good job as governor, and we have a reputation of integrity of honesty and being a hard worker, and I guess that's what's really important." In prepared remarks Perpich told reporters that some of his greatest satisfactions as he left office were the "excellent condition of Minnesota's economy" and "opening up the governmental process to the media." He urged the news media to make sure the next administration would be open to the public and press. If he had been re-elected, Perpich said, "it was my intention to remove the doors from the governor's private office. I'd have done it before the election but certainly a few would have called it a political ploy."

Bob Aronson, Perpich's communications director, said, "That was Rudy in the first term, and Rudy in the others was different. I wasn't with him in the others, so I don't know what the heck went on, but I know in that first term that was the real Rudy." If there ever was a charismatic person, it was Rudy Perpich, Aronson said. "Whoever he was with at the time was his best friend in the whole world. He made you feel like a king."

That first term in office was not a political one, Aronson said. There was no political plan. "I think Rudy's thought was, 'I will be so popular by all the things I do, I don't have to raise money, and I don't have to campaign.'" Without Fraser, Short, and Wendy Anderson, it just might have worked.

Chapter 9

Rudy Perpich Goes to
"Control Data University" in Vienna

Once Perpich had recovered from the painful experience of "falling off the chair" of elective office, he took a job as a trade representative for Control Data Corporation in Europe, and he and Lola moved to Vienna. "I had every intention of coming back," he later admitted. "I knew I was going to run again. Nothing could have stopped me. I knew I hadn't been given a chance to show what I could do."[1] He made the most of his nearly three years abroad. He learned a lot about the global economy, and his appetite was whetted for world trade. He and Lola would always say these were the happiest years of their lives. They enjoyed traveling and soaking up the history and culture of Central Europe.

Back in Minnesota, it was time for another reapportionment of legislative districts, but once the boundaries had been redrawn, with turf being lost and won, and veteran legislators finding themselves with new and unknown areas and constituents, almost one-eighth of them decided to retire. The liberal architects of many of the landmark social programs enacted during the 1970s departed. George Perpich was among about a dozen senators who announced they would not run again. DFL Senator Edward Gearty of Minneapolis, an 18-year legislative veteran and the genial president of the Minnesota Senate, also quit.

After 18 years in the Senate, Nicholas Coleman left at the end of 1980, saying that times were changing, and he no longer had the heart for the job. "The current cycle of ultra-conservatism [and] the political myopia have created a climate that I do not suit, nor do I wish to." Urging his caucus to keep concern for principle above a concern for self-preservation, he told his colleagues in his farewell message, "The continuing fight to keep our state progressive, to protect the poor, to create opportunities for all our citizens but particularly to cherish those without power, I leave in your able hands." A year later, at age 56, he died of acute leukemia.

Rudy Perpich slipped almost unnoticed in and out of Coleman's funeral in the St. Paul Cathedral. A year later, on the anniversary of Coleman's death, Rudy and Lola sent an orchid to his widow, Deborah Howell. A commemorative bust of Coleman, the first DFLer to be senate majority leader, was placed at the foot of the stairway leading to the Senate chamber in the Capitol, the only such memorial to a state legislator. Each year afterward, Howell sent roses to be placed at the bust on Coleman's birthday and the anniversaries of their wedding and his death; his sister, Rose, did the same on St. Patrick's, Christmas and Easter.

Others among those titans of the 1970s were leaving. In 1982, Jack Davies of Minneapolis, an 18-year legislative veteran and senior member of the Senate, was defeated by a fellow DFLer, Representative Donna Peterson, following a bitter campaign. Davies had run as an independent after losing party endorsement to Peterson, who wooed and won many Independent-Republican votes in the district, which took in much of the Longfellow and Powderhorn neighborhoods of Minneapolis and parts of the Nokomis and University of Minnesota areas. Davies, a law professor at William Mitchell College of Law in St. Paul, was chairman of the Judiciary committee, where he battled for passage of the state's no-fault insurance law and drunken-driving legislation and against the taconite amendment.

As early as mid-1979, Rudy Perpich began dropping hints publicly that he would run again for his old job as governor.[2] Privately he was calling friends in Minnesota, engineering a comeback campaign. When Connie Motherway and George Perpich were married in January, 1980, and went to Paris on their honeymoon, Rudy showed up, and in their room at the Hotel International he told George and Connie he was going to run again, and that he wanted Mark Dayton, DFL activist and an heir to the Dayton department store fortune, for his running mate.[3] Perpich and Dayton had stayed in touch after the former governor went to Europe, and Perpich broached the idea of a Perpich-Dayton ticket to him in 1979. But Dayton had his sights set on challenging U.S. Senator David Durenberger, and the day after the 1980 election, Dayton began making courtesy calls to DFL leaders, informing them of his intention.

Later Perpich said he wanted former state Senator Emily Anne Staples of Plymouth as his lieutenant governor candidate. Rudy wanted

George to orchestrate a "groundswell" for him. Connie Perpich later recalled that George was cool to the idea because he didn't think Rudy had much chance of winning. Eventually George did come around, but in the beginning only a handful of Perpich stalwarts, including St. Louis County Commissioner Tom Anzelc and Frank Ongaro Sr., signed on.

Perpich called his friend Ron Gornick in Chisholm and asked him to come to Croatia, saying he wanted to talk about their going into international trade business together. Perpich was at a trade seminar in the Croatian city of Dubrovnik, on the Adriatic Sea. Gornick met him there, and Perpich introduced him to political and business people. Perpich, big and tall, stood out at the Yugoslavian seminar. Eyes turned when he and Lola entered a room. Perpich was able to speak Croatian with many who were there, and he was a good salesman for Control Data, Gornick thought.

One sunny afternoon, as the two sat on a dock on the Adriatic Sea, their pants legs rolled up, their bare feet dangling in the water, Gornick asked Perpich, "Rudy, do you really want to be a businessman? Or do you want to be in politics?" Perpich replied, "Oh sure, I want to get in politics. But I'm dead meat. They beat me. I'm an outcast." Gornick said, "No, Rudy, you weren't beat. You were a victim of circumstances. The circumstances were just lousy. The economy was bad…I don't think you had a fair shake…Anderson went up there [to the Senate]. You got in there. They took it out on Anderson, and at the same time you got beat. People don't feel that way towards you, believe me. What do you want to be? Do you want to be a dentist?"

Perpich said, "Never. I'll never be a dentist again in my life. I wouldn't look at another mouth for all the tea in China." Gornick asked, "Do you want to be a senator? Do you want Oberstar's job? Do you want to be a Congressman?" "No, I can't stand Washington. I don't want to be in Washington." "Do you want to be governor?" "Sure, I want to be governor. I had so much unfinished business. I didn't get the chance to do it."

Gornick assured him, "Rudy, you've got the chance. You can be governor." The timing was perfect, Gornick told him. "If you want to be the governor, you've got to make up your mind you want to be the governor. If you'll do that, I'll tell you what I'll do, Rudy. I'll spend all my time that I have to see that you get elected governor. I'll go back, and I'll test the market. I go down to the cities once a month for two or three days, see different reporters, I'll check." Perpich gave him the go-ahead to go back to Minnesota and start organizing.

Gornick went home and started a small export-import business dealing in Yugoslavian goods and called it CarRon, a blending of his first name and that of his Croatian-descent wife, Carol. Gornick told Perpich loyalists—Ongaro, Gary Lamppa, Doug Johnson and others, "Hey, I think Rudy's ready to go." They were excited about Perpich's prospects and began holding meetings to make plans.

One day, at a Sports Commission meeting in Minneapolis, Associated Press reporter Gene Lahammer asked Gornick about Rudy and Lola. Gornick, whether naïve or astute about baiting the press, told Lahammer, "Gene, this is off the record, but we are going to have a meeting tomorrow night in Chisholm, downstairs at my motel, a bunch of Perpich cronies, to see if there's a groundswell of support for Rudy Perpich for Governor."

When Gornick came home from the meeting the next night, his phone started ringing. Lahammer had put a story about the Perpich for Governor meeting on the AP wire. "I really had people get mad at me," he said, for not telling them about the meeting. Sixteen Perpich backers, including George Perpich, were at the meeting to plan a comeback strategy.[4] Gornick and others held a press conference the next day, and the Perpich campaign was launched.

Gornick had caps and campaign buttons made that read, "Rudy Perpich for Governor. X Jobs [Vote for Jobs]." The buttons cost 50 cents each, and the enterprising Gornick sold them for $1, so there was a 50-cents profit for the campaign. At the same time Gornick was building an office above his RonSon Deep Rock service station, going out of the service station and motel business, and going into franchising new SuperDuper stores. But before long Gornick had become heavily involved in politics, and got no farther than a single store in Hibbing. Politics also spelled the end of the export-import business, because Gornick no longer had time for it.

Monday night campaign meetings were held in the half-finished offices above the service station. Representative Joe Begich of Eveleth would be there, and also Doug Johnson, who took time off from his school counseling job to work on the campaign, though he had a hard time getting up the stairs with his leg brace. The office had neither air conditioning nor bathroom, and the temperature often rose to 90 degrees. The group would usually have a few beers, and Gornick brought a pail for Johnson so he wouldn't have to go up and down the stairs to the bathroom. Gornick joked to Perpich later, "Governor, I carried it for you."

Gornick got a lot of razzing from friends in the Twin Cites for his all-out effort for the long-shot Perpich campaign. He went out to dinner with labor leader Richard Radman, a fellow member of the Sports Commission and a staunch supporter of Warren Spannaus, who was also preparing a gubernatorial campaign. Radman told Gornick he was "goofy" for thinking Perpich could beat the attorney general and insisted that "no way" could Perpich win. Spannaus was Mr. Minnesota. He had all the credentials to be governor.

However, a Minnesota Poll published by the *Star Tribune* in early April, 1981, galvanized Perpich's supporters. It showed Perpich and U.S. Senator David Durenberger were the best-known politicians in the state. Of those surveyed, 93 percent knew who Perpich was, compared with 86 percent who knew Attorney General Spannaus. Forty-seven percent said they had a favorable impression of Perpich compared with 39 percent for Spannaus. Durenberger, who was up for reelection in 1982, had a 91 percent name identification, a 51 percent favorable, and 15 percent unfavorable impression.

Joe Perpich and his wife Cathy were visiting Rudy and Lola in Vienna when the poll came out. While Joe was talking about the delights of Vienna, Rudy was waxing enthusiastically about visiting county fairs and coffee shops in his forthcoming campaign for governor.[5]

In May, 1981, Perpich was back in Minnesota for a visit, urging his friends not to make commitments to other candidates for governor, because he might jump into the race. The sly Perpich loved to tease the press and knew that tantalizing tidbits were an irresistible lure. "I haven't made a final decision yet," he told Bill Salisbury of the *Pioneer Press*.[6] But sounding like a candidate, he said, "I've learned more and have gotten a lot of new ideas in the past two-and-a-half years that would be very helpful to this state."

On June 10, 1981, Warren Spannaus formally announced for governor. The Mr. Nice Guy of the DFL Party, he was one of the few DFL survivors in the 1978 Massacre. He described himself as "a work horse, not a show horse." and he may have looked like an ordinary guy with his thinning gray air, medium height, rumpled suits, low-key style, and soporific speeches, but that was part of his appeal. Warm and friendly, Spannaus could enter a room full of strangers, spend an hour shaking hands, and come out with a room full of friends. He was always available to campaign for DFL candidates. He had put more than 150,000 miles on a '67 Olds, attending weddings, wakes, fundraisers, and, it was said, any meeting of two or more DFLers around the state, collecting countless political IOUs. He held liberal positions on abortion, civil rights, and gay rights. His views were more conservative on fiscal and law enforcement issues, however, and he was sometimes at odds with DFL liberals. For example, he opposed the legalization of marijuana and favored tougher sentences for drunken driving and other crimes. "I will run for Governor because I love this state," Spannaus said in his announcement. "I believe in it, and I want to fight to preserve its future. Minnesota, for my money, is the finest state in the Union."

A year before the election and six months before the state DFL endorsing convention, Spannaus had already secured the backing of much of the party establishment, including former Vice President Walter Mondale and former Governors Wendell Anderson and Karl Rolvaag, Congressmen Bruce Vento and Martin Sabo, Secretary of State Joan Growe, State Treasurer Jim Lord, Mayors Donald Fraser of Minneapolis and George Latimer of St. Paul, Speaker Harry Sieben, and Senate Majority Leader Roger Moe. Spannaus also had the support of labor leaders, including David Roe, president of the Minnesota AFL-CIO, and Jack Jorgenson, president of the Minnesota Teamsters Joint Council. There was little doubt that DFL Party endorsement was his for the asking.

On the other hand, a Minnesota Poll taken in October and published in the *Star Tribune* presented Spannaus with a less encouraging picture. It showed Perpich running two-to-one ahead of Governor Quie. According to the poll, Perpich would have the support of 52 percent of those surveyed if the election were held then. Quie, whose popularity had plummeted as the state's financial problems worsened, would have only 24 percent. Spannaus did not do quite as well as Perpich. He would have the votes of 49 percent of those surveyed, compared with 25 percent for Quie.[7]

Minnesota still was in a recession. The farm economy and farm land values were collapsing. In late 1981 there was an estimated $600 million state budget deficit. Governor Quie, plagued by a recession, was forced to call a series of special sessions to cut the state budget time and again, and under fire by leaders of his own Republican party for raising taxes, announced on January 25, 1982, that he would not run for re-election. The governor, with tears in his eyes, made the surprise announcement at a press conference at the Capitol, after a weekend at his farm in Washington County praying and deliberating. There was little mourning within the Republican Party hierarchy. U.S. Senator Boschwitz and Minnesota's three Republican Congressmen, Arlan Stangeland, Tom Hagedorn and Vin Weber, said they feared Quie would be a millstone around the neck of every Independent-Republican candidate on the ballot.[8]

His announcement rocked the political landscape and re-opened the long-festering rift between conservatives and moderates in the IR Party. Quie "wholeheartedly" endorsed the conservative Wangberg as his successor, and the lieutenant governor immediately began lining up support from party leaders, but other Independent-Republicans also expressed an interest in running, including State Senator Robert Ashbach of Arden Hills, State Auditor Arne Carlson, and State Representative John Ainley of Park Rapids. Perpich, reached in Austria, said he was surprised by Quie's decision, but said it would not alter his plans. Perpich was ready and waiting in the wings. He had formed a campaign committee but had not officially announced.

At the end of March, 1982, Perpich told the *Pioneer Press* in a telephone interview from Vienna, that he planned to return to Minnesota the next week, "listen to the people" for a few weeks, and then make up his mind about running for governor, no matter what the DFL did at its June 4-6 state endorsing convention in Duluth. The former governor rejected a scheme which the Spannaus camp came up with to prevent a damaging primary battle. The plan would have Congressman James Oberstar move to a new, north suburban

Sixth Congressional District, so Perpich could run for Oberstar's Eighth District seat or have Perpich run for the U.S. Senate against Republican David Durenberger. Perpich said he was absolutely not interested in either federal office.[8]

Chapter 10

The Iron Ranger Returns.

Rudy Perpich came home to the Iron Range to run for governor and found abandoned open-pit mines, shut-down taconite plants, and unemployed steelworkers. He also found a hero's welcome in depressed northeastern Minnesota, where many voters looked to him as their saviour. But in the state-wide governor's race, the Mesabi Messiah remained the underdog against Warren Spannaus, the well-financed DFL favorite.

Yet Perpich also had a few things weighing in his favor. Many who had moved to the Twin Cities from the northeast part of the state to find jobs remained Perpich supporters. And many Minnesotans throughout the state had fond memories of the colorful governor who had been in office during relatively good economic times, a sentiment that was reflected in opinion polls giving him high name identification and favorable ratings. Even in southern Minnesota, Sandy Keith found Perpich support. Many felt that he had been "done in" in 1978, through no fault of his own. And Spannaus was not exciting voters.

Perpich had also grown during his sojourn abroad. Working for Control Data in Austria, he had witnessed great changes in the world economy and entered into competition with Asian businessmen who were vigorously developing new overseas markets. In the process, he had developed a fiery new message: By making the state of Minnesota more competitive in world markets—a novel concept at that time—many new jobs would be created. Perpich asserted that rural areas could step up the production of food to sell abroad, and he envisioned a world-class University of Minnesota as a center for the development of high-tech products and expertise. In order to meet its potential, however, Minnesota would need well-educated citizens. He was confident his theme of "Jobs, Jobs, Jobs" would resonate with Minnesota voters.

On April 12 Perpich met with eighteen advisers in his first formal campaign meeting.[1] With $6,000 in his campaign fund and no professional staff, he had negotiated his final contract in Europe for

Control Data, resigned from his job, reportedly giving up a six-figure salary, and shipped his household goods back to Minnesota. On April 22, at a press conference at the Minnesota Press Club in Minneapolis, he formally announced he would run for governor. He said if he were elected, he would seek to improve the state's economy by finding new markets for Minnesota products. "I want to be Minnesota's number one salesman, number one fan, and number one promoter."

Perpich had soon hired a professional fund-raising firm and opened a St. Paul campaign headquarters, though his staff had little experience in statewide campaigns. George Perpich organized the northern half of the state for Rudy's gubernatorial campaign on a shoe-string. In the course of the campaign Perpich was outspent by Spannaus two-to-one, but other factors—Perpich's name recognition, his charisma, his strong support on the Iron Range and in northeastern Minnesota, and support from zealous and well-organized antiabortion and anti-gun control people—played to his advantage.

The Rudy Perpich who returned to run for governor had not only changed his views, but also his appearance. His previously salt-and-pepper hair was now a youthful-looking reddish brown. He had decided to dye his hair while in Yugoslavia, he said, when people began asking him if Lola was his daughter. After news stories began to appear about his rejuvenated appearance, Perpich let some of the gray return, but later darkened it again.

At the state party convention June 4-6 in Duluth, Spannaus was endorsed with 81 percent of the vote. "That's about as close to unanimity as Democrats get," a jubilant Spannaus aide said at the time. Perpich was setting his sights on the September 14 primary, however, and had made no effort to win party endorsement.

His announcement that he would name a woman as his running mate, a first in a major campaign, was a brilliant move, and it put Spannaus on the spot. Polls indicated that voters were ready for the idea. The "women's vote" might well be a key to victory. Feminists in both the DFL and Independent-Republican Parties were pushing for a women's rights agenda that included legalized abortion, the Equal Rights Amendment, and pay equity.

During the Christmas holidays in 1981, Rudy and Lola invited former state Senator Emily Anne Staples, a prominent feminist, to breakfast at the Leamington Hotel in Minneapolis.[2] She had been elected to the state senate in 1976 and was one of two women in the senate. The other was Independent-Republican Nancy Brataas. Staples had lost her senate seat in the 1980 election to Republican Jim Ramstad.

She had told Spannaus she would support him for governor in the 1982 election and was surprised when Perpich asked her to be his lieutenant governor candidate. "Why are you running?" asked Staples, who didn't think he had a chance of winning. Perpich said he wanted to finish the job he'd started in his first term as governor, and he wanted to redeem himself. Staples told him she was interested but would be unable to accept the role on the slate because she had been awarded a Bush fellowship that year to study at Harvard's John F. Kennedy School of Government and wanted to finish it.[3]

Perpich then approached Secretary of State Joan Growe.[4] Growe, a petite, gracious woman, divorced, and mother of four children, was a former school teacher, former state legislator, and savvy politician. She had been elected secretary of state in 1974, defeating Republican incumbent Arlen Erdahl. Now in her third term, she was a respected role model for women in politics. She had championed election law changes to open up the political process and increase voter participation, and in the process had helped make Minnesota the highest voter registration and highest voter turnout state in the nation.

Rudy and Lola had breakfast with her in downtown Minneapolis. "He asked me [to run with him], and Lola pitched me also. He told me I was the very first person he had asked. I said 'no,' much as I liked and respected him, but I was very flattered." Growe told him she had something else in mind—the U.S. Senate race in two years. She thought it would be better to run from her secretary of state office rather than as lieutenant governor. Perpich was not taken aback by her refusal; perhaps he half expected it, and said he understood.

At the same time, Growe wanted her name out as a possible lieutenant governor candidate with Spannaus, and many Spannaus supporters were putting pressure on him to ask Growe to be his running mate. Growe didn't expect him to do that, but, "I wanted to put Warren on the spot and in a position of having to say 'no,' to a woman," said Growe. She had been a founder of "All The Good Old

Girls," a feminist group that delighted in tweaking "Good Old Boys" like Spannaus and Wendell Anderson.

With increasing public speculation about a Spannaus-Growe ticket, "Warren ended up in a position where he had to call me up [to stop the speculation]. I went to a meeting where he had to say 'no,' he didn't want me for that position." Growe said, "Warren was scared to death of women," said Growe, recalling that on the campaign trail, he would never be seen traveling alone with her although that would have been logistically convenient at times.

Even Spannaus' wife, Marjorie, wished he would select a woman as his lieutenant governor candidate. But the cautious Spannaus, who had resisted having his wife go to work as a part-time, salaried church-education director once their three children were in school, wasn't ready to accept a woman running mate. Growe discouraged a draft-Growe movement at the convention. "I wanted no part of it. I felt the gubernatorial candidate had a right to choose whomever he wanted. I left the floor, sat up in the balcony, because I didn't want to be seen as advocating that [draft]."

Many who wanted a woman candidate then backed State Representative Arlene Lehto of Duluth. While she was a student at the University of Minnesota at Duluth, she had been the chief organizer and first president of the Save Lake Superior Association and a fiery leader of the effort to stop Reserve Mining Company from discharging taconite tailings into the lake.

It took two ballots, and feminists were angry because Spannaus didn't pick a woman, but delegates endorsed his choice for lieutenant governor, Carl Johnson, 48, a St. Peter farmer, eight-term member of the Minnesota House and chairman of the House Education Committee. Spannaus felt at ease with Johnson, a genial, well-liked, short, balding man with a flair for telling Swedish jokes. Besides, Johnson opposed legalized abortion, which Spannaus supporters hoped would balance Spannaus' pro-choice position on that difficult issue. When Spannaus and Johnson appeared before a convention caucus of 325 delegates who called themselves Democrats for Liberal Issues, Spannaus was uncertain when asked if he believed selecting a woman might increase his chances to win the November election. "Not necessarily, because I think that, the fact that—who knows?" he said.[5] There were many women qualified to be governor and lieutenant governor, he added, but he selected Carl Johnson primarily because he was a bona fide farmer.

Meanwhile, Perpich, in his efforts to find the proper running mate, turned to Marlene Johnson, 36, the owner of a St. Paul advertising agency, Split Infinitive, and active in the DFL feminist movement. He asked her to meet him at The Brothers restaurant at Southdale, and when she arrived, he was eating a triple-scoop chocolate sundae. She sat down, and he said, "Do you want to run for lieutenant governor with me?" She did.

As a matter of fact, Johnson, tall, reddish-haired, composed, tastefully dressed, had been thinking of running for statewide office for some time. She was young and articulate, knew the issues, and had a good Scandinavian name. He needed someone from the Twin Cities, and her background in small business was also a plus. "It was a perfect fit, almost like a computer model," he said.[6]

Keith had expressed support for Perpich's decision to seek out a woman as his running mate, but he had mixed feelings about the choice of Marlene Johnson as a candidate. He asked Perpich if he knew that Johnson had been arrested for shoplifting. Perpich assured Keith that Johnson had told him exactly what happened. She had been depressed over the recent death of her father (an old friend and supporter of Keith's) and simply forgot to pay for the merchandise. Keith also warned Perpich that because Johnson had never been married and would be the first woman in that spot on the DFL ticket, she would be accused of being either a lesbian or a whore.

Spannaus had hit the campaign trail long before Perpich returned from Austria, accusing the Quie-Wangberg administration of fiscal mismanagement, for example. And it was true that the Quie administration had turned a $200-million surplus into a $195-million deficit. During a Spannaus-Wangberg debate sponsored by the Minnesota Public Interest Research Group, Wangberg attempted to lay the blame for the drastic turnaround on President Carter's credit policies and pointed out that Minnesota was not the only state with large budget deficits.

Spannaus's campaign organization was the best Minnesota had ever seen, in the eyes of many observers. He had far more money and staff, a much larger network of volunteer workers, and more campaign paraphernalia—computers, phone banks, television and radio commercials, pamphlets, press releases, buttons and bumper stickers—than Perpich. But state DFL Chairman Michael (Mike) Hatch acknowledged that DFL Party leaders and candidates were nervous just the same. Perpich had become something of a folk hero. Voters had fond memories of his exciting, unpredictable style as governor, and there was a nostalgic view among voters that things were better during his three-year tenure as governor than at present.

After receiving the DFL endorsement, Spannaus focused his energies on the September 14 primary, where he would face Perpich. Reaching out to still-angry feminists, he stressed his support for the Equal Rights Amendment and other women's issues. When Spannaus promised that if elected half of his major appointments would be women, Marlene Johnson countered, "His ticket isn't 50 percent women."

But with 140,000 Minnesotans out of work, the campaign soon became a bidding contest between Perpich and Spannaus for job programs, particularly economic recovery proposals for Minnesota's DFL-voting, depression-stricken Iron Range.[7] Both said they would take $5 million for jobs from the Iron Range 2002 Economic Recovery Fund, which had been created with mineral production taxes, and was earmarked for long-range investment in economic diversification when the iron mining industry fell into decline. Spannaus said he'd match the fund withdrawal with $5 million from the state treasury, if money were available, to create jobs for unemployed steelworkers. Perpich said he'd put money from the fund into development of peat, willows, cattails and other alternative energy sources. Spannaus topped that by proposing the construction of two small steel plants in the region, along with alternative energy development. Spannaus also called for tax breaks and incentives for small business expansion, and outlined his "Minnesota Jobs Plan" in radio ads.

As the weeks wore on, the campaign rhetoric escalated. In an August 5 debate Perpich accused Spannaus, the state's leading advocate of gun control, of "politicizing the state" with his "harping" about the issue. Spannaus retorted that the measure he sponsored as attorney general was excellent legislation that kept pistols out of the hands of irresponsible people. In a TV follow-up Perpich said that he opposed gun control, even though he had signed Spannaus's handgun-control measure in 1977. Spannaus said Minnesota was paying a heavy price now for a lack of economic planning during Perpich's years as governor, and that Perpich had no energy plan, no jobs plan, no export plan. Perpich countered that he did have such plans, and that Spannaus, as the top DFL official in state government, had dropped the ball by not fighting for the continuation of the governor's energy, property-tax relief, and education programs. Perpich said he "wouldn't oppose" a constitutional amendment restricting or outlawing abortion. Spannaus opposed any constitutional restraint on abortion.

Spannaus released his income-tax returns for the past three years and challenged Perpich to release his, something Rudy had done in three previous statewide races. Perpich accused Spannaus of running a "smear campaign" and said his tax returns were too complicated to release. But just before the primary election Perpich did make a summary of his salary and taxes public. The documents revealed that during his final year at Control Data, Perpich had a federal adjusted gross income of $215,940, upon which Control Data had paid Austrian taxes totaling $83,874, and U.S. income taxes totaling $31,044 on his behalf. Though somewhat more complex, Perpich's state tax situation appeared to be above board as well.

Marlene Johnson refused an invitation to debate her primary opponent, Carl Johnson. Her campaign spokesman told the Urban Concerns Workshop of St. Paul, which was trying to set up the debate, that her campaign schedule was too full.

The Perpich campaign was rapidly gaining momentum. And in a novel tactic, Gornick stuck campaign signs on his new Winnebago motor home and drove around the state. Drivers of other cars would blow their horns and yell, "Rudy, Rudy, Rudy." It was so effective the campaign rented a second motor home. Six or eight people would ride and sleep in the motor homes, driving all over Minnesota, and people would see the Perpich signs and think Perpich himself was there. By the end of the campaign Gornick's Winnebago had traveled 30,000 miles, the signs had torn the paint off, and he had to have it repainted. He later speculated that Paul Wellstone, who campaigned for the U. S. Senate in 1990 in a dilapidated green bus, might have been inspired by the Perpich motor homes.

Gornick was surprised and disappointed, though, with Perpich's choice of Marlene Johnson for his running mate. "I don't think she moved fast enough for Rudy Perpich. She didn't bring anything to the campaign at all that would make it exciting."

Before long the under-funded campaign began to run out of money, however, and Rudy was reluctant to borrow. He became pessimistic and told his campaign manager, Eldon Brustuen, that he was going to lose. He warned Brustuen not to go into debt. "We have internal problems. We have external problems. No money. Spannaus is so strong. Mondale is against me," he said. But Brustuen remained confident Perpich was going to win. He saw the many believers in Perpich like his apolitical mother, Cleone, who stood at the Yellow Medicine County fair in a driving rain for hours, handing out Perpich brochures that she kept dry under her raincoat. He told Perpich that he was drawing a lot of people to his campaign who felt ignored by traditional party machines, and that they would push him through.[8]

Brustuen, whose wife, Sharon, was Perpich's cousin, had kept his regular job at Honeywell Inc., where he dealt with international trade. He worked on the campaign early in the morning before going to work, and also in the evenings and on weekends. He and others already were using their credit cards to help finance the struggling campaign. When Perpich heard the campaign had a $100 check from Elmer Benson, former Farmer-Labor governor (1936-38), he was so elated he didn't want to cash it. "Frame it," he said, but the campaign was desperate for money, and the check had already been cashed.

Just before the primary election, George Perpich and Brustuen, without telling Rudy, went to about twenty Perpich friends on the Range and asked for a $1,000 loan from each to pay for last minute TV and radio ads. The ads hammered away at the fact that the DFL-endorsed ticket headed by Spannaus had no candidates living north of University Avenue in St. Paul.

On the day before the primary, Gornick drove his motor home across the Range from Chisholm to Grand Rapids to Gilbert, Biwabik and Aurora, with the sound system playing polka music. He sat in the back, saying on the loudspeaker, "We need your vote for Rudy Perpich tomorrow. This is a vote for the Range. Don't forget to vote." He made a similar swing on Election Day.

When the polls closed that evening, supporters packed the Rustic Rock Inn in Eveleth for a victory party. Early returns from the Twin Cities were not good for Perpich, however. The cases of champagne under the tables remained unopened, as the news kept getting worse. People were in shock and blaming Gornick. Gornick was with Connie and George Perpich in the bar: "We sat there and actually bawled, and said, 'What did we do wrong? What should we have done to win this thing?'" Rudy Perpich's father, Anton, was there and tried to comfort his son George, "Don't feel bad, George. You do good job." People started walking out before midnight.

Meanwhile, Spannaus and his supporters, including Minneapolis Mayor Don Fraser and St. Paul Mayor George Latimer, were optimistic at a victory party at the Sheraton-Ritz Hotel in Minneapolis. But as the evening wore on, they became uneasy: Spannaus was losing outstate. After midnight the dance band went home, and the dwindling group of people in the red-carpeted Cotillion Room began talking quietly about why Spannaus was now in serious trouble. About 4:45 a.m., the official word was out. Perpich, the Iron Range underdog, had won.

Around 3 o'clock in the morning, about thirty Perpich supporters remaining at the Inn in Eveleth realized the vote count was starting to turn their way. Eighth District returns began to come in, and Rudy was gaining. At 3:30 a.m. Doug Johnson happily told the weary supporters on the Range, "It appears Rudy Perpich is going to win the election." Pandemonium set in. The few jubilant campaign leaders on hand decided they had better get Rudy there because he might have to make an acceptance speech. Tired supporters who had gone home in sorrow returned reinvigorated and exuberant to the Rustic Rock Inn, where the bottles of champagne were now being opened. About 6 a.m. Perpich came in and thanked everybody. He and Gornick and a few others went to breakfast at the Holiday Inn, and people there were "just bananas." He stopped at a bakery and met more excited well-wishers. The people of the Iron Range were ecstatic.

Keith had been watching the Twin Cities metro area where Spannaus was winning 60-40. He was angry with Terrence O'Toole and other Fourth District DFLers who promised they would carry St. Paul for Perpich. Nor had St. Paulite Marlene Johnson, his running mate, given Perpich the boost there he had expected. But Keith's spirits were lifted when later that night the first returns began dribbling in from southern Minnesota, where Keith had given heart and soul to an all-out drive. They showed Perpich in the lead. The trickle turned into a flood, with reported returns running two-to-one, three-to-one for Perpich. Toward morning, when Keith heard that votes from the Iron Range hamlets and villages were pouring in overwhelmingly for their native son—four-, five-, six-to-one over Spannaus—the elated Keith told his wife, Marion they were going to win.

When the votes were totaled, with almost half-a-million votes cast, Perpich had scored an upset, winning the DFL gubernatorial primary by a 51 percent to 46 percent margin. Perpich's vote total was 275,820; Spannaus's was 248,218.

Perpich had inserted earplugs and had gone to bed at 10 p.m. at his cottage on Lake Esquagama, near Gilbert, at a time when news reports had him trailing Spannaus by scores of thousands of votes. Lola was in New York enrolling their daughter, Mary Sue, at Fordham University. Rudy Jr. was at Stanford University. When Perpich got up the next morning at 5 a.m. he heard a radio announcer declare him the winner. Calls poured in. He was wanted by TV stations around the state. He called Lola, who had heard about it 15 minutes before because she had a call from Rudy Jr. "It was the biggest day of my life," Perpich told Jim Klobuchar of the *Star Tribune*. "The greatest thing about it was that the old man [his retired father, Anton] and my mother lived to see it. When I lost four years ago, it just broke them up." Before leaving for a press conference in Duluth, Perpich washed the dishes in the sink and changed a tire on the car where Rudy Jr. had hit a curb, according to Klobuchar.

The election of 1982 was a serious blow to the party-endorsement system, with voters rejecting the choices of both the DFL and Independent-Republican parties in the primaries. Not only did Spannaus lose out to Perpich, but Republican-endorsed Wangberg also lost to Wheelock Whitney, a moderate Republican who favored legalized abortion. Whitney, like Perpich, had bypassed the party endorsement convention to go straight to the primary. In that election he and his running mate, Lauris Krenik, a Madison Lake farmer and University of Minnesota regent, garnered 185,801 votes to 105,696 for Wangberg and his lieutenant governor candidate, Bloomington Mayor James Lindau. Whitney, who said he would be "a governor who can manage," put more than $700,000 of his own money into his $1 million primary campaign, which relied heavily on TV and other advertising. Wangberg spent roughly $270,000 and wound up deeply in debt.

DFL-endorsed U.S. Senate candidate Mark Dayton, 37, won the primary by a huge margin over Eugene McCarthy, the 65-year-old former senator (1960-1972) and unsuccessful 1968 presidential candidate. McCarthy had been living in Virginia since leaving the senate, and after the primary he said he was through with the DFL party. "I thought I should give them [DFL party leaders] one more chance," he said. "But I think this ends my relationship with the DFL in Minnesota."[9]

Spannaus was stung by the defeat that not only shattered his dream of becoming governor, but ended his political career. Yet he played the good soldier and endorsed Perpich. The most difficult task he faced the morning after the election, he said, was waking his 14-year-old son, David, and 10-year-old daughter, Laura, and giving them the bad news. "They took it pretty hard," he said. At the end of his term as attorney general, Spannaus joined Dorsey and Whitney, Minnesota's largest law firm.

After the primary, DFL state chairman Mike Hatch worked to unite the fractured party and persuaded reluctant party leaders, angry over the defeat of their endorsed candidate Spannaus, to endorse Perpich in the general election campaign. He had to persuade an even more reluctant Perpich, who felt like an outsider with the DFL, to accept that grudging support. The Republican Party was also less than totally united behind its nominee. Representative Glen Sherwood of Pine River, a leader of the Independent-Republican conservatives and an unsuccessful candidate for the party's gubernatorial endorsement, refused to endorse Whitney. Sherwood was a Ph.D. wildlife biologist, a devout religious fundamentalist, lay minister and elder in the Riverview Independent Tabernacle in Pine River. First elected as a DFLer, he switched parties, saying DFL policies were eroding moral values. He helped organize a "Pro Family, Pro Decency, Pro Life," caucus, a bipartisan group of legislators who held weekly prayer breakfasts and championed antiabortion, anti-pornography and "family" legislation.[10] Sherwood said he could not back the moderate candidate for governor because of Whitney's repudiation of the party's platform, which opposed both abortion and the proposed Equal Rights Amendment and supported capital punishment. Sherwood supporters promoted him as a write-in candidate in the November election.

Whitney was a likable, unorthodox millionaire who sat through council meetings lasting until midnight twice a month for $240 a year when he was the three-term mayor (1962-68) of Wayzata. "Every responsible citizen, if he has time, should take part in local government," he said.[11] Whitney, whose great grandfather settled in Minnesota in the mid-nineteenth century, was a native of St. Cloud. He was a graduate of Yale University and had served in the U. S. Navy. Active in bringing the Twins major league baseball team and other professional sports to Minnesota, he was selected as the 1959 Outstanding Young Man of Minneapolis by the Junior Chamber of Commerce. He failed in a bid for party endorsement for lieutenant governor in 1962 and was an unsuccessful candidate for the U.S. Senate against Senator Eugene McCarthy in 1964. At the Republican national convention in San Francisco that year he sharply criticized presidential nominee Barry Goldwater in a ten-page statement to the GOP Platform Committee. In 1972, at age 45, he left his job as chief executive of Dain, Kalman and Quail, a Minneapolis-based investment firm, to begin a second career as a university instructor and a social activist specializing in chemical-dependency treatments.[12]

In the general election campaign Whitney accused Perpich of participating in a DFL "spending spree" in the 1970s which he identified as the root cause of the state's current economic difficulties. Calling Perpich a "career politician," Whitney said he was an experienced business executive who could better manage the state. Perpich responded that when he was governor from 1976-79 he had saved $50 million through a freeze on state hiring and a crackdown on waste. His cost-saving and economic development programs were unwisely dropped by the Quie administration, Perpich said. His own experience as a small business owner (dentist) and international trade representative better qualified him to be governor, Perpich argued, and to develop the new industries and markets that would boost Minnesota's economy.

In a strange sidelight to the impending election, Dan Cohen, a Whitney supporter and former Minneapolis City Council member, contacted Capitol reporters for the *Star and Tribune*, the *Pioneer Press*, Associated Press and WCCO-TV on October 27. In exchange for promises of anonymity, he gave them court records showing that in 1970, DFL lieutenant-governor candidate Marlene Johnson had been arrested and convicted of stealing $6 worth of sewing materials, a misdemeanor.[13]

The next morning stories about Johnson's shoplifting conviction were published in Twin Cities newspapers. Johnson countered by explaining, as she had earlier explained to Perpich himself, that the incident had taken place during a time when she was depressed over the death of her father; she had simply forgotten to pay for the merchandise. She informed the press that Perpich knew all about the incident when he asked her to be his running mate, and both had agreed it had no bearing on her qualifications to be lieutenant governor.

Star Tribune and *Pioneer Press* editors overruled reporters' promises of anonymity to Cohen, saying the source of the documents was as newsworthy as the contents, and Cohen was named in articles in those newspapers. The Associated Press did not use Cohen's name, and WCCO-TV did not use the story at all. Cohen was fired from his job as public relations director for Martin-Williams Advertising Inc., where he had been handling advertising for the Independent-Republican gubernatorial campaign.[14]

Meanwhile, Perpich and other DFLers accused Whitney's campaign of eleventh-hour muckraking. Perpich said he was proud of his running mate and had absolute confidence in her. "In the last 12 years, she's been in business, a taxpayer, a good citizen, a very meaningful contributor to society. I just feel Minnesotans judge people on these things," he said. Whitney and his campaign manager, Jann Olsten, said Cohen had acted without knowledge of the campaign or its staff, but added that such information about a candidate's past ought to be available to the public before the election.

On December 15, Cohen filed a lawsuit against Cowles Media, parent of the *Star Tribune*, and Northwest Publications, parent company of the *Pioneer Press*, claiming fraud and breach of contract for naming him as the source in the Johnson story. Newspaper attorneys called

Cohen "a dirty trickster" who was trying to defeat Perpich by feeding the information on Johnson to reporters. The case was appealed all the way to the U.S. Supreme Court, which ruled 5-4 in a landmark decision that reporters' promises of confidentiality are legally enforceable. The Minnesota Supreme Court, which had previously ruled that the newspapers were not liable for damages, reinstated a $200,000 award to Cohen by a Hennepin District Court jury.

On Election Night, November 2, three minutes after the polls closed, CBS News declared Rudy Perpich the winner, based on exit polls. When the official vote tally was in from the state's 4,066 precincts, Perpich had won the race for governor with a landslide victory, carrying 78 of Minnesota's 87 counties, including some Independent-Republican strongholds in southern Minnesota. His total vote-count was 1,049,104 to Whitney's 711,796.

Minnesota voters split their tickets, re-electing Republican David Durenberger to a full six-year term in the U.S. Senate over DFL challenger Mark Dayton. Dayton, wealthy heir of a department store family, had spent $7 million of his own money in the losing campaign.

The Minnesota Poll published later by the *Star Tribune* identified improving the economy as the most important issue among voters.[15] But other factors were also at work. Whitney's somewhat negative campaign offended voters with fond memories of their colorful DFL governor. And his candid, and perhaps fiscally prudent, admission that he would not give schools any increase in state aids in the 1984-85 school year did not go over well with many teachers and parents. His plans to freeze popular property-tax-relief programs and remove property-tax levy limits on real estate for local governments were displeasing to homeowners, farmers and local officials. Perpich had argued that property taxes would skyrocket if that happened, but Whitney said it would force local governments to tighten their belts and be responsive.

Perpich was snowbound at his lake home in Gilbert the day after an ecstatic election night victory party at the Sawmill Saloon in Virginia and was unable to get to the Capitol until Friday. When he did finally arrive, the enthusiastic governor-elect began working in a transition office on the east end of the first floor of the Capitol, setting the fast pace that he said would be the hallmark of his administration. He met with Governor Quie, who told him more cuts might be needed to keep the state budget in balance.

Though Perpich had shunned out-of-state travel during his first term as governor, saying he didn't have the time, he immediately disclosed plans for several trips. He would be flying to Boston the following Tuesday with leaders of the Minnesota Business Partnership to look at Massachusetts public/private partnerships that brought the state new technology jobs. He also announced plans for a 10-day trip to Japan later in the month with an itinerary that included signing a contract with a trading company to sell local products in Japan. He and Lola also planned to fly to Park City, Utah, to attend a conference of newly elected governors, sponsored by the National Governors Association.

He was losing no time in his efforts to bring his vision of Minnesota as a leader in the developing world marketplace to life.

Chapter 11

Jobs, Jobs, Jobs

Breaking with tradition, Perpich took the oath of office as the state's thirty-sixth governor 189 miles from the state Capitol. He was sworn into office at Hibbing High School, the first time a governor had made his inaugural speech outside of St. Paul. Perpich's communications director-designate, Gerry Nelson, cobbled the address together in Jack DeLuca's office in Hibbing, spending the New Year's weekend up there, and finished barely in time for the event.[1] Because of the limited seating, invitations went only to family, friends, and teachers and students from Hibbing High School, where the four Perpich brothers graduated, and Nashwauk-Keewatin High School, where Lola Perpich graduated. More than two dozen former teachers of the Perpiches were in the audience. The governor thanked them for making an extra effort for "a bunch of kids from a ghetto." Minnesota Supreme Court Associate Justice Rosalie Wahl administered the oath of office to the new governor, and his longtime friend, Frank Ongaro Sr., was master of ceremonies in the elegant high school auditorium. The Hibbing High School band and mixed chorus provided music including the "Yugoslav Polka" and Aaron Copeland's "Fanfare for the Common Man." Rudy's three brothers were present. Their mother and father, Mary and Anton, watched the swearing-in and speech on television in their Hibbing home.

The theme of his inaugural speech was education, and it was a symbolic setting for the governor who often said education was his passport out of the poverty of his Iron Range childhood. "It's not my intention to move the state capitol to the Range," he said, "But it is my intention to insure that all of Minnesota's students receive the same high-quality education I received in this high school." He called for strengthening school programs in foreign languages, computers, and science to enable Minnesota graduates to compete better in the world marketplace. After the speech Governor Perpich had lunch—chicken soup and peaches—in the school cafeteria and then headed back to St. Paul to go to work.

Marlene Johnson was sworn in at the Capitol with her mother, Helen, holding the Bible for her. She recalled later, "I had an incredible sense of making history, of realizing that now it was up to me to figure out a role that would make a difference. I was both terrified and excited—and determined to do my part well."[2] Johnson felt she had received a gift, enabling her to pursue a vision of "opening up opportunities to other women and people of color...and to improve our response to the needs of children and their families."

On January 6 a reception was held at the Landmark Center in St. Paul sponsored by a citizens' inaugural committee. The proceeds from the $50-per-person event were to fund the restoration of the Governor's Residence. Perpich declined the traditional inaugural ball, saying times were too tough to spend money on such an event, but Gornick organized an inaugural party for the new governor on the following Saturday night at the St. Paul Civic Center. More than 3,000 people attended, including busloads from the Range, dressed in everything from blue jeans and leisure suits to black tie. The admission price was only $5, so any-

©2000 Star Tribune/Mpls. St. Paul
Lieutenant Governor Marlene Johnson being sworn in by Ramsey County municipal judge Harriet Lansing

one could attend. The guests drank beer, mixed drinks, and wine and were entertained by local groups including the Mesaba Button Box Band and the Sabathani Baptist Church Choir of Minneapolis, and there was a grand march featuring couples in ethnic garb from more than a dozen countries. Proceeds were donated to emergency-food shelves. "We're all one people, and we're going to help each other," Perpich said in a brief address.

The need was great. Minnesota's unemployment rate had soared to 10.4 percent. State tax revenues were falling, and there was a $734-million budget shortfall. The state had lost its top AAA credit rating.

"The state of our state is not good," Perpich said in his State of the State speech to the Legislature on January 4. He asked business to work with him on economic recovery and proposed business subsidies and tax incentives to create jobs. "As long as I am governor, government and business are partners—not adversaries—in Minnesota," he said.

Labeling his new business-friendly approach "progressive pragmatism," Perpich presented the Legislature with a $10-billion proposed state budget for 1983-85. It was designed, he said, to create jobs in growth industries with state investments in "businesses of the future" and to lay the groundwork for making Minnesota a world center of high technology, health care, and tourism. It would be the state's first double-digit budget, compared with $8.3 billion for the 1981-1983 biennium. At the same time, the governor promised to hold down taxes and impose tough spending restraints on both social programs dear to the DFL Party and property-tax relief for homeowners and renters. It all sounded strangely similar to the platform that had brought defeat to the Republican candidate Wheelock Whitney a few weeks earlier.

To balance this new fiscal conservatism, with its heavy echoes of traditional Republican philosophy, Perpich also reasserted his commitment to listening to ordinary people around the state. He and other DFLers had been defeated in 1978, he remarked, because "there were a lot of arrogant people in our party who refused to listen to the public."

The outlook was not as bleak as it might have been, however. When Perpich took office, he benefited from the tough tax-increase and spending-cut decisions already made by former Governor Quie and the Legislature to balance the budget. Furthermore, there were signs of economic recovery.

Aides said a new Perpich had returned to the governor's office, more confident, sophisticated, and disciplined.[3] "It's like the difference between day and night," said Tom Triplett, Perpich's policy adviser. Gerry Nelson, communications director, said Perpich's three-and-a-half years in Europe were "sort of like going to Control Data University and getting his graduate degree." Yet the new Perpich was, if anything, even more of a paradox than the old one: He was a DFL governor who aggressively sought alliances with business to create jobs, while remaining staunchly loyal to his friends in organized labor. He opened up state and judicial appointments to women and minorities, but also took care of pals who "brung us to the dance."

Some of the governor's liberal friends were not happy with this new business-stroking version of Rudy Perpich. Senator Allan Spear said, "When he came back from Vienna he had kind of lost that populist touch he once had." Perpich defended his new perspective, however. "I have not lost the feel or the sight of helping the poor and other people who are down and out, or of making sure that our young people get an even break at the starting gate. But I recognize now that without the business community, we're not ever going to meet our objectives of putting people back to work and providing equal educational opportunities."

One of the new governor's first efforts to court business was the appointment of Gus Donhowe, a former Pillsbury Company executive recommended by business leaders, to be commissioner of finance. Donhowe was not a "yes" man but a long-range thinker who became a top policy adviser to the governor and contributed a good deal to shaping state policy during his time in the Perpich cabinet. Perpich also created eleven economic-recovery commissions and recruited top business and political leaders to serve on them—men and women who would continue as valuable contacts throughout his administration. Commission chairmen included prominent business CEOs like William Norris, chairman of Control Data Inc. and Harold Zigmund, president of Blandin Paper Company of Grand Rapids. Each commission focused on one topic from a list that included high technology, medical technology, agri-processing, mineral development, tourism, wood products, small business, international marketing, film and graphic arts, investment and banking, and the expediting of state contracts. The governor asked each commission to develop proposals for the 1983 Legislature that would facilitate the formation of economic partnerships between government, education, and business institutions.

That public-private partnership principle was exemplified in the centerpiece of what Perpich called his "Investment Budget" for economic recovery, a $75-million, one-year jobs program. The Legislature passed the Minnesota Emergency Employment Development Act (MEED), which provided subsidies to businesses which contracted to hire unemployed Minnesotans in new jobs for at least six months. Perpich also proposed loan guarantees and other financial assistance for small businesses that retrained unemployed workers. He quadrupled the state tourism budget and established two new engineering schools, one at Mankato State University and the other at the University of Minnesota at Duluth.[4] Saying Minnesota should be the energy research center for North America, he vowed to make Minnesota as energy-independent as possible. He asked for a $30-million program to stimulate development of home-grown alternative energy sources, such as peat, biomass, and solar and to encourage energy conservation, an endeavor he said would provide thousands of jobs.[5] The Legislature agreed to much of Perpich's conservation and energy initiatives, including a new natural resources research center in Duluth and the establishment of a separate state energy agency.

Terry Montgomery returned as Perpich's chief of staff. Likable, methodical, unflappable, he was remembered from Perpich's first term as a shrewd tactician whose forte was figuring out how to help make the governor's ideas work. The chemistry between the two was positive, and it often resulted in effective strategies.

A behind-the-scenes facilitator, Montgomery began to pull together opinion leaders and powerful businessmen, enlisting their help largely through accommodation rather than confrontation. With the governor on the road much of the time, Montgomery wielded considerable power; people who wanted the governor's ear found Montgomery accessible and were confident that the friendly chief of staff could get things done. Indeed, Perpich affirmed, "He's right after Lola." Perpich said it was Montgomery who had advised him to push pro-business legislative initiatives during his second term and also helped him build a close relationship with the business community. It was Montgomery's idea to appoint prominent business leaders to study commissions, which not only gave Perpich easier access to corporate boardrooms, but also were tapped for and drew large contributions for Perpich's travel and campaign funds. Montgomery introduced Perpich to Carl Pohlad, and the governor and the powerful Minneapolis banker were allies throughout Perpich's administrations.

The governor named Earl Craig, president of the Minneapolis Urban Coalition, to head a task force on long-range state planning. He appointed Mike Hatch, the DFL state chairman who had rebuilt the party and paid its debts after the 1978 disaster and secured party endorsement for Perpich in the 1982 general election, to be commissioner of commerce.

The other Perpich brothers returned to the Capitol. Rudy Perpich appointed his brother Tony to be temporary head of the state Consumer Affairs Office, which he planned to abolish as a separate agency and transfer to the office of Attorney General Humphrey. Tony and his wife, Irene, then an anesthesiologist at the Veterans Administration Hospital, had moved to St. Paul. The governor said his brother would lobby for his energy proposals. In June Mark Dayton, whom Perpich had named commissioner of the new Department of Energy and Economic Development, appointed Tony as his deputy commissioner for energy sources, the state's highest energy official. Tony was a firm believer in the governor's notion of using Minnesota's vast peat bogs and wood chips from wood-processing industries as new energy sources for the state, although many observers didn't take the idea seriously. A skilled carpenter, he had built his own house in Eveleth, employing his energy-saving expertise in the construction, and after he retired he built another house in Sunrise Township, north of the Twin Cities. He said that along with his legislative experience, his building experience was helpful in his new energy job. Later the governor appointed Tony to head the Department of Public Service.

George Perpich sold his dental practice, and he and his wife Connie moved to Vadnais Heights, a St. Paul suburb. George plunged into a new career as a lobbyist with an impressive list of clients including Iron Range municipalities and school districts, the Canterbury Downs race track, the First National Bank of Minneapolis, the Fond du Lac Indian tribe, and the Minnesota Dental Association. George's wife, Connie, was a lobbyist for Planned Parenthood, an advocate for legalized abortions.

In 1987 Minnesota Power Company of Duluth hired George to fight legislation supported by Iron Range lawmakers who said it would save 600 taconite mining jobs. The proposed legislation would have permitted the National Steel Corporation, operator of a taconite plant in the Hibbing-Keewatin area, to drop Minnesota Power as its power source at the end of 1988 without having to pay more than $90 million in lost future revenue. National Steel said that unless it could get less expensive power from outside the state, it could not be competitive and would have to close the plant. George succeeded in killing the National Steel bill, but later Minnesota Power reduced its large taconite plant customers' rates to help the company cut costs and make it more competitive. Some legislators thought George was working against the interests of taconite workers. Senator Doug Johnson, an author of the bill, said, "I think he's on the wrong side for what's best for the Iron Range." Republican critics accused George of trading on his relationship with the governor, which Rudy and George denied. "I don't have the governor's ear to the point where I can turn his head," said George.[6]

Like Rudy, George had changed. Though he had once railed at big business on the Senate floor, he now adopted Rudy's "Progressive Pragmatism" theme. Business people needed to lobby effectively to present their case to busy legislators and to produce good legislation, he declared.[7] "Lobbying is a form of continuing education for legislators who need and want to hear all sides of an issue before legislative decisions are made."[8]

Perpich named Joe Samargia, a welder and steelworkers' union leader from Gilbert, to head the new emergency jobs program. Samargia had been President of Local 1938 of the United Steelworkers of America for seven years and was an early activist in Perpich's 1982 gubernatorial campaign. The jobs program provided short-term jobs through state subsidies for private employers and through temporary jobs in the public sector. Minneapolis legislators who were among sponsors of the legislation had asked Perpich to appoint Earl Craig, longtime president of the Urban Coalition of Minneapolis, to head the program, arguing that he was the best-qualified candidate. Representative Randy Staten, like Craig an African-American and Minneapolis DFLer, felt that Perpich's appointment of Samargia was a political appointment that would damage the program and said he was concerned that the Iron Range would be favored in handing out the jobs.[9] Samargia denied that he would favor northeastern Minnesota over the Twin Cities or any other area of the state.

The program was highly popular, and the next Legislature, satisfied with the operation, approved its expansion. During the first two years more than 100,000 people applied under the program, and about 24,000 were placed in jobs.

Yet Perpich was not shy about rewarding loyalty and appointing Iron Rangers and other political friends, along with relatives and campaign contributors, to posts in his administration, and this naturally triggered charges of cronyism. The *Star Tribune* reported nine months after Perpich took office that half of the top state employees hired by his administration had personal, family, financial or party ties to the DFL governor. And many others with such ties, the newspaper added, had been appointed to non-salaried jobs on boards and commissions that governed or promoted special interests in the state.[10] When asked about the high number of DFLers, friends. and relatives in his administration, the governor replied: "It is not illegal for any governor to appoint people he knows and trusts. It is not illegal or unexpected for a DFL governor to appoint DFLers."

Montgomery attempted to keep the governor focused on a few big projects, instead of remaining transfixed by the myriad of ideas that were perpetually surfacing in his ever-active imagination—but he never quite succeeded. As Jim Nichols, commissioner of agriculture, put it, "Rudy had millions of ideas, and some of them weren't workable. The trick was to get him to follow through on the good ones."[11] In contrast to his first term in office, however, Perpich delegated much of the running of government to commissioners, acting on the advice of Montgomery in a four-page, "Strategic Long-Range Plan." In that memo Montgomery cautioned the governor not to become preoccupied with hour-to-hour crises and fighting brushfires, "thereby losing sight of the big picture." He suggested the governor bring in a small group of his most capable and trusted cabinet officials to advise him on governmental policy and to flesh out a vision of where Minnesota should be in the next four to eight years, as well as a plan for how he intended to get there. That policy council might be headed by State Planning Director Tom Triplett, Montgomery advised.[12] Montgomery, his eye on the 1986 reelection campaign, urged the governor to begin building a political operation and raising money. "There is nothing that will discourage opponents more than a strong rating in the polls and money in the bank," said the chief of staff. He suggested Perpich also select a small group of political advisers "with whom you are totally comfortable and whose political judgment you trust."[13]

It was extremely important to establish a close and harmonious relationship with the DFL Party, said the memo. It called for a systematic effort to reward helpful legislators, particularly by appearing at fundraisers or campaign appearances in their districts. And Montgomery, hinting at an even bigger national agenda for the governor, said, "we should consciously orchestrate your activities, both locally and nationally, for maximum media impact." That they did. When there was good news or a major announcement, it was timed to accommodate TV prime time and newspaper deadlines, with the governor carefully positioned in center stage and on hand to take a bow. Bad news and politically sensitive disclosures often came via press releases brought down to the Capitol press room by an aide late in the afternoon, when reporters were ready to go home—especially on Friday afternoons when reporters were working on weekend "thumbsucker" pieces; by then the governor and other sources had left the Capitol and would be unavailable for comment.

Perpich's office door was not as open to the press as it had been in his earlier term. Many meetings were closed. Still he was easily accessible and candid with reporters during the early years of his second term. When aides tried to shield Perpich from reporters pursuing controversial issues, they would stake out the parking place on the northwest corner of the Capitol where the governor's car was parked, and he was almost always willing to talk with them. Throughout his terms as governor, aides knew that the biggest source of news leaks in the administration was the governor himself. Commissioners and staff crowded around when Perpich was talking with reporters because that might be the first time they would hear about his newest idea. Once, when a reporter pressed the governor for the name of the soon-to-be appointed commissioner of finance, Perpich couldn't resist playing Deep Throat and suggested the reporter look inside his coat pocket on the coat rack in a few minutes. Sure enough, there was a slip of paper with "Peter Hutchinson" written on it, and a page one story in the *Star Tribune* the next morning revealed the appointment that was not scheduled to be announced until a press conference the next day.

Governor Among Governors

A "border war" erupted in late 1982, when Perpich threw down the gauntlet to the Republican governor, William (Bill) Janklow, and other South Dakota officials, who were trying to woo business away from Minnesota by portraying it as a high-tax state with an unfavorable business climate. Perpich declared that South Dakota couldn't begin to compare with Minnesota's quality of life and belittled it as "fiftieth in everything" among the states. "I concede they're Number One in prairie dogs," Perpich jabbed. Janklow, a lawyer, ex-Marine, and flamboyant politician, was quick to butt heads with opponents, Democrat or Republican, and he challenged Perpich to a debate. Perpich accepted the challenge, drawing national publicity, and the two met on March 18, 1983, in Chicago, on public television's *MacNeil-Lehrer Report*. With the cameras rolling, they traded insults in a rapid exchange that continued after they were off the air.

Later the two became friends, traveling together on a National Governors Association trip to China, where Perpich, because of his dental background, was tapped to give Janklow occasional shots of adrenaline for an allergic condition. Perpich quipped when he was asked to do the injections, "Given our history, I'd give Janklow a shot, and it'll kill him, and I'd get blamed for it." They later worked on education matters and other cooperative ventures for their states.

At an October 1983 meeting of the Midwestern Governors' Conference in Lawrence, Kansas, Perpich led a panel on international trade. At the end of the conference, he was elected chairman of the thirteen-state organization.

But he got into trouble on another count. Governors of the fifty states, banded together in the National Governors Association (NGA) and regional groups, met several times a year around the country and discussed issues publicly and privately, and were entertained and fawned over by local hosts and throngs of special-interest lobbyists. The last thing they wanted to do was to get into a public controversy. When the governors took a position on an issue, it was usually carefully sanitized and scrutinized by their staffs to avoid adverse repercussions back home. So when Perpich, the "new kid on the block," proposed in Lawrence that governors adopt a tough stand on acid rain, it was voted down. Instead, the governors adopted a carefully-worded resolution expressing concern about the problem and calling for research on the topic. The next year, when the Minnesota governor again threw out a controversial initiative at an NGA meeting in Nashville, calling for governors to go on record in favor of equal pay for so-called women's jobs in public employment, some of his colleagues were not pleased. It seemed like a radical step at the time. The governors approved a watered-down resolution to avoid argument and public embarrassment, but it cost the Minnesota governor. When it came time to hand out NGA committee assignments, both then and later, Perpich received no plums. Meanwhile Nina Rothchild, commissioner of employee relations, was given an award by the NGA for her work on pay equity. Rothchild, a former Mahtomedi school board member and a magna cum laude graduate of Smith College in mathematics, had fought hard for pay-equity legislation in Minnesota, going back to the time when she was executive director of the Council on the Economic Status of Women (1976-82). With strong support from women legislators, the State of Minnesota had enacted first-in-the-nation "pay equity" or "comparable worth" for all state employees in 1982, a far-reaching victory for women. In 1984 Perpich and Rothchild spearheaded the Local Government Pay Equity Act, requiring local governments to put pay equity into effect.

At the same meeting in Lawrence—to the consternation of the surprised Commissioner of Finance Gus Donhowe and other officials back home in Minnesota—Perpich unveiled the agenda he intended to push in the 1984 Legislature to reporters who had followed him down there. (Donhowe, who was vacationing in Canada, called a reporter to learn what the governor had announced would be his agenda.) His proposed legislative initiatives included 1) removal of the onerous 10 percent income-tax surcharge which had been passed during the budget crises of the Quie administration, 2) a reduction in the size of the Minnesota Legislature, and 3) a reduction in the number of constitutional officers elected on the state ballot. He also spoke about the possibility of reducing the number of cabinet heads and changing the Metropolitan Council from an appointed to an elected body.

The day after the Kansas conference Perpich traveled to Portland, Oregon, to talk with executives of two wood-products companies about the possibility of building plants in Minnesota. With the frequent comings and goings, a number of Perpich's cabinet members and staff, as well as some members of the press who accompanied him on his travels, were finding that the best opportunity to talk with the busy governor was en route. Perpich would hold meetings with his entourage in a coffee shop or hotel room, sometimes at seven in the morning, at other times late at night, during which he would take care of state business. These meeting were also open to any reporters who happened to be in the vicinity.

In 1982 voters had approved a constitutional amendment creating a new Court of Appeals to ease the workload on the Supreme Court. The twelve judges were to be appointed by the governor, one from each of the eight congressional districts and four at large. Perpich had the rare opportunity to pick an entire court. The Legislature had also created more than a score of other new judicial positions. It allowed Perpich to have an enormous impact on the court system for years to come.

At the request of then-House Speaker Harry (Tex) Sieben, Perpich named Sieben's brother Michael, a Newport lawyer and former legislator, to head a judicial selection commission—a prize plum for a lawyer.[14] Sandy Keith was a member and informal secretary of the commission which recommended to the governor appointees for both the Appeals Court and the district courts. The first question was whether there should be any Republicans appointed. Keith said Perpich felt strongly that "We won it. We get it," and Michael Sieben also leaned that way. That one-party philosophy reflected Perpich's northeastern Minnesota view, Keith said, that "where one party dominates they kind of think of everything, all appointments [as opportunities] to help our friends and make sure we stay in office." The Sieben family dominated a political machine in Dakota County with a similar view.

Perpich named his good friend and fellow Croatian, Peter Popovich, chief judge of the new court. Popovich, a workaholic former state legislator, took on the job of organizing the new court with zest. Among those Perpich appointed to the Appeals Court was Don Wozniak of St. Paul, a former member of the Minnesota House. Wozniak, a DFL Party maverick like Perpich, had supported Perpich in his primary election challenge to Warren Spannaus. Wozniak found out about his appointment when *Pioneer Press* reporter Robert O'Keefe called him and said the governor had told him to tell Wozniak that Perpich wanted him on the new Appeals Court.[15] (In 1987 when George Scott retired and there was an opening on the Supreme Court, Perpich moved Popovich up to the high court, and named Wozniak chief judge of the Court of the Appeals.)

Another issue with the new Court of Appeals was the appointment of women judges. Perpich appointed three women to the twelve-member court, who were recommended by the advisory committee, but Keith lost his battle to have Republican representation on the bench: "I wanted Rudy to pick the best people. Rudy almost always insisted his judicial appointees be DFLers, and he and I fought over this. Thirty-five percent of the state identify as Republicans. The whole Court of Appeals were DFLers. I thought that was wrong, that there should be a mix. He didn't agree with me."[16] Women's activists were furious when Daniel Foley of Rochester was appointed to the Appeals Court from the First Congressional District, instead of a woman they favored.

The *Minneapolis Star Tribune* reported in October that Governor Perpich had dismantled the system designed by his predecessor, Independent-Republican Al Quie, to restrict the influence of politics, and had filled nearly half his judgeships with former DFL officeholders and activists.[17] Former Governor Quie had joined a growing national trend by allowing local bar associations and judges to name members of his screening panels which tended to be bipartisan. As many as a third of the forty-five judges the scrupulously nonpartisan Quie appointed (to the dismay of many Republicans) were DFLers, the newspaper reported. In contrast, Perpich appointed each member of his judicial selection commission, and it was therefore dominated by people with ties to the DFL or to Perpich. But the newspaper reported that nearly all of the lawyers interviewed for the article, both friend and foe, said the Perpich appointees they knew were well qualified, and spokesmen for Perpich said that's what counted.

Allan Spear, chairman of the Senate Judiciary Committee for many years, gave Perpich good marks for appointing more women and people of color to the bench. "But there were some blatantly political appointments, no doubt about it." The worst, Spear said, was the naming of Sean Rice, who suffered from a manic-depressive disorder, to be a Hennepin County District judge in 1987. "It was unfair both to the judiciary and to Sean Rice to put somebody with his kind of mental-health problems on the bench. It was a reward to Sean's father [Representative James Rice, chairman of the House Appropriations Committee], and you just don't do that."[18]

William Kennedy, Hennepin County chief public defender and a member of Perpich's kitchen cabinet, defended the judicial appointments of Rice and former House Speaker Fred Norton against the charges of political payoffs. Rice was condemned for having past medical problems that required medication and for being his father's son, said Kennedy. Norton was a good lawyer with a reputation for fairness, under attack by elitist lawyers, said the public defender. Later Sean Rice was suspended by the State Board on Judicial standards for sixty days for being abusive to his staff.[19] The State of Minnesota paid $150,000 to settle a lawsuit alleging that he screamed insults and threw objects at two female clerks. Rice was defeated for reelection in 1994.

Spear also remembered that Perpich was heavily criticized for appointing his campaign manager, John Stanoch, to the Hennepin County District Court, on his last day in the governor's office in 1991: "John Stanoch turned out to be a wonderful appointment. He was an outstanding judge."

Governor Abroad

In 1983 Minnesotans got their first exposure to Perpich's overseas travels. During his first term as governor, Perpich had restricted travel by state officials with a directive that, "Department and agency heads should attend out-of-state meetings only if they are of significant importance to the state." Now that he had developed an interest in the global economy, Perpich traveled abroad extensively. He claimed that he was promoting Minnesota and bringing new jobs to the state. And indeed, late that summer of his first year back in office, Perpich went on a twenty-six day trip knocking on doors of European businesses accompanied by William Dietrich, his trade representative, and Representative James Rice. While overseas he arranged to open a Minnesota trade office in Stockholm,

Sweden, making Minnesota the first state to open such an office in Scandinavia.[20]

A Minnesota Poll published in the *Star Tribune* in the summer of 1983 found Perpich's approval rating at a record high for that stage in a governor's term. Seventy-two percent of the respondents in the poll approved of his performance. Perpich received a standing ovation on September 13 when he was introduced to the Minnesota Business Partnership and painted an upbeat picture of Minnesota's economy.

"My problem is that I've got so many things going that I might get too much in the pipeline and clog it up," an exuberant Governor Rudy Perpich said as he ticked off a long list of his new ideas at the beginning of 1984.[21] Putting people back to work was still his top goal, he said. But he also wanted to hold an annual college football bowl game at the Hubert H. Humphrey Metrodome, lure a major national golf tournament to the state, create an international K-12 music school in the Twin Cities, study the feasibility of installing domes over tennis courts for year-round use, and provide low rent for studios for beginning artists in order to build a thriving community of artists in the metro area. He suggested that a statewide mosquito-control program might help the state's tourism economy. And he asked state agencies to explore the feasibility of a winter amusement park for Minnesota—an indoor-outdoor facility based on winter sports and outdoor recreational activities similar to the famous Disney parks in California and Florida.

Sensitive to criticism of the state's business climate, Perpich held press conferences around the state urging Minnesotans to "accentuate the positive" about their state. News articles in the *Star Tribune* showed that Minnesota had outpaced many of its neighbors, he said. The governor said Minnesota was known throughout the world for its high technology and medical expertise, but it also could lay claim to being the "agricultural capital of the world."[22] But it all seemed to be so much overblown hype when 3M, the state's largest private employer, announced in February of 1984 that it planned to locate a major research and development center in Texas instead of Minnesota. Lewis Lehr, 3M chairman, and Robert Adams, senior vice-president of technology services, said the general direction of the Legislature and the state's tax and regulatory policies had made it difficult for 3M. "I think we're mostly taken for granted," said Adams.[23]

When Whirlpool Corporation closed its St. Paul manufacturing plant and moved production to Indiana, House Minority Leader David Jennings called that "further evidence that Minnesota tax policies make it impossible to be economically competitive."[24]

Perpich announced plans for a national labor history interpretative center in Minnesota, and he hired retiring Minnesota AFL-CIO President David Roe to head a task force to carry out the project. The center would be the first of its kind in the U.S., Perpich said, and would be a major educational institution where research, literature, and conferences would focus on the workers' role throughout American history. Minnesota would be an appropriate site for the center, said the governor, because every labor group was represented in the state, and labor's struggles for equity and human decency were played out here. "Minneapolis truck drivers in their successful fight for union recognition in 1934 played a pivotal role in national acceptance of peaceful collective bargaining." And Perpich recalled that populist Ignatius Donnelly helped found the Minnesota Federation of Labor in 1890.[25]

Perpich also wanted Minnesota to be in the vanguard of an effort to substitute corn-based ethanol for lead as an octane booster in gasoline, and as soon as he took office in 1983 he ordered all gasoline-powered state vehicles to switch to "gasohol," a blend of corn-based ethyl alcohol and unleaded gasoline. It cost 6 to 10 cents a gallon more than regular gasoline. The governor asked cities, counties, and school districts to follow the state's example. At Perpich's request, the Midwestern Governors' Conference meeting in Lincoln, Nebraska, adopted a resolution urging the farm states in the conference to pass tax and incentive programs for the use of ethanol. Perpich said he would ask the 1985 Legislature to raise the state gas tax on leaded gasoline, already one of the highest in the nation, and reduce it on ethanol in an effort to get drivers to switch. That would encourage eliminating lead additives for health reasons, the governor said, and at the same time provide a new market for corn and make Minnesota more energy-independent. He said he planned to talk with companies that might be interested in constructing ethanol plants in Minnesota.

In 1985 the Minnesota Energy and Economic Development Authority approved a $3 million loan guarantee for an ethanol plant in Mankato. Later Governor Arne Carlson also supported economic incentives for the ethanol industry. By 1999 there were 15 ethanol plants operating in Minnesota, producing 218 million gallons of ethanol and using 84.5 million bushels of corn valued at $260 million, according to the Minnesota Department of Agriculture and other state sources. With a state-mandated law, the 15 percent ethanol-oxygenated gasoline replaced 200 million gallons of traditional gasoline. Consumers paid an estimated $42 million annually in higher gas prices, and the state spent an estimated $25 million annually for ethanol programs. The estimated annual benefit to the state from the ethanol industry was $350 million in 1999.

Gene Hugoson, Carlson's commissioner of agriculture, said there was clear evidence that ethanol had improved the air quality in the Twin Cities. Jim Nichols, Perpich's commissioner of agriculture, called the effort "an incredible success story." On the other hand, a legislative auditor's report questioned the wisdom of providing major support for a single industry.

Independent-Republicans made what they called the state's "disastrous" business climate a major election campaign issue, saying high taxes and high spending had driven businesses and jobs out of the state. House minority leader David Jennings wrote letters to newspapers around the state, calling Minnesota the "Land of 10,000 Taxes." Jennings wrote, "There's a billboard south of the Twin Cities, purchased by an irate businessman. It says, 'Will the last business leaving the state please turn off the lights?'"

Perpich, incensed by Jennings' attack, appealed to Minnesotans to stop "knocking Minnesota." The State of Minnesota is like a family, he said. "When you go around knocking the state, it's the same as knocking your own family." In fact, Minnesota was prospering and setting all-time employment records, he said. The governor noted that *TIME* magazine in an article headlined "Minnesota's Magic Touch," cited Minnesota as a breeding ground for new technology enterprises.[27] And the New York *CITYBUSINESS* magazine reported that Minneapolis and Cincinnati were listed as the "two favorite U. S.

cities for doing business" by William May, dean of the graduate school of business administration at New York University.[28]

The retirement of Speaker Harry Sieben and House Majority Leader Willis Eken, and the consequent jockeying by other would-be leaders vying for those posts, put the House DFL caucus in disarray at a crucial time. A score of races looked very close, and DFLers were nervous about whether they could hold onto their 74-57 majority. In the summer of 1984 Perpich, who had previously shunned his role as head of the DFL Party, traveled the state campaigning vigorously for DFL legislative candidates, promising that tax cuts would be his number one priority in the 1985 session and saying he needed a comfortable DFL majority to help pass his legislative program. He told reporters on a plane with him that he'd leave the governor's office before the end of his term if he had to deal with a Republican House obstructing his programs.

Perpich also became chairman of the Mondale presidential campaign in Minnesota, which caused the vice president some discomfiture. On a campaign swing down into Iowa, Perpich said that Geraldine Ferraro of New York, Mondale's running mate and the first woman to be the vice presidential candidate by a major political party, was the wrong choice for the Democratic ticket. He had advised Mondale, he said, to pick someone from the South.

Independent-Republicans needed eleven new seats to take control of the Minnesota House, and David Jennings, House Independent-Republican minority leader, was cautiously optimistic: "I think Mondale is going down in flames at this point, and if that happens, our chances improve to fifty-fifty. I'm feeling real good about it now."[29]

In the November election Independent-Republicans, helped by the heavy voting for President Reagan and Boschwitz, who were elected to second terms, picked up thirteen seats and took over the House with a 69-65 majority, their first time in control in fourteen years. Walter Mondale was crushed by Reagan. The former vice president and Ferraro carried only the District of Columbia and Mondale's native state of Minnesota, where he won by only 3,761 votes. Growe was swamped by Boschwitz who won 1,199,926 votes to her 852,844. Jennings said the election returns were an indication that voters "endorse the Independent-Republican agenda of lower taxes and smarter state spending."

Though he was not up for re-election himself, the results were a personal setback for the DFL governor who had made eighty-five campaign trips on behalf of sixty-five DFL legislative candidates. Perpich did not resign as he had threatened, but girded up to do battle with an old adversary, Jennings, who would be the new House Speaker.

Chapter 12

The Education Governor. $1 Billion Tax Cut.
Perpich Meets the Ghermezians and Finds
an Austrian Castle.

M
any Minnesota farmers were in deep financial trouble. On January 21, 1985, ten thousand suffering rural citizens came to the Capitol in St. Paul to rally for farm relief. Some carried signs demanding an emergency moratorium on foreclosures of farm, home, and small-business mortgages.[1] The Reverend Jesse Jackson, national civil rights leader and 1984 presidential candidate, made an appearance, encouraging farmers to support Groundswell, a liberal farmers-rights group seeking a ban on foreclosures.

With the taconite industry in a slump, the Iron Range also was hurting. Northeastern Minnesota's unemployment rate was 17.4 percent in January, more than double the state and national rate. Duluth's unemployment rate was 9.1 percent, but St. Louis County outside of Duluth was even more hard-hit with 22.9 percent of its workforce unemployed.

Saddened and worried over the suffering of so many, Perpich promised in his 1985 State of the State speech, "We will not turn our backs on the thousands of Minnesotans who desperately need our help." The farm crisis and the severe problems of unemployment would require a massive, bipartisan effort and a major commitment from Washington, however. "The state can help, and we will...pull together in this time of economic disaster in rural Minnesota." But the problem went far beyond the state's control, Perpich believed. He was careful not to promise more than he thought the state could deliver and avoided the issue of a mortgage foreclosure moratorium. Furthermore, he was disturbed by what was increasingly apparent—that Minnesota was becoming a two-economy state, with widespread prosperity in the metropolitan area and depression in many rural areas.

Perpich's 1985 State of the State speech was perhaps his finest, and one that best spelled out his vision of the great state he wanted Minnesota to be. The DFL governor gave his speech at seven o'clock in the evening, January 10, instead of the traditional noontime, before a joint House-Senate session. It was broadcast live by commercial television stations in the Twin Cities and by public television throughout the state. Earlier that week Perpich had slipped into the empty Minnesota House chamber one night to practice his speech, reading it from a new TelePrompter.

Setting a fiscal conservative tone, Perpich called during the speech for a 1985-87 budget that made state government "lean, not mean." He said he was determined to establish Minnesota as a national leader in excellent fiscal management. His department heads would be judged by their ability to reduce spending and streamline state government. "It is my hope that by the time I leave the office of Governor, our state will be run with such efficiency and such foresight that stockholders throughout the United States will ask, 'Why can't business be run like government in Minnesota?'"

He reiterated his belief that foreign trade was the wave of the future and that Minnesota must cultivate new markets. "International trade means expanded business for Minnesota, and business expansion means more jobs for Minnesota's workers. I will travel to any community in this state, to any city in this nation, any corner of the world, to bring jobs to Minnesota."

He called for a $604 million individual income-tax cut and a drop in the maximum tax rate from 16 percent to 9.9 percent, which, he said, would remove Minnesota from its Number One rank in all personal income-tax categories. He also proposed to simplify the state's three-page income tax form by reducing it to one page with only sixteen lines, all in large print.

Perpich also made a strong push for a $500 million state budget reserve or "rainy day fund," saying that would be good, sound business practice and would help restore the top bond rating which the state had lost during the recent series of revenue shortfall crises. The governor said his 1985-87 budget would hold average spending increases to less than six-percent a year, the smallest in twenty years. Had Washington operated like Minnesota for the past two years, he said, the federal government might be operating in the black instead of the red.

New House Speaker David Jennings was as much a libertarian as a conservative Republican. He strongly believed that government should do less, not more, and he was therefore repeatedly at odds with the governor's wellspring of ideas on how government should do more to help people. A carpenter from the small town of Truman, in southern Minnesota, Jennings was a former Marine and a 1976 magna cum laude graduate of Mankato State University with a degree in political science and history. He had been among the "New Right" conservatives who were swept into office in the 1978 Minnesota Massacre.

Tall and lanky, he customarily wore checked shirts with rolled-up sleeves, jeans, and cowboy boots during the early years; after he became Speaker, he found it prudent to wear a jacket and tie in the House Chamber. He was articulate and irreverent of any political establishment, be it DFL or Republican. Critics found him arrogant, friends thought of him as brilliant. The news media found him delightfully candid and a good quote. When he learned he was the only legislator who rated a zero from Minnesota's Americans for Democratic Action (ADA) in the liberal group's 1985 legislative survey, he quipped, "That's the best news I've had all day. Some days I think I'm softening, and then I get my ADA ratings."[2] As a high school student, he had worked for Republican Barry Goldwater's presidential campaign.

As a young legislator, Jennings had crossed swords with powerful Minnesota AFL-CIO President David Roe, scuttling a bonding bill for state building construction that Roe wanted for the jobs it would bring union workers. In the early 1980s he was also an irritant to Governor Al Quie and one of the "Gang of Four" Independent-Republican legislators who refused to give the Republican governor the votes he needed in a special session for borrowing authority to cover a shortfall, thus forcing Quie to call another special session. He also battled the powerful Christian Right of the IR Party and former House Minority Leader Glen Sherwood, the hero of the party's Christian conservatives. Jennings said that Perpich was "a nice guy" and that he liked him, but he also referred to the governor as "a totally unpredictable, loose cannon," and a "flake."[3]

The new 1985 House Independent-Republican majority surprised even itself that year by choosing the first woman majority leader, Connie Levi. The moderate Levi and the conservative Jennings made a good team. She and her husband Arlo, corporate vice president and secretary of 3M, lived in the affluent suburb of Dellwood. Smart, feisty, dressed fashionably in Ultrasuede suits and high heels, she was well-liked and won the respect of both caucuses in leading the sharp floor debate for her caucus.

House Republicans, exercising their new majority clout, called for a $10.8 billion budget for the next two years, $500 million less than Perpich's budget, which Jennings referred to as a "a monstrous mishmash." Health and welfare, with increasing caseloads, were the Republican budget targets; the new majority proposed to freeze state spending for those programs at current levels for the next two years. Perpich stormed that he'd rather "chop off my hand" than sign a House bill cutting thousands of people deemed employable from general assistance rolls. "It would be just like spitting in the face of my father and mother to sign that bill," the governor said, recalling the long periods of unemployment his father went through.[4] Yet by the time the end-of-the-session horse-trading was over, Independent-Republicans felt they had gotten meaningful welfare reform, and Perpich supported the legislation, saying he believed that "everyone will be taken care of." But 45 of the 65 House DFLers voted against the bill and accused the IR majority of cruelty toward the poor.[5]

The Independent-Republican-controlled House and the DFL-controlled Senate failed to pass major tax and spending bills before the Legislature adjourned its regular session May 20, and Perpich was forced to call his first special session in June. Both Perpich and the Independent-Republicans had promised tax cuts to voters in the 1984 campaign. It was only a question of how much and what taxes to cut. Republicans had vowed to give $1 billion back to income-tax payers. Lobbyists for major business groups pushed for a 20 percent income tax cut, more than a billion dollars, and about twice the amount Perpich had initially proposed. But their aggressive "Boston Tea Party" promotion, in which they sent tea bags to lawmakers signifying a protest against high taxes, antagonized many legislators, who said the business people had not identified what programs they would cut to fund the large tax cut.[6]

In the special session, the Legislature passed and Perpich signed legislation for what was eventually calculated as a $920 million tax cut, the largest in Minnesota history. It included an individual income-tax cut of 25 percent over two years for middle-income taxpayers. Independent-Republicans and DFLers both took credit for the tax cut. The tax cut dropped Minnesota from its ranking as second-highest among the states in individual income-tax collections per capita to fifth, according to the Minnesota Taxpayers Association, a lobbying and research group, while dropping the top tax rate from 16 percent, the highest among the states, to 9.9 percent, fifteenth highest, as Perpich had proposed. It also decreased the number of rates and the gaps between them, making the system less "progressive," critics noted. On the other hand, because of closed loop-holes, many high-income people complained that their taxes had gone up, while thousands of Minnesota's poorest citizens were pleased to find they no longer had to pay state taxes at all. Perpich got the simplified one-page state income-tax form and $450 million of the budget reserve he had demanded.

However, the Legislature had ignored or rejected a number of the recommendations of the Minnesota Tax Study Commission. This eighteen-month $500,000 study headed by St. Paul Mayor George Latimer had proposed a more progressive rate system. (Under the approved legislation, some of the largest income-tax cuts went to those with high incomes, as St. Paul DFL Representative John Tomlinson, former chairman of the House tax committee, pointed out.) The commission also proposed a fundamental reshuffling of the three major tax sources—sales, income, and property taxes—to finance state and local governments. It said less reliance should be placed on personal income taxes, which the commission considered too high, and more on the sales tax, which it said would be a more stable source of revenue in bad times. The Legislature had also retained politically touchy credits and deductions that the commission would have scrapped to achieve simplification and equity. Latimer, chairman of the Tax Study Commission, and other critics argued that lawmakers missed a golden opportunity for reform by paying too much attention to politics and too little to policy. Don Paterick, executive director of the Minnesota Taxpayers Association, said, "It's tax relief without reform, and it's not simple [simplification]." DFL Representative John Brandl of Minneapolis, a University of Minnesota economics professor and a member of the House Tax Committee, pointed a finger at business lobby groups who, he said, argued that "We have to cut the heck out of income taxes and leave it at that."

But the widespread criticism and a Department of Finance warning a month later of a significant budget shortfall ahead did not stop the Legislature or the governor from trumpeting the massive tax cut they'd engineered.

Education Governor

Since his earliest days in politics on the Hibbing School Board, education had been central to Perpich's vision. And educational reform remained high on the Perpich agenda throughout his years as governor. He vowed more than once that Minnesota would become "the brainpower state," and he wanted to be known as the "Education Governor." In pursuit of this ideal he presented the 1985 Legislature with a bold new "open enrollment" proposal, allowing high school juniors and seniors to attend any school regardless of where they lived. Many came to believe that Perpich's campaign for school choice was his finest crusade, and when it was eventually approved by the Legislature it was hailed as a national model for education reform.

The idea grew out of the time when he was lieutenant governor and lived in a Twin Cities suburb, and was not satisfied with the schools where his children had to go; at the time the system forced students to go to the nearest school, whether it met their needs or not.[7]

It was a big change, however, and it met with resistance from the powerful Minnesota Education Association and the Minnesota Teachers Federation. The teachers' organizations predicted it would result in chaos. Senate sponsor Tom Nelson said, "Changing education is like trying to rearrange a cemetery. The establishment does not want changes it cannot control." The governor, joined by 3M Chairman Lewis Lehr (who had sparred with Perpich over the state's business climate) held press conferences around the state selling the program. Connie Levi, the House Independent-Republican majority leader, became an ally, sponsoring the bill in the House. Former Governor Al Quie publicly endorsed the proposal. The legislation "put Minnesota in the forefront of educational policy," he declared.[8]

The Perpich "choice" proposal stirred debate across the country, and state and national lawmakers seized upon the idea. President Reagan adopted the choice idea in his education programs, and President George H. W. Bush also promoted it in his 1989 nationally televised budget address. The public was wary at first, however, and polls showed that only 30% approved of the idea. Many associates advised Perpich to drop the idea, in fact, but Rudy kept at it, and in 1988 his program for letting patents and students, rather than school districts, decide which schools children would attend, became law.

That session, Perpich also got legislative approval for a first step of his "access to excellence" initiative, which gave high school juniors and seniors the opportunity to take college classes at state expense. Perpich chose the Anoka-Ramsey Community College as the site for the ceremony at which he signed that and other education bills, to highlight his administration's emphasis on education.

Perpich had tried unsuccessfully to sell a smaller legislature to lawmakers when he was a state senator. In 1985 he promised to "hit the road hard" to promote the idea to voters. "There are too many people up there," the governor remarked, referring to the House and Senate chambers on the second floor above the governor's office. "They've just been going too far. Someone had better bring them under control, and one way to bring it under control is to reduce the size of the Legislature." Again, legislators, DFLers and IRs alike, who had no intention of giving up their seats, rejected the idea.

When, early in 1985, General Motors announced it was looking for a site for a new $3.5 billion Saturn automobile plant to build as many as 500,000 subcompacts each year to compete with the Japanese in the American small-car market, Perpich went after the prize. Twenty-seven other states also entered the competition for the plant, which would result in thousands of well-paying jobs. Independent-Republicans went along with the Saturn quest reluctantly but said the governor would do better to improve the general business climate rather than try to buy jobs with incentives for selected businesses. David Jennings, the House speaker, balked when Perpich asked him and Roger Moe, the senate majority leader, to authorize a package of subsidies for a site in Cottage Grove or Duluth, without telling the legislative leaders or the public what was in it.[9] "He had met with Saturn officials. He promised them some outrageous amount of money, over a billion dollars. [He wanted us to] 'Just trust me' on money. I wasn't going to do that," Jennings said. When Mark Dayton, commissioner of Economic Development, refused to disclose the "highly confidential" details of the subsidy package, saying that would tip off competitors, Jennings threatened to subpoena him before the House Budget Committee, where Dayton would have to "tell God and everybody" what was in it. Dayton gave Jennings enough information to satisfy him, and the legislation was passed, although Jennings grumbled, "They didn't know if General Motors would take the money or not. It was one of those deals that if this and this and this happened, the governor was authorized to do this and this and this."

Perpich and Dayton flew to Detroit with the hastily-passed $1.2 billion package of thirty-year tax breaks and other incentives and presented their bid for the small-car plant to the automaker executives in a private meeting. Afterward Perpich was euphoric over the meeting, which he thought had gone well. Although other competing states were guarded about their offers, Minnesota appeared to have made the largest bid of any state, according to an industry analyst familiar with many of the proposals. "I've never seen an offer this big, and I've seen a lot of offers," said Robert Ady, executive vice president of Fantus Companies of Chicago.[10] Nevertheless he and other analysts predicted that General Motors would reject the Minnesota offer in favor of building the auto plant in a central location nearer its suppliers and customers.

A few months later General Motors executives announced they would build the new Saturn plant in a small town in Tennessee, a state that offered relatively little in the way of incentives to the auto manufacturer but was more centrally located.

Perpich put a positive spin on the failed Saturn mission, however: "It became obvious that Minnesota was a state that wanted business and all that anti-business [talk], those editorials nationally, really slowed down. You just don't read those in the press any longer. And I think that was a result of the presentation we made to Saturn, where the national press had the opportunity to see what Minnesota is all about."[11]

The Perpich administration also launched a $1.1 million nation-wide advertising and marketing campaign to promote business development, touting the millions of dollars in tax incentives and loans at below-market rates available to businesses that expanded in Minnesota. Minnesota is "The Land of Cool Blue Water and Cold Hard Cash," said one advertisement.

What legislators failed to do in the regular session, they worked early and late to finish up in the three-day special session. After it was over and they had settled their differences, everyone declared a victory. Jennings said Republicans had kept their campaign promises: "I got my way in terms of a big tax cut, keeping spending down, meaningful welfare reform." The only thing they hadn't gotten was unemployment compensation reform, a top business priority for 1985, and Jennings blamed that on Perpich and Senate DFLers. Perpich called it a "genuine landmark" session despite the partisan split between the House and Senate. He cited, in addition to the big tax-cut bill, a dozen economic development and job-creation initiatives passed. "We have made our whole job climate much more competitive than we were," he said.

On the other hand, the Legislature failed to approve partial state funding for the construction of a new "world-class" convention center in the Twin Cities for which Perpich had fought hard, and that was a bitter disappointment. Asked if he could take credit for the tax relief bill, expected to total $866 million (which was $124 more than he had recommended in April), Perpich said: "I was headed that way. I had made that a priority a long time ago." Independent-Republicans challenged Perpich's claim, pointing out that they had first called for a $1 billion tax cut the previous October when hardly anyone gave it a chance.

Perpich had also failed to get the go-ahead for light-rail transit in the Twin Cities. The governor had become a fan of light-rail transit—the modern version of the old street cars that used to clatter down the streets of Minneapolis and St. Paul—when he rode the tram in Vienna. When he became governor again in 1983, he pledged that construction of a Twin Cities light-rail system would begin during his term and said if the Legislature complied, it could be operating by

1989. Otherwise, he warned presciently, "The freeways are going to be so clogged, you wouldn't believe it." But the 1985 Legislature denied money for detailed planning of a light-rail streetcar line to run on University Avenue from St. Paul to Minneapolis. Suburban legislators argued that basic bus service should be provided for the suburbs before the cities got the expensive light-rail system.

Business gave the governor and the 1985 session mixed reviews. Bruce Atwater, chairman of the Minnesota Business Partnership, said Minnesota still was not fully competitive. He said unemployment-compensation reform and a reduction in employers' rates were "absolutely critical" to put Minnesota on a par with other states.

Megamall

The Twins baseball team and the Vikings football team had long since played their last games in Bloomington's Metropolitan Stadium at the southeast corner of Interstate Highway 494 and Cedar Avenue, and a previous deal to sell the 100-acre site for $25.9 million had already fallen through, when Bloomington reached an agreement to sell that prime but now-vacant real estate to Triple Five Corporation of Edmonton, Canada, for $20.4 million. The owners of Triple Five Corporation, Raphael, Eskander, Nader and Bahman Ghermezian, proposed to build a $1.3 billion complex that would include an 800-store shopping mall, a 2,000-room hotel, two office towers, a large convention center, and an indoor amusement park with a 2 ½-acre lake. The Ghermezians were Iranian immigrants who had built a billion-dollar empire in North American retailing and real estate. They envisioned the Bloomington project as "the Eighth Wonder of the World," and they sought state tax breaks and highway improvements for the construction.

The massive scheme sounded like a pipe dream to many Minnesota legislators, however. The Ghermezians were businessmen who had already built the largest mall in the world, yet as they waved their arms in excitement, rolled their eyes, nodded their heads, and expounded enthusiastically upon the anticipated marvels of the proposed mall, few could resist thoughts of the Marx Brothers' comic antics. Meanwhile, news stories about the "G-Men" reported that they had been accused of ruthless and unethical business practices in their secret operations but portrayed themselves as victims of conspiracies and harassment.[12]

Perpich was intrigued by the idea of bringing such a large development to Bloomington, and he traveled to Edmonton numerous times with Bloomington Mayor James Lindau and a contingent of Bloomington officials to examine Triple Five's West Edmonton Mall and meet with the Ghermezians. The Minnesota governor liked what he saw, and he became an enthusiastic supporter of the Bloomington project. The clincher for Perpich was a promise by Eskander Ghermezian to include in the plans a precast concrete plant in northeastern Minnesota to supply the megamall construction.

The plant was announced first as costing $400 million, but that figure was corrected the next day to $9 million. Eskander Ghermezian said it would provide 1,100 jobs on the economically distressed Iron Range. The governor held a press conference in Edmonton to endorse the mall proposal and call for state assistance for the Ghermezian development. Perpich said, "You're hurting so for those [unemployed Iron Range] people. They're not only losing their homes; they're losing their furniture. I'd walk barefoot from Minneapolis to St. Paul for 100 jobs for them."

The mall proposal rekindled the old war between Bloomington and Minneapolis that had first flared up over the location of a new sports stadium, which ended up in downtown Minneapolis. Downtown Minneapolis had also been picked as the site for a proposed new state-financed convention center by a state commission, and Mayor James Lindau charged that the commission was skewed against Bloomington.[13] Bloomington officials felt it was now their turn to get something, but Minneapolis city officials launched an intense lobbying campaign to block the Bloomington proposal. Minneapolis Mayor Don Fraser and St. Paul Mayor George Latimer railed at the governor's insistence that a world-class convention center must be part of the Bloomington project. "Why is the state being asked to subsidize a third downtown?" Fraser asked, saying it threatened the economic centers of both downtowns. "I don't think we're prepared to tear our convention center down and make a memorial to Governor Perpich." Latimer agreed that the convention center should be in downtown

Minneapolis for the good of the entire region. House Majority Leader Connie Levi warned, "The day this opens, Southdale will be obsolete." (Southdale, a large shopping center in Edina, opened its doors in 1956; it was the first indoor shopping mall in the world.)

But former Governor Elmer L. Andersen, owner of a chain of newspapers in the suburbs, defended the Bloomington mall and took issue with Fraser and those who said there shouldn't be a third downtown.[14] "Why not?" Andersen asked in an editorial. "Two thirds of the people of the metropolitan area live in the suburbs. Aren't they entitled to a downtown? In fact, 28 percent of all the people in the state live in the metropolitan suburbs and yet there are those who want that large segment of the population to just be vehicles to channel money and activity into the central cities." Andersen lectured the anti-Bloomington forces: "One of the oldest caveats in business and many other activities is that you don't build your own situation by tearing down the other fellow's. St. Paul and Minneapolis should join in saluting Bloomington's good fortune, encourage it all they can, and adjust to it with some clever new plans of their own. There's room for all."

James McComb & Associates, a Minneapolis-based marketing consulting firm, undertook a study on behalf of the Minnesota Retail Merchants Association, which speculated that more than half of the business of apparel, accessory and specialty retail stores in the Twin Cities area would be lost to the proposed megamall if it fulfilled its projections. Southdale and Burnsville Center would be particularly hard-hit, the study contended. The firm also did a study for the City of Minneapolis that was highly critical of tourism projections made by Triple Five Corporation. Leonard Inskip, *Star and Tribune* Associate Editor, called Perpich's endorsement "intuitive and impulsive," saying the decision might have been the right one, "but so far there's been little state planning and analysis to support it." Inskip wrote: "Instead, events in the past two weeks have resembled the six-foot man-made waves the Ghermezians propose [in a megamall lake]: shifting positions, murky assumptions, tidal exaggerations."[15]

The Ghermezians lobbied intensely to win over Minnesota legislators, organized labor, and other opinion leaders. They spent an estimated $25,000 to charter a plane and fly interested parties to Edmonton, wine and dine them, show off the mall there, and extol the economic benefits that would come to Bloomington if they built an even larger one. Nader Ghermezian declared, "We are talking about something that will change the face of your state." But Minnesota legislators remained skeptical of the Ghermezians' claims that the proposed new mall would add an estimated 40,000 jobs and bring 11 million tourists to the state every year.

On one occasion David Jennings, House speaker, and Roger Moe, Senate majority leader, were invited to the governor's office to meet with Perpich and a couple of the Ghermezians. There was more hyperbole than specific information, Jennings recalled, some years later. "They start talking to me about a submarine, an indoor golf course. They were all sort of feeding off each other's enthusiasm. I'm kind of looking at Moe, rolling my eyes, wondering what the hell is this all about. I am sure he shared [my] feelings. He didn't say a word, but Roger Moe is not exactly the wide-eyed dreamer. I'm sure the submarine concept flabbergasted him as it did me." It was, Jennings said, "like every-day Perpich was being taken to a whole different level, time warp or something. Rudy was always a little bit farther out than the rest of us, but on that particular day, he was just way out ahead of everybody else."[16]

Moe said the governor "bought in too early" on the project. The Senate majority leader had flown with Perpich to Edmonton to talk with the Ghermezians. "I saw the original seduction. I mean his eyes kept getting bigger and bigger as the day went along." On a more practical level, other legislators, particularly in the Twin Cities metropolitan area, were simply fearful that the proposed highway improvements for the megamall would take away money from pet projects in their districts, and that retail shops would siphon shopping revenues from their merchants.

In the end Perpich concluded there weren't enough legislative votes to approve state subsidies for the project, and he wisely dropped plans to call a special session to take it up. In September he traveled to France on a trade mission and said he was putting the mall behind him. "I cannot put all my eggs in one basket," he said. Jennings took the opportunity to make some political hay, suggesting that dropping the controversial project in the middle of the brouhaha was classic Perpich style. He had conveniently failed to recall that he, the influential

House speaker, had been adamantly against the plan from the first, had said "no" to state subsidies, and had even declined the Ghermezians' invitations to look at what they had done in Edmonton.

Perpich felt he had done all that he could personally, but he warned that the state might lose the project unless Jennings and Moe exercised "strong leadership" to get agreement on mall legislation for a special session.[17]

Throughout the early negotiations, Bloomington Mayor James Lindau had been involved closely in the megamall negotiations but had been overshadowed by Perpich. When the governor abandoned the project, Lindau and Bloomington city officials, with the help of Representative John Himle, an Independent-Republican legislator from Bloomington, and DFL state Senator Michael Freeman of Richfield, who also represented that part of Bloomington, continued efforts to work out a mall deal. Eskander Ghermezian had said, "We will not build the project without the convention center," but in December, at the urging of Lindau, the Triple Five Corporation dropped the convention center proposal, which would have competed with the downtown Minneapolis center. In exchange, Minneapolis officials pledged to halt their opposition to the project. The City of Bloomington offered financial help and advanced money for highway construction.

But the 1986 Legislature rejected the Ghermezian brothers' request for direct subsidies, and Perpich said, "That thing is dead." Legislators did authorize Bloomington to raise money for highways and other improvements relating to the project by selling bonds to be repaid with a one-percent sales tax on goods sold at the megamall, and they also authorized a loan from the metropolitan property-tax-sharing pool. Perpich signed the bill.

New developers took over the construction management, and the flamboyant Ghermezians assumed a lower profile. Though scaled down from its originally-proposed size, the Mall of America was still huge, with 4.2 million square feet. There were 520 stores and room for further expansion. In the end it cost $625 million to construct, and it opened on August 11, 1992, minus a convention center but with a spectacular Knott's Camp Snoopy amusement park.

The Mall of America billed itself as the largest indoor shopping center in the U.S and the second largest (after West Edmonton) in the world. Its early success exceeded even the optimistic expectations of its advocates. During its first five years of operation, more than 100 million tourists, 6 percent of them from outside the U.S., visited the Mall, many coming just because of its bigness. It boasted of having created more than 11,000 permanent jobs. A new light-rail line was completed in 2004, running from downtown Minneapolis to the Metropolitan Airport and the Mall, something Perpich and the Ghermezians had dreamed of doing. "It's become a draw for tourism more than anyone expected," said Judy Cook, president of the Minnesota Retail Merchants Association. Nor did the gloom-and-doom predictions that the Bloomington mall would be the death of other Twin Cities regional shopping malls come to pass. Seven years after the Mall of America opened in 1992, regional malls were still mighty "cathedrals of commerce," and looked stronger than ever, Dave Beal, *Pioneer Press* business columnist wrote.[18]

Meanwhile, Perpich, always eager to embrace new ideas, persuaded the University of Minnesota to help establish a private, nonprofit Center for Victims of Torture on East River Road in Minneapolis, close to the University's medical facilities. Although the governor credited his son, Rudy Jr., for coming up with the idea for the center—the first of its kind in the country and at the time only the third worldwide—the governor's son, then a law student at Stanford, had, in fact, merely suggested to his father that Minnesota might do something to support Amnesty International of London, an organization he had learned about on campus. At Perpich's behest, Tom Triplett, then the governor's chief policy aide, discussed the idea with people in Minnesota who were knowledgeable about international human rights, and they suggested the torture victims treatment center. The governor, after visiting similar centers in Copenhagen, Denmark, and Toronto, Ontario, appointed a task force which studied the idea and recommended establishment of the Minnesota center, supported by private contributions including foundation grants and a house donated by the University.

Since the center was founded in 1985, hundreds of torture survivors from around the world have come there for treatment from

Bosnia, Sierra Leone, Turkey, and many other countries. Thirty other states have now followed Minnesota's example, and the United States Congress appropriates money regularly to promote the center's work worldwide.

Another initiative that captured the Governor's attention that fall was that of establishing a center for East European studies in Austria. He had discussed the matter with professor William Wright, director of the Center for Austrian Studies at the University of Minnesota, after Count Otto Traun, owner of a castle in the village of Petronell, offered to give the University a 99-year-lease on the castle at no charge. The count's architect had estimated it would cost about $4 million to modernize the 200-room castle and renovate it for educational uses.

Professor Wright later said he had been told it would cost $1 million for renovation costs, and he had actually contacted other colleges and universities in the state about forming a consortium to sponsor the project. While the schools had no money to fix up the castle, Wright had expressed the hope that businesses in Minnesota might be interested in financing and making use of the center as a training and meeting place for their central European operations and possibly as a trade office for the state.

On the last Sunday in October Perpich and Lola set off for Austria to take a look at the facility. They found that the castle, about 40 kilometers east of Vienna, was too far out of town to be practical for a University of Minnesota program. They also visited a castle near the Hungarian border which was even farther from Vienna, about 60 kilometers.

It was noted in the press that Perpich had undertaken the trip without informing his staff of his intention to do so.[19] In fact, it was the third visit Perpich and his wife made that year to Vienna—where they had lived for three years before he ran for governor in 1982—and the governor's tenth trip overseas since returning to office in 1983. Travel costs for the Perpiches' trip to Austria were paid from the governor's special economic development fund, which came from private donations rather than the public coffer, but Independent-Republicans, seizing the opportunity, criticized the governor for going to Europe again in the middle of a farm crisis. Even Senate Majority Leader Roger

Moe expressed surprise that the governor had taken off on a foreign trip so soon after saying he'd curtail his travels to work on the state's farm problems.[20]

The farm crisis had worsened. It was not only hurting banks and other businesses in small towns around the state, but adversely affecting the Twin Cities business community. Attorney General Hubert (Skip) Humphrey III proposed a farmer-lender mediation program which included mandatory intervention by state mediators in all farm foreclosure proceedings and the possibility of a one-year delay in foreclosures. But on Thanksgiving Day, when the Capitol was shut down, Perpich called a surprise press conference and endorsed a 90-day voluntary suspension of farm foreclosures and a farm-debt mediation program agreed to by major money lenders who were trying to avoid a state-imposed moratorium. Perpich, who had been under pressure to issue an executive order mandating a moratorium similar to action taken by Depression-era Governor Floyd B. Olson, said the voluntary action would give troubled farmers a temporary reprieve until federal and state rescue legislation could be passed. He said David Jennings, the House speaker, Fred Norton, the House minority leader, and Glen Taylor, the Senate minority leader, endorsed the plan. Roger Moe, the Senate majority leader, could not be reached.

Moratorium advocates called Perpich's plan "a cruel blow to farmers," pointing out that it covered only land foreclosures and not those on equipment and machinery. Minneapolis banker Carl Pohlad had suggested a similar plan earlier and was given some credit for being a catalyst in putting the voluntary plan on the table in negotiations.[21]

A Minnesota Poll conducted in mid-December and reported in the *Star Tribune* found that Perpich's approval rating had slipped slightly from 64 percent in August, 1985, to 60 percent in December, while those who disapproved of how he was handling his job had climbed from 25 to 30 percent. A majority of Minnesotans still viewed Perpich as a strong, intelligent, innovative leader, but they clearly doubted whether his overseas travel was producing new businesses and jobs, as he claimed.

Chapter 13

Hormel. The George Latimer Challenge.
Friend of Business.

In the fall of 1985, 1,400 workers at the George A. Hormel plant in Austin went out on strike in response to company demands for deep wage cuts. The strike drew national attention and was seen by many militant union members as a symbolic battle for all organized labor against concessions and attempts to break unions. Perpich had met separately with Hormel employers and leaders of the Local P-9 of the United Food and Commercial Workers International Union in a personal effort to negotiate a compromise, but without success. As the strike wore on and the new year dawned, he proceeded cautiously, consulting often with both the Minnesota attorney general's office and local authorities in an attempt to project an evenhanded image to the public.

On January 4, Hormel mailed letters to striking employees announcing that the plant would reopen in nine days and offering them the opportunity to return to work. If they refused, the company would start hiring replacements on January 20. Governor Perpich decided it was time to intervene again, and he tried to initiate mediation efforts, but P-9 President Jim Guyette insisted on a face-to-face meeting with Hormel executives. Hormel reopened the packinghouse on Monday, January 13, a trickle of strikebreakers drove past the picket lines throughout the week, and the company began handing out job applications. On January 20, true to its word, Hormel opened up jobs to all comers. It was Martin Luther King Day, and hundreds of Twin Cities activists and sympathizers joined union members in a massive picket and car blockade of the plant. Some in the crowd put a padlock on the gate. Windshields were smashed, and tires were slashed.[1]

Fearing that an angry mob was on the verge of a major riot, Mayor Tom Kough and other officials in Austin and Mower County called the governor for help in keeping peace. Faced with the threat of unmanageable violence, Perpich ordered nearly 500 members of the

National Guard to Austin and increased the number later to nearly 800. Acting on an attorney general's opinion, he put them under the sheriff's command, making them in effect sheriff's deputies, which enabled the governor to stay in the background. On Tuesday, January 21, the company kept the plant closed, but the Guard cordoned the area, allowing the company to reopen the plant on Wednesday, using replacement workers—"scabs" in union lexicon—and P-9 defectors who had crossed picket lines.

It was a politically sticky situation for the governor, who faced a tough re-election campaign in the coming fall and knew that his actions were likely to antagonize union members in Austin and elsewhere, particularly the heavily unionized Iron Range. Three Independent-Republican gubernatorial candidates took issue with Perpich's handling of the meatpackers' strike, though their views differed radically as to what *should* have been done. State Auditor Arne Carlson said the governor should have intervened earlier, former State Representative Cal Ludeman of Tracy criticized Perpich for turning control of the National Guard over to local officials, and former State Senator Marion (Mike) Menning of Edgerton said Perpich had sent National Guard troops in too early.

Paul Wellstone, a Carleton College professor of political science and social activist who later became a U.S. senator, rushed to the governor's office to berate him for bringing in troops and urged Perpich to use his influence to force a settlement. He also counseled the union to return to work and continue bargaining. Perpich and members of his administration denied accusations that ordering out the National Guard amounted to union-busting. Public Safety Commissioner Paul Tschida said the Guard was there to "keep the peace, not keep the plant open." But Perpich, whose father had been a union organizer, had gone on strike and walked picket lines, later described the decision as one of the hardest he ever had to make. [2] "It was like going against my father."

The governor continued to seek a settlement between the striking members of Local P-9 and management, and he eventually got the two to agree to call in an independent fact-finder to make recommendations for a settlement. He also met with Minnesota AFL-CIO President Dan Gustafson and other Minnesota labor leaders, seeking advice and urging them to press for a settlement. P-9 President Jim Guyette accused the international union office and state labor leaders of working in tandem with Hormel to break the Austin local, but Gustafson denied the charge, saying Local P-9 had received more than $1.6 million in financial aid from organized labor since the strike began August 17.

On March 14, with workers streaming across the picket line, including approximately 460 P-9 members, the parent union called the walkout a lost cause. It withdrew its sanction for the strike and on June 2 obtained a federal court order allowing it to put the local in trusteeship and oust P-9 leaders. The Austin workers ratified a new contract; the strike was broken, and about seven hundred strikers lost their jobs.

The Department of Finance had first warned of a sizable revenue shortage the previous July, just a month after Perpich and the 1985 Legislature had agreed on a nearly-$1 billion cut in state taxes. The shortfall had continued to develop, and when the Legislature convened on February 3, the governor called for $277 million in budget cuts. Unemployment was still high—more than 100,000 people were without jobs. Farmers squeezed by high debt and interest rates of 15 percent to 17 percent were going bankrupt, facing foreclosures, and being forced off their land. Twenty-seven Minnesota counties had been declared agricultural disaster areas, making farmers there eligible for low-interest federal loans.

The voters were pessimistic about the state's economy. A Northstar Poll published February 16 in the *Pioneer Press* showed 43 percent of those surveyed believed the economy was getting worse, while only 19 percent thought it was getting better. Senate Majority Leader Roger Moe, whose northwestern Minnesota district had been hard hit, said rural Minnesota was hurting and needed help. Moe and Governor Perpich continued to press for federal action, arguing that the real solution to the serious economic problems of rural Minnesota could not be found in St. Paul. Perpich declined an invitation to appear at a farm protest rally, saying he didn't want to raise any false expectations of what state government could do. "We can help at the state level, but the big decisions have to be made in Washington," he said. The governor traveled to Washington numerous times to lobby Congress and the White House in support of farm aid legislation.

Perpich did, however, threw his support behind a $9.3-million rural-recovery package designed by Moe, who emphasized the importance of diversification in rural farm areas. The package included rural-development revolving-loan funds and economic-recovery grants. The governor crisscrossed the state promoting the short-term, farm-relief program, the Rural Development Act of 1986, and a constitutional amendment for a state lottery to finance both that program and job programs in the Twin Cities area. A state-operated lottery would be "a long-range solution to the problems experienced in our rural areas," he argued, estimating that a lottery would raise $120 million a year. Of that, $80 million would go to a new Greater Minnesota Fund for rural and farm relief, patterned after the 2002 Fund in northeastern Minnesota, which was used to create jobs there after the long-anticipated decline in the iron ore mining industry. The other $40 million would go to the Reinvest in Minnesota (RIM) conservation program, supported by sportsmen's groups, that would pay farmers to take less desirable agricultural land out of production and convert it to wildlife habitat. Taking poor land out of production would also reduce crop surpluses, Perpich said, and drive up commodity prices.[3]

Pressure continued for the governor to order a moratorium on farm mortgage foreclosures by executive order, but Perpich said such an action on his part would be illegal, though he supported legislation for a limited moratorium. Later the governor said he would sign a moratorium bill if the Legislature passed it with bipartisan support, which was unlikely to happen in the Minnesota House. Perpich's refusal to emulate the late Governor Floyd B. Olson in leading the charge for a moratorium on mortgage foreclosures and other major relief measures disappointed some liberal farm activists including Paul Wellstone, an organizer of the Groundswell movement.[4]

In the 1986 session about 250 farmers, many of them members of Groundswell, rallied at the Capitol, calling for a one-year moratorium on farm foreclosures. The Senate narrowly approved the plan, but the House opposed it, and it did not pass. Instead, the Legislature established a new mediation system for farmers facing mortgage foreclosure, designed to get them together with lenders to work out repayment plans that would allow them to keep their farms. The governor and legislators agreed on other measures to help farmers, including the sale of $50 million in general-obligation bonds to back up new farm loans by private lenders, $5 million to continue an existing "buy down" program to help finance interest payments on distressed loans, and the RIM initiative. But the Independent-Republican-controlled House refused to put a state-operated lottery on the ballot. Later the new Greater Minnesota Corporation established an Agricultural Utilization Research Institute in Moe's district in Crookston that proved successful in developing new uses for farm products.

President's Day, Monday, February 17, 1986, was a holiday, and the Capitol seemed quiet. But over the weekend House Independent-Republicans had quietly prepared budget-cutting bills at Jennings' direction, which they moved on Monday through IR-controlled subcommittees. Protesting DFLers railed against the "Presidents' Day Massacre" and "slash-and-burn" program cuts. They complained that because of the holiday and because there was no public announcement, many state agency heads and employees and others affected by the IR "steamroller tactics" were off work and had no opportunity to respond. The budget bills were quickly approved by the IR majority in the House. They cut welfare benefits by up to 19 percent for 150,000 women and children receiving Aid to Families With Dependent Children, a policy that was immediately denounced by clergymen and charitable, religious and labor groups. Independent-Republicans called for keeping more money in education aids and property-tax relief than the governor had proposed.[5]

DFLers called the Republicans "mean-spirited" toward the poor and needy. Representative Lee Greenfield of Minneapolis lamented, "How can you balance the budget by stealing food from children?" State Auditor Carlson, a former Republican legislator, broke ranks with the House Independent-Republican majority, saying their proposed drastic cuts in welfare benefits made them look heartless and cruel. "There is a very deep notion in segments of the Republican Party that welfare is a sin, that lack of success is a sin," he said. "Well, I don't think it's a sin."[6]

But Jennings said the public wanted welfare reform: "They believe welfare benefits are too high. So do I." IR Representative Joel Carlson of Moorhead, who led the battle for welfare cuts, said the program had gotten out of hand. He said Minnesota's average AFDC benefits were seventh highest in the country, 38 percent higher than neighboring Iowa, 42 percent higher than North Dakota and 60 percent higher than South Dakota, but slightly lower than Wisconsin for a single parent and one child. Republicans also demanded the abolishment of Minnesota's Department of Energy and Economic Development, headed by Commissioner Mark Dayton and the governor's brother Tony. "It has not been effective as a department," said Jennings. "It has not created many new jobs that would not have been created anyway." Dayton called it a Republican vendetta.

The IR House majority's insistence that deep cuts be made in welfare-benefits and other similar spending had the effect of stalemating conference-committee negotiations with the DFL-controlled Senate. On March 18, at 5:21 a.m., after meeting nearly 18½ hours, the House adjourned the 1986 session in an uproar, with DFLers hooting, hollering, pounding on their desks and standing on chairs, making House Speaker David Jennings' final hammer of the gavel inaudible. Despite pleas from the governor and Senate to continue the six-week session until an agreement was reached on the 1987-89 budget, Jennings said it was a waste of time to continue the session. He blamed Senate DFLers for the failure of conference committees to reach a compromise on budget bills. Three days later, with no House to negotiate with, the Senate was forced to adjourn also.

The governor called the Legislature back for a one-day special session on April 2. After approving $174 million in budget cuts and revenue increases, the Senate and House again failed to resolve differences over welfare benefits and adjourned with the budget still out of balance. House and Senate leaders and Perpich agreed that the governor should finish the job, which he did, cutting $109.8 million in the executive branch and generally adhering to an informal agreement with legislative leaders.

Representative John Brandl called the decision to adjourn without finishing the budget an "abdication of responsibility," and House Minority Leader Fred Norton of St. Paul called it "fiscal incompetence." On the other hand, Speaker Jennings said it was "the best possible agreement under the circumstances." Benefits for 50,000 poor women and their 100,000 children remained intact, including a scheduled one-percent increase to go into effect July 1. "The people that are hurting, the people that need help, they've been protected," Perpich said. Nor was the Department of Energy and Economic Development abolished.

At an end-of-the-session press conference, Perpich pointed to a flower sent to him by the Children's Defense Fund and read the note: "Rudy, on behalf of all the little children, who you stood so firm for, thanks, you did it." The governor said, "This is going to be on my tombstone. That's what this session is all about, we protected these people."

Jennings, in a surprise announcement, said he would not run for re-election to the Legislature and was quitting politics.

The $5 million appropriated by the 1986 Legislature for an interest "buydown" program to help distressed farmers with high interest costs had quickly been exhausted, and Perpich was under pressure to call a special session of the Legislature to authorize more money for the program. But that posed a dilemma for the governor. If he called a special session, Republicans would insist upon reconsideration of unemployment-compensation legislation opposed by the AFL-CIO. Perpich did not want to jeopardize the union's badly needed support in his primary election contest with St. Paul Mayor George Latimer, who had announced in March that he would run against Perpich. Perpich had vetoed an unemployment compensation bill passed in the Legislature with the help of "wood ticks" in the DFL, a rump sub-caucus of mostly rural legislators, who had broken ranks to vote with Independent-Republicans for unemployment and workers' compensation reform and other small-business interests. Organized-labor leaders said the unemployment compensation bill gutted the program and stripped 23,500 working men and women of coverage, while small-business spokesmen said a reduction in the taxes for the state unemployment compensation fund, operating with a deficit as maximum weekly benefits rose, was vital to hard-pressed main-street businesses.

Mike Hatch, commissioner of commerce, who was in charge of disbursing the buy-down funds, figured a way out of the quandary.[7] When Montgomery called a meeting of state finance officials and lawyers to discuss the problem, Hatch proposed that the Commerce Department simply continue accepting applications and issue chits which lenders could redeem after the 1987 Legislature provided more funding. Finance officials and lawyers from the attorney general's office were aghast, saying it would be unconstitutional to encumber the next Legislature, and that there was no guarantee that banks would honor the chits or that legislators next year would make them good. But Perpich approved the plan, and bankers, fearful of worse sanctions, such as a moratorium on farm mortgage foreclosures, went along.

Foreign Travels

Early in 1986 the *Pioneer Press* reported that the governor's travels had taken him out of Minnesota 213 days in the past two-and-a-half years and provided a variety of financial details.[8] The Perpiches and staff members had traveled to San Francisco over Super Bowl weekend to try to persuade the National Football League to hold the 1990 Super Bowl in Minneapolis.(It came in 1992). The Perpiches and Montgomery then flew to Copenhagen to complete plans for cheese and ethanol plants in Little Falls (the cheese plant fizzled; the ethanol plant was built) and to tour the International Rehabilitation and Research Center for Torture Victims, in preparation for the center that was later built in St Paul. It listed a $1,270 trip in a state plane to Winnipeg for the governor and Minneapolis banker Carl Pohlad, described as a major contributor to Perpich's campaign, for a meeting with Triple Five Corporation to discuss the Bloomington mall. Perpich and his wife also traveled to New York to meet with David Stern, president of the National Basketball Association, about a professional basketball franchise in Minneapolis, and to Hyannis, Massachusetts, to participate in the National Academy of Sciences annual meeting. They traveled to Detroit, Michigan, for a presentation on the Saturn auto manufacturing plant and to Cleveland, Ohio, to meet with mining and steel companies. In addition, Lola Perpich, an interior designer, and her assistant made several trips to shop for antiques and other furnishings for the refurbishing of the governor's residence.

The governor was incensed that his wife had been mentioned in the articles. "That woman has worked like you can't believe on that house [the governor's residence.] She's been working day and night, and I don't think any member of the Legislature has even said 'thank you' or written a letter, and that's the state's responsibility," he told the *Pioneer Press*. Perpich said he had accomplished much of what he wanted to do, and would be cutting back on his travels. He said a new World Trade Center to be opened in St. Paul would be "a natural calling station" for international contacts and said he was getting tired of spending time in airports and on airplanes.

The *Star Tribune* reported in late 1985 that private contributions to the travel fund exceeded expenditures by almost $50,000.[9] Host countries and host companies also paid many thousands of additional dollars for Perpich's foreign travels. The fund was handled by the Department of Administration and audited and accounted for the same as state funds, with the business purposes of the trips indicated on state expense claim forms.

Nevertheless, Independent-Republican candidates for governor, looking for campaign issues, zeroed in on Perpich's travel fund—which they called a personal "slush fund." It was argued that the travel fund came primarily from Minnesota corporations prohibited by state laws from contributing to campaigns but not from supporting the governor's travels. Arne Carlson said most of the business donors had received favors or did business with the state: "It raises the very broad question of whether or not government is for sale."[10] The state auditor also criticized Perpich for accepting rides on private corporate jets.

The governor replied that those who contributed to the travel fund did so because they recognized the importance of international trade, not because they expected anything in return. As governor he could open doors, have access to corporate executives, and let potential investors and markets know about Minnesota, which others couldn't do. Perpich denied that he lived a lavish lifestyle when traveling. He said he often asked executives of corporations he visited to make dinner reservations, and they did so at expensive restaurants. He said he was one of the few governors in the nation who did not take a security guard with him on travels, and because of that he stayed in good hotels in safe areas of cities.

Others also defended Perpich's travels, including Republican Congressman Bill Frenzel and George Latimer, Perpich's DFL opponent, who said the travel issue was overrated and "a silly issue." Latimer said, "Only in Minnesota can a governor be criticized for staying in a first-class hotel with his wife."

In response to the criticism of Perpich's travels, his office produced a thirteen-page list of firms that had begun or expanded investments in Minnesota after Governor Perpich met with company officials. Louisiana-Pacific Corporation, a wood products firm, selected Two Harbors for a new hardboard siding plant with 150 jobs. American Telephone and Telegraph announced plans for a new billing center in the Twin Cities with 550 jobs. IBM Corporation had added about 1,000 jobs in Minnesota. Harcourt Brace Jovanovich Inc., a major publisher of educational books, began major expansion in Duluth with 400 jobs. Ford Motor Company completed a $250 million expansion of its St. Paul truck plant with 500 jobs.

The list included a dozen foreign companies, and the governor's office was especially proud of a proposed new Danish dairy processing plant in Little Falls, a plant expected to create 185 jobs in 1987, which Perpich spokesmen said was a direct result of his foreign travels. Unfortunately that project never got beyond the highly publicized groundbreaking.

Several years later, *Pioneer Press* business columnist Dave Beal wrote, "His zeal in urging Minnesotans to recognize the realities of the global economy helped him go into the history books as more of a visionary than a quack."[11]

© 2005 STAR TRIBUNE/Mpls-St. Paul

Chapter 14

Run-up to the Election

With economic crises facing the state, both urban and rural, the governor's popularity began to drop. A Northstar Poll published in the February 16 *Pioneer Press* showed DFLers only marginally in favor of Perpich over Latimer, 38 to 34 percent. The governor's approval rating had dropped from 51 percent the previous October to 45 percent. Fifty percent gave him unfavorable marks. On the other hand, none of the three announced candidates on the Republican side appeared to have significant strength. Carlson, the most moderate, was favored by just 24 percent of the Republican respondents, and Mike Menning and Cal Ludeman trailed far behind. Carlson charged that "power brokers" in the Independent-Republican Party were trying to drive the three out of the race to clear the way for House Speaker Jennings. Carlson named U.S. Senators Rudy Boschwitz and David Durenberger and U.S. Representative Vin Weber as those power brokers.

A month after David Jennings said he was bowing out of politics, he changed his mind and said he would run for governor. Although he had urged his close friend Ludeman to run earlier, Jennings said, "There is no question but that I have the best chance to win of any

Republican." Jennings declared he could beat either of the "big government, big spending" DFL candidates, Perpich and Latimer. He was encouraged to enter the race by both Weber and Boschwitz, who said none of the announced IR candidates were "catching fire."

At the state Independent-Republican convention in June, Jennings had the backing of many of the party's big names and wealthy contributors, renewing the long-harbored resentment of many party members from the St. Paul area and outstate against the "Lake Minnetonka, Gold Coast crowd." Ludeman, 34, a Tracy farmer, was 6-foot, 3 inch, handsome, and a former All State football player. Although he had been in the Legislature for three two-year terms, he was the least known of the leading candidates. He had run the lowest-budget campaign and was considered the underdog. But Ludeman, a strict conservative, was many delegates' second choice, and he emerged the winner in a five-ballot contest for the endorsement, defeating Jennings and Menning, who had switched from the DFL Party and was the hero of the Christian Conservative faction of the IR Party. Jennings and Menning said they would abide by the party endorsement and not go to the primary.

Perpich went on the offensive early in the 1986 campaign, launching a series of paid TV and radio ads in May portraying his record as one of "Moving Minnesota Forward." The ads credited Perpich with tax cuts, new jobs, education, and farm assistance. One said, "Last year Governor Rudy Perpich slashed state taxes by $1 billion. He cut taxes on businesses and farm machinery, increased homestead tax credits, and provided property tax relief. But best of all, he cut Minnesota individual income taxes by twenty-five percent." House Independent-Republicans were quick to protest that the $1 billion tax cut had been their initiative going back to the 1984 election and had passed while they held the House majority. Tom Berg, chairman of the Perpich campaign, acknowledged that the Legislature also had a hand in the tax cuts and other legislation for which Perpich claimed credit, but he said the governor's leadership made these things happen.

Stung by a Minnesota Business Partnership poll which gave the state's business climate a poor rating, Perpich issued a list of accomplishments for business during his administration, including the $1 billion tax cut in 1985. But if the Perpich list included legislation that

IR and DFL legislators had crafted and passed, and reflected the rising economy in large part, it was an impressive list all the same, showing that the state was making progress under an activist, albeit divided state government. It included major tax simplification and over $70 million in tax relief to allow the taconite industry to become more competitive in world markets; an improved business climate resulting in 190,000 more Minnesotans working than were working in 1983, with 16,000 of those jobs in 225 businesses created with help from a revitalized economic development department; special financing and technical assistance programs to help timber, agriculture, mining, medical and technology development in the state; a jobs program (MEED) which helped 17,500 Minnesotans find jobs using wage subsidies and other support programs; $479 million in state-assisted housing construction; and increased funding for all levels of state education. All this had been done, the governor said, with the lowest budget increase in 20 years, and was a start toward fiscal stability through creation of a budget reserve and the upgrading of the state credit rating to AA+.

"That's a record I'm proud of." Perpich said. He had kept his promise to work day and night to help put Minnesotans back to work, he said.

His claims of job growth were challenged by his opponents, however, who said Perpich was trying to take credit for something he had less to do with than the economy in general. Furthermore, Latimer and Ludeman said, Perpich didn't take into account the thousands of jobs lost during his time in office because of businesses who had left the state or did not grow because of the failure of unemployment-compensation reform legislation and the state's anti-business climate. Also, Perpich's opponents said, 5,000 farmers and their families were out of business because the governor had failed to help them with their problems. Perpich in turn hailed a report by Alexander Grant & Co. that Minnesota had improved its ranking in the firm's annual business climate study. The state was ranked thirty-fifth out of the 48 contiguous states, compared with its forty-third place the previous year. The reported improvement was attributed to a slowdown in local government spending, a decline in union membership, a high percentage of residents with high school education, and a decline in work time lost due to strike or other labor disputes. The two big negative factors were a rise in state and local taxes and a decline in vocational-school enrollment. "We feel good about the business climate in this state," said David Abramson, managing partner for Alexander Grant's Minneapolis office.

Independent-Republican Chairman Leon Oistad called Perpich a liar and said the governor was claiming credit for policies which were never his and taking credit for spending cuts he had opposed during the 1985 and 1986 legislative sessions.[1]

However, when St. Paul Mayor Latimer tried to make the case that Perpich's record wasn't good enough, he found he had a tough sell. "I believe we can do much better," he said, but Perpich responded: "I'm the best governor St. Paul ever had," and he even chartered a bus to take reporters on a tour of the capital city, pointing out improvements made with state assistance during his administration.

The bearded, genial, witty George Latimer, 51, a native of New York and a labor lawyer, had been on the St. Paul School Board and had been a University of Minnesota regent before becoming mayor of St. Paul. During his six terms as mayor, he was lauded for obtaining substantial federal assistance and private venture capital for city projects and development. He gained national visibility as president of the National League of Cities in 1983-84. In 1983 Governor Perpich named Latimer to head the prestigious Tax Study Commission. When Latimer talked about running for governor early in 1986, Perpich bristled at what he felt was a betrayal. He couldn't understand why a DFLer he regarded as an ally and friend would do this to him and vowed, "I'm going to win that one going away. You better believe me. I'll be in there fighting from early morning until late at night." He privately told Mike Hatch, who was helping his campaign, that, "George's beard is going to cost him 5 percent of the vote. You cannot have a beard in Minnesota without losing five percent of the vote."[2]

Perpich named his brother George re-election campaign manager, formalizing the adviser role that George had played for years. It was frequently said, however, that "Perpich campaign manager" was an oxymoron since the politically astute, independent governor always did his own thing.

Though he had thumbed his nose at DFL endorsement four years earlier, Perpich now made peace with his party with the help of state DFL Chair Ruth Esala[3] and went after that prize. Latimer, critical of party endorsement, bypassed the process and the June 13-15 state DFL convention in Minneapolis, where Perpich won a respectable but not overwhelming endorsement with 72 percent of the 1,250 delegates supporting him. The margin was comfortably above the 60 percent required for endorsement, but short of the 81 percent that Spannaus had won in 1982. During the convention Perpich, who courted and won the support of some of the party's leading feminists, stressed his record of supporting programs helping women. "From appointments of women and minorities to protection of families in need, to Minnesota's leadership on child care and pay equity, the Perpich/Johnson team has a strong and reliable record of working for us," said a campaign flyer. Perpich said, "I am very proud to have appointed more women and more minorities to judgeships than any other governor in the history of this state. I am very proud of the first woman lieutenant governor, Marlene Johnson, in the history of Minnesota."

In his acceptance speech Perpich boasted that he had balanced the state budget, reduced income taxes, restored the state's credit rating, and held state spending growth to the lowest level in twenty years. He took credit for 100,000 more Minnesotans employed than ever before, the "best farm bill of any state in the nation this year" passed in the 1986 legislative session, his success in keeping a nuclear-waste dump out of the state, and blocking cuts in Aids to Families with Dependent Children. He was interrupted by applause twenty-five times, and at the end of the speech the delegates gave him a standing ovation and cheered and paraded for more than five minutes. It was a good send-off for Perpich's primary campaign.[4]

Latimer's campaign made mistakes. The St. Paul mayor's attacks against the endorsement system and references to "political hacks" offended party regulars. His proposal to extend the sales tax to clothing and personal services was so unpopular Latimer was forced to dump it in mid-campaign. Latimer's choice of Arvonne Fraser, a prominent Minneapolis feminist and wife of Minneapolis Mayor Donald Fraser, as his running mate reinforced the perception of Latimer as a big city liberal and hurt him in the rural areas.

Perpich, on the other hand, worked to avoid the kind of activities that critics had called quirky in the past, and as a result, the image that stuck in voter's minds was of a strong, decisive leader who had improved the state's tax and business climate while also showing compassion for the needy. While Latimer issued position papers that were thoughtful though not exciting, Perpich employed a "Rose Garden" strategy, shunning most debates, where he might have been pinned down on hard issues. When he did appear at ceremonial events, he touted his record of creating jobs.

Campaigning on the Iron Range, Perpich and his workers urged voters to flock to the polls as they had done four years before to keep their native son in the governor's office. Perpich supporters on the Range played hardball politics, painting Latimer as "the metropolitan candidate." They played up the fact that he had helped lead a gay-rights march in St. Paul in 1978 and had recommended collecting a sales tax on clothing and eliminating the homestead credit on property taxes, references to the "Latimer Commission" recommendations. Congressman James Oberstar, signaling that the feud with the Perpiches was over, campaigned for the governor, saying, "We stand behind Perpich one hundred percent." (When Perpich learned that campaigners on the Range were using the gay rights issue against Latimer, he told them to stop and invited gay-rights activists to lunch at the governor's residence to apologize.)

Perpich, recalling that Spannaus in 1982 had made his income-tax return a campaign issue, released his state and federal income-tax returns for 1985 and called upon Latimer to do the same. He said Minnesota voters deserved a full accounting by candidates for major office, and how they earned their income was part of that full disclosure. Perpich's return showed the governor and his wife had a total income of $71,424, and paid federal taxes of $12,519 and state taxes of $4,443.

At first Latimer refused to release his income tax return; when he changed his mind and did so, the return revealed that he had been late in filing and made substantial use of real-estate tax shelters to shield his income from state and federal taxes.

As the primary approached, Perpich continued to build a hefty war chest, while Latimer went deeply in debt. A $50,000 contribution to Latimer from Independent-Republican Wheelock Whitney, Perpich's unsuccessful 1982 opponent, financed a radio ad campaign making a direct pitch to IR voters to cross over and vote for Latimer in the DFL primary.[5] Post-election analysts found that the ads had backfired, antagonizing many DFLers without generating a significant crossover vote.

On the Friday before the election, a Minnesota Poll published in the *Star Tribune* showed Latimer twenty-seven points behind Perpich. It also showed Ludeman with an overwhelming lead over his principal Independent-Republican opponent, Bloomington Mayor James Lindau. Lindau was hampered by a late start and lack of money, and polls showed he was damaged by his association with the megamall and the Ghermezians' unpopular quest for state subsidies.

The September 9 primary election was a reaffirmation of the party-endorsement system which had been under fire in recent elections, with the endorsed candidates of both the DFL and Independent-Republican parties winning handily. It was an election, however, with less than one-fifth of eligible voters participating. Ludeman easily won over Lindau, 147,674 votes to the Bloomington mayor's 30,768. Perpich defeated Latimer by a landslide, 293,426 votes and 57 percent to 207,198 and 41 percent, carrying 84 of the state's 87 counties, with Latimer winning only in the St. Paul-area counties of Ramsey, Dakota and Washington.

But a Northstar Poll published by the *Pioneer Press* revealed that many voters were actually critical of the governor's performance in office.[6] The statewide survey of DFLers who voted in the primary found that by a margin of more than two-to-one, DFL voters were critical of Perpich's handling of the Bloomington mall issue. Nearly as many doubted that Perpich's efforts to promote trade had produced new jobs for Minnesota, and many were not convinced that the state economy had improved much during his first term in office. Still, DFL voters remained confident that Perpich, not Latimer, understood their needs and could do a better job of alleviating the economic problems for farmers and on the Iron Range.

Latimer immediately endorsed Perpich and said that he had known from the beginning that he was an underdog running an uphill battle against the popular incumbent governor. When his term as St. Paul mayor ended in 1989, Latimer became dean of the Hamline University Law School. In 1993 he went to Washington to work for Housing and Urban Development Secretary Henry Cisneros as director of the Office of Special Projects. Later he returned to Minnesota to join Macalester College as "distinguished visiting professor in urban studies." In 1990 and again in 1994 he said "no" to friends who wanted him to run again for governor.

Just after the 1986 primary election Perpich spoke to the Minnesota Business Partnership, made up of the chief executive officers of the state's largest businesses. It was an opportunity to cast himself as a business-friendly governor before a powerful audience that leaned Republican, although some had worked with Perpich on job programs during the past four years and had contributed to his campaign. Perpich credited his administration for turning Minnesota around from a state drowning in a sea of red ink, a state with a lowered credit rating, high unemployment, and a weakened educational system, to a state that was moving forward and resolving its problems.

"I believe very strongly in the idea of [business-government] partnership," he assured them. Stressing his efforts to help businesses already in Minnesota, he said his administration had established an aggressive program to reach out to Minnesota businesses of all sizes and was spending $22 million a year on business incentives. His first priority was to create the best possible climate for all business, Perpich declared, and he had stopped the flight of business out of Minnesota to South Dakota and other states. He praised the business community for its contribution to a robust economy: "The single biggest factor in Minnesota's recovery in the last four years has been the ability to produce new jobs. And the credit goes to Minnesota employers, large and small, who have started new business and expanded with the confidence that state government is working with them—not against them."

Perpich also took the opportunity to defend his veto of the unemployment compensation overhaul bill favored by business, saying it was neither a fair bill nor a reform bill. "It was a political year, and that bill was an early maneuver in the race for governor," he said, promising to push for passage of a fair and balanced bill in 1987. He pledged another look at workers' compensation in 1987. Perpich told the business executives, "I'm not a miracle worker, but I am a hard worker. I love this state."

Many of the business leaders in the audience had been appointed to commissions, task forces and "blue ribbon" panels created by the governor. In addition to 190 citizens' commissions established by state law, Perpich had named more than a hundred special commissions, task forces, and panels since he became governor, dealing with such wide-ranging issues as noise pollution, economic depression, drought, government mismanagement, prejudice and violence, pipeline safety, and curling.

The commissions, heavily loaded with business executives and leaders in civic, education, labor and other areas, also helped build a broad base of support for the DFL governor, not only among traditional DFLers but also among independents and Republicans. Members often received letters soliciting contributions to his campaign committee. "You can't get elected staying within the boundaries of one political party," Perpich said. "You need that middle ground." And the commissions created a firewall for the governor, who tossed them politically hot issues. Triplett said, "Citizens commissions are a terrific way to bring ideas into government. It's also a nice way of building a consensus among people with a variety of interests."

Independent-Republican leaders Leon Oistad and Marge Gruenes issued a tongue-in-cheek press release saying they would request to be appointed to a commission. "We read that they're looking for the last eight people in the state to name to a commission, and we want to do our part," they quipped. "We would also seek out, if possible, business leaders who haven't yet served on any other commission. We believe we met one down in Pfingsten who hadn't yet been asked, although we may have to resort to asking a former business leader who has relocated in Sioux Falls."

In the fall campaign Ludeman said he would focus on Perpich's style. He called Perpich's economic-development spending misguided and wasteful, using as an example a state-assisted chopsticks plant in the governor's home town of Hibbing. Ludeman flew a planeload of reporters to visit Lakewood Industries, whose Canadian owners raised nearly $4.5 million from state and local industrial revenue bonds and loans to manufacture chopsticks for sale to Japan. During its first year of operation the company sold only a hundred cases of chopsticks to U.S. customers and was in financial trouble. Ludeman ran television and radio ads lampooning the chopsticks venture, showing people with chopsticks fumbling with fried chicken and Jell-O. The Perpich administration said the controversial plant, which at one point employed about a hundred people, was an effort to use wood products and create jobs on the depressed Iron Range.

Lakewood did eventually start selling chopsticks to Japanese customers who liked the white wood from Minnesota aspen.[7] Initially the firm had problems producing the smooth, uniform, disposable chopsticks acceptable to the Asian market but that was fixed. Then the company found that it couldn't compete with China, where the government used prison labor. The plant closed down in 1989 after piling up more than $7 million in debt.[8] Canadian developer Ian Ward, head of the venture, said the plant had been used as a political football "to kick at Rudy Perpich."

In the general campaign voters found Ludeman's pet themes unexciting. Meanwhile, Perpich hammered away at Ludeman's conservative voting record during his six years in the Legislature. The DFLers were largely united, while Ludeman's conservative views did not play well with IR moderates, many of whom stayed home on Election Day. Few were surprised, therefore, when, on November 4, Perpich and his running mate, Marlene Johnson, were re-elected to four more years in office by a landslide, 56 percent to Ludeman's 43 percent. Aided by a low Republican turnout, DFLers also swept back into control of the Minnesota House, gaining 18 new seats and an 83-51 majority in a rout described as "the firestorm" of 1986. Among the 17 defeated Independent-Republicans were prominent champions of deep spending cuts in welfare and other programs. The short-lived House IR majority had gone too far to the right too fast. DFLers increased their state Senate majority by four seats to 48-20.

DFLers also held onto all but one of the state's constitutional offices; IR State Auditor Arne Carlson, who was re-elected to a third term, blamed his party in part for its loss in the governor's race and said, "We have to become a more centrist party, more of a people party." DFLer Collin Peterson almost upset IR Congressman Arlan Stangeland, who won by a razor-thin 121 vote-margin in the Seventh District.

On the national level Democrats regained control of the U.S. Senate, and Minnesota's Republican senators, Durenberger and Boschwitz, found themselves in the minority and lost their chairmanships of high profile subcommittees.

At the DFL election night victory celebration at the Radisson Hotel Metrodome, euphoric DFLers sported "Rudy Perpich On To Iowa" buttons, alluding to the upcoming precinct caucuses in that state and the beginning of the presidential campaign. Asked whether he might consider running for President, Perpich said, "I want to be governor, and that's it for me." The fact that voter turnout in the election was a record low, about 46 percent of the state's eligible voters, didn't dampen the celebration.

His tremendous re-election victory strengthened Perpich's hand with the DFL Party. He had headed the victorious DFL ticket and could claim some credit for legislative victories, which would give him friendly majorities in both houses when the Legislature convened in January. This year there had been no Hubert H. Humphrey II or Walter Mondale with coattails to help carry the party candidates. Perpich now looked like a middle-of-the-roader and not the liberal firebrand that critics had cast him as in the early days of his political career. He had earned his place as head of the party.

And he lost no time in exercising that clout. The governor endorsed newly re-elected Attorney General Hubert Humphrey III for the U. S. Senate against Durenberger in 1988 and told other potential candidates to stay out of the way.[9] Perpich had advised Humphrey to step aside in 1984 and let Joan Growe run against Boschwitz. Humphrey in turn praised Perpich for bringing the DFL Party closer to the ideological mainstream.

Perpich wanted to spend more time working to create jobs, traveling the state and focusing on individual communities rather than traveling the world and said he would delegate more of his responsibilities to others. The day after the election he announced in Hibbing that his chief of staff, Terry Montgomery, would take over the day-to-day responsibility of administering state agencies, becoming in effect a deputy governor. Montgomery's $71,823-a-year salary made him the second-highest paid state official after the governor. Perpich also expanded the role of Lieutenant Governor Johnson, who had previously, aside from representing the administration at many ceremonial occasions, been a leader on tourism and some social issues. Perpich said she would take a more prominent role in shaping his 1987 budget and would be the administration's leading lobbyist at the Legislature. Johnson was pleased. The increased responsibility would enhance her candidacy for governor when Perpich stepped down at the end of this term, as he had said he would do.

Perpich also reorganized his cabinet, rewarding some favorites and moving one commissioner because of a complaint from organized labor. Perpich transferred Steve Keefe from his job as commissioner of labor and industry to head the Metropolitan Council. Keefe, a former state senator from Minneapolis, reportedly did not get along with Minnesota AFL-CIO President Dan Gustafson, who urged the governor to remove him. Ray Bohn replaced Keefe as Commissioner of Labor and Industry. Bohn had been finance director for Mark Dayton's unsuccessful 1982 Senate campaign, had worked for the DFL Party, and had been owner and publisher of the *Nobles County Review* newspaper. Perpich named his longtime favorite, Sandra Gardebring, who had been chairwoman of the Metropolitan Council, to head the Human Services Department, the largest of the state agencies and the overseer of care for the needy and aged in Minnesota. The governor called Gardebring "probably the best person we have in state government."[10]

Tony Perpich, the governor's brother, was named Commissioner of Public Service, and the department, which represented consumers in public utilities cases, was expanded to include energy programs. Tony had been deputy commissioner in charge of the energy division in the Department of Energy and Economic Development. He took a pay cut from $60,000-a-year to $52,500 to assume the more visible and powerful position with the Public Service Department, which dealt with utility rates and regulations involving many millions of dollars. The governor moved Leonard Levine from his post as Commissioner of Human Services (formerly called Welfare) to Commissioner of Transportation, a job Levine, a former St. Paul City Council member, had long desired. He succeeded Richard Braun, an engineer, who resigned. (Highway builders were not pleased to have a non-engineer in the top job.)

The governor appointed Joseph Pavelich of Babbitt to be chairman of the Waste Management Board, succeeding William Walker whom Perpich appointed to a judgeship. Pavelich, a geologist, was a retired Reserve Mining Co. purchasing supervisor. David Speer, co-founder of the Padilla and Speer public relations firm, replaced Mark Dayton, who stepped down as head of the Department of Energy and Economic Development. Dayton said he wanted to spend more time with his two young sons.

Mindful that during the 1986 campaign, Perpich had said this would be his last term, potential 1990 candidates immediately began showing interest in running for governor: Roger Moe, Marlene Johnson, Mike Hatch, and Hennepin County Commissioner John Derus.

Chapter 15

Greater Minnesota Corporation.
The Sports Governor. Rudy for President?

T he 1987 inaugural was like none other—a week-long celebration, the theme of which was "The Best of Minnesota." Phillip Brunelle, acting music director of the Ordway Theatre, directed the inaugural week musical events. Sixteen searchlights and four hot-air balloons were part of the week-long festivities, as well as receptions, concerts, visits to the elderly and handicapped, press conferences statewide, and a ball. The inaugural week colors were royal blue, white, and gold. Everyone was invited, and most events were free.

On Thursday night Perpich hosted a teen concert at the Prom Center, admission $2 or a food-shelf donation. The next night he held a $1,000-per-couple dinner at the Plaza Hotel in Minneapolis, and the following morning Archbishop John Roach delivered the inaugural Mass homily at the St. Paul Cathedral before the noon swearing-in at the Capitol for the governor and other constitutional officers. Chief Appeals Court Judge Popovich administered the oath of office to the governor, who, on December 29, had become the longest-serving governor in state history. Afterward, guests were invited to pass down a receiving line and greet the officeholders. A Polaroid photo was taken and given to each guest standing with the governor and his wife; the 3M Company paid for the film. Rudy and Lola stayed in line until 5 p.m. Meanwhile, choirs and musical groups from Minnesota schools performed on the second floor of the rotunda throughout the afternoon. Catering students from Minnesota area vocational-technical institutes provided food for the reception. That evening the Perpiches hosted a private dinner party at the governor's residence for $10,000 contributors to his campaign and their spouses.

The final event described by coordinator Paul Ridgeway as a "wowser" was a $12.50-per-person "People's Inaugural Celebration" on Saturday night at the spacious IDS Crystal Court. Rudy, wearing black tie, and Lola, wearing a black and silver lamé gown bought in New York, made a grand entrance, descending from the top of the court on the escalator illuminated by a spotlight as the University of Minnesota's seventeen-piece brass band played a fanfare written especially for Perpich by Twin Cities composer Libby Larsen. Two Minnesota dance bands, the Sentimental Journey from Virginia and the Wolverines from the Twin Cities, played, while outside, a 3.2-billion-candlepower display of colored searchlights waved back and forth over downtown Minneapolis.

Ridgeway estimated the cost of the six-day extravaganza at $25,000 with $5,000 to be paid with state funds for the nonpolitical events. There were three high-priced events, including a $100-per-person fundraiser in the Orion Room at the top of the IDS Tower which was attended by about 400 people. Perpich raised about $100,000 from those two events and $100,000 at the private dinner at the governor's mansion on January 5, according to Vance Opperman, finance chairman of the governor's campaign committee.[1] He said the money would be used to help sell the governor's legislative program, possibly with radio and TV ads, to pay DFL Party debts, and to finance Perpich's political and nongovernmental activities.

"I think we have done a good job of balancing between elegant and overly elegant," Ridgeway said. But despite the food-shelf benefit, the week of free events open to all, the visits to the elderly and handicapped, and the five hours spent greeting any and all who wanted to say hello to their governor, Dane Smith of the *Star Tribune* wrote that the production "may have left some people wondering what happened to their down-home, slightly rumpled, but lovable governor." And it was true that Perpich himself had a new look for the inaugural. He had returned in December from a vacation in Hawaii, tanned, trimmer, and looking younger, and his hair, which had been mostly-gray, was now a deep brown.

Although there was grumbling about the scale of the inaugural festivities, the 1987 legislative session went well for Perpich. Of particular importance, the Legislature approved Perpich's proposed Greater Minnesota Corporation (GMC), which he envisioned as his long-term jobs legacy to Minnesota. This new agency was designed to provide financing to businesses through grants, loans, loan guarantees, and equity investments, but its main focus would be on applied research and new product development. Such activities wouldn't constitute a "quick fix" for rural Minnesota's economic misery and population exodus. Rather, they were intended to help establish permanent diversity and stability for the rural economy. Perpich and Moe flew around the state hailing the passage of what they called historic legislation, and Perpich predicted, "In twenty, thirty years, they'll be saying this is the most significant legislation of this decade, for sure." He called the GMC the "missing link" that would turn the rural economy of the state around.

The governor chose Terry Montgomery, his chief of staff, as interim GMC president, though he acknowledged that Montgomery's departure from his staff that fall would leave a big hole in the administration. When a new Perpich-appointed GMC board of directors met, it named Montgomery as the first permanent president. Lynn Anderson, deputy chief of staff, replaced Montgomery as the governor's chief of staff.

Along with an initial appropriation of $12.5 million plus up to $120 million in state surplus money, Perpich wanted to build a $1 billion endowment fund for the new corporation. His plan was to give the GMC one-half of the lottery proceeds for five years, if voters approved a constitutional amendment for a state-operated lottery in 1988.

In line with his promise to help struggling farmers, Perpich also earmarked $3.5 million for research to find new ways to use and sell the state's farm products, along with money for development loans on the Iron Range, forestry and mineral programs to help economically depressed northern Minnesota, and $9 million for redevelopment projects in poor neighborhoods of St. Paul and Minneapolis.

A *Star Tribune* editorial cautiously endorsed the new economic development scheme, but it also warned, in light of Perpich's past record of failing to follow through on programs, "Taxpayers who provided the seed money, deserve assurance from Perpich that he intends to take this strategy from drawing board to fruitful execution." On the other hand, Senate Minority Leader Duane Benson described the new agency as a statewide version of the Iron Range Resources and Rehabilitation Board, which, in his view, had already wasted millions of taxpayer dollars.

In the legislative sessions of succeeding years, there were recurrent battles over how heavily to fund the corporation, while envious legislators repeatedly attempted to raid its coffers for their own projects. The Legislature refused to include the dedication of proceeds for the GMC in a proposed lottery constitutional amendment that appeared on the 1988 ballot—an amendment that voters approved. And two years later, in mid-1989, Perpich unexpectedly divorced himself from the project, saying he was tired of fighting the Legislature over the agency, which he said had become a political pawn. "I don't care what they do" with the corporation, Perpich said. "I don't intend to spend any more of my time for the GMC. It's there for Greater Minnesota. If they don't want to defend it, so be it."[2]

Perpich's declaration on June 15, just after the 1989 Legislature adjourned, that he would end his support of his long-cherished centerpiece rural economic program stunned legislators and associates. In order to avoid the continual haggling of the legislature over the future of the GMC, Perpich announced, he would go to the private sector to get money for an independent "Class A" research institute. "We are going to have a private institute where the Legislature can't get their hands on it." This surprise announcement, which came two weeks after the governor had vetoed the omnibus tax bill passed by the DFL-controlled Legislature, caught even GMC president Terry Montgomery unaware, and it widened a growing rift between the governor and DFL leaders.

But although the GMC was embroiled in controversy at the time, after Perpich's death *Pioneer Press* business columnist Dave Beal noted that it had proved to be "an enduring asset for the state and its economy" and praised Perpich for his vision in creating it [3]; and *Star Tribune* editorial writer Leonard Inskip wrote in 1999 that with assistance and seed money from the agency for research and development, the state was outpacing most others in manufacturing growth.[4] Minnesota was reaping "jobs, jobs, jobs" as a result of the program, just as Perpich had predicted.

In the midst of the initial controversy surrounding the his GMC initiative, Perpich in 1987 turned his attention once again to another aggravating problem, unemployment-compensation reform. True to

193

his promise to the business community, he called together key DFL lawmakers and asked them to draft an unemployment-compensation-reform bill. Joe Samargia, Jobs and Training Commissioner, negotiated a compromise between business and labor, and the Minnesota Business Partnership called the resulting legislation "a good first step." It reduced unemployment-compensation insurance premiums for employers who used the system less, increased them for heavier users, and reduced unemployment benefits. The following year Perpich and Samargia announced that the state unemployment-compensation fund was at $165 million, so employers would not have to pay a surtax, which they would have been charged if it had fallen below $150 million. In 1983 the fund had been $352 million in debt, and the state had be forced to borrow money from the federal government at interest to cover unemployment claims. Perpich said his veto of the 1986 bill, which he termed "inadequate," had forced the Legislature to come back with a better bill which, together with the growth of the state economy under his administration, had "restored the health of our unemployment-compensation system."

On the Iron Range many people were still out of work and desperate. Every day there were more layoffs. So when Endotronics Inc., a Coon Rapids-based technology firm, claimed to have made a miraculous breakthrough in developing a cancer treatment and asked the 1987 Legislature for $24 million from the taconite-tax fund to create hundreds of new jobs on the Range[5], Perpich and legislative leaders quickly backed the proposal. In March, before the bill came up for floor action, the governor's chief of staff, Terry Montgomery and an FBI representative came to Roger Moe privately to inform him that the firm was being investigated by the FBI for possible securities fraud, but Iron Range legislators assured Moe that there was no reason to worry. The majority leader let the bill go through the Senate without informing members of the FBI investigation, as Iron Range authors of the bill requested, and sent it on to the House, which had already passed a different version of the measure. Senator Doug Johnson, an author of the bill, said the FBI investigation might have been spurious, and public disclosure would have hurt the ultimate goal of providing jobs on the Iron Range.[6]

But word of the investigation leaked out, and the next day, Friday, March 13, 1987, the story of the FBI investigation was splashed across the front pages of Twin Cities newspapers, which also reported that Moe had known about it. Perpich, who had worked to help Endotronics get financing, said the FBI investigation would not affect the legislation because the bill would allow the money to be used for other projects if it were not given to that firm. Perpich insisted the bill was never intended as a boost for the Coon Rapids company and said he would sign the measure if it reached his desk. The bill authorized money from taconite taxes only for Iron Range development, although it had been presented as a bill to help Endotronics.

After getting beat up in the press, Moe spent a miserable weekend back home in Erskine. He returned to the Capitol on Monday and stood up on the floor of the hushed and somber Senate chamber, where he apologized to his colleagues for bowing to the wishes of the two Iron Range sponsors of the bill, who had requested that fellow senators be kept in the dark about the FBI probe. "That was wrong, and I admit it, and I apologize to the Senate for that action," said Moe, who said he accepted full responsibility for allowing the bill to pass out of the Senate. "I was following my heart and not my head," he said. He called the Senate-passed bill back from the House and shelved it.

Perpich could not be reached for comment that day and was undoubtedly hurt and embarrassed himself, feelings he never displayed publicly. He had gone up north and was ill, his staff said; he refused to talk with reporters on the phone.

Senate Independent-Republicans questioned the timing of the Endotronics initiative, noting that twelve days before the hard-fought Perpich/Latimer primary in 1986, the *Hibbing Daily Tribune* had broken the story that an unnamed "international high-tech medical company is considering building a major bio-technical plant in the Hibbing area." The article said the company had been working closely with the governor and his staff and said the decision to explore the Iron Range as a potential plant site was influenced by the governor.

At that time, Hibbing city officials had met with Endotronics executives at the governor's urging to discuss the company's interest in building a 750,000-square-foot biomedical plant that would employ up to 5,000 people producing "killer cells" to fight cancer. Jubilant Range folks had high hopes for the new enterprise. On October 25, just before the general election, more than 3,000 attended an

"Endotronics Forum" in the Hibbing High School gym. Endotronics stock sold heavily in the area, and the value of the stock plummeted after the disclosure of the FBI investigation. (Three years later, on October 31, 1990, Endotronics Inc. founders Eugene Gruenberg and his son, Michael Gruenberg, were convicted of fraud and other charges in federal court.[7])

Perpich, in an unusual appearance before a state senate committee on March 30, denied that he had made a commitment of public funds to Endotronics. The next day the *Star Tribune* reported that Gary Lamppa, Perpich's appointee as commissioner (administrator) of the Iron Range Resources and Rehabilitation Board (IRRRB), in a December 1, 1986, letter to Eugene Gruenberg, the company's chief executive, had pledged $27 million to help Endotronics finance a "cancer-treatment" plant at Perpich's home town of Hibbing. Although the IRRRB administered development programs in northeastern Minnesota, legislative action was required to release the funds.

Roger Moe was Norwegian, one of five children raised on a modest Red River Valley farm, a champion wrestler in college, and a former school teacher. He was elected to the Legislature in 1970 when he was 27, joining his older brother, Senator Don Moe of St. Paul. He became the protégé of Senate Majority Leader Nick Coleman and later his successor as majority leader. He was esteemed by both DFLers and Independent-Republicans as a consensus builder and widely respected by the press. He generally had good relations with all the governors under whom he had served. He had become particularly close to Republican Governor Al Quie during the bleak recession days of the early 1980s while the two were working together to make up shortfalls and keep the state operating in the black.

But now, uncharacteristically angry over the Endotronics embarrassment, Moe declared he would not continue to lead the charge for Perpich's legislative programs, the traditional role of legislative leaders of the same party as the governor.[8] Moe said he no longer felt "any responsibility to be the governor's water boy." Perpich had promised too much too often, raising expectations of the public, Moe said, and leaving legislators exposed to criticism when they responded to the governor's legislative requests and something later fell through. The Senate majority leader said the governor had a track record of backing away when a venture became controversial. As examples, he cited Perpich's enthusiastic but short-lived pursuit of the Bloomington megamall, his talk of a world-class convention center for Minneapolis (both of which initiatives Moe had personally been against), and the Endotronics fiasco.

Meanwhile, the governor had turned to other issues. Perpich was a former basketball and football player, but he was not an avid sports fan. All the same, he saw the potential of attracting people, dollars, and prestige to the state by promoting Minnesota as a sports center. In the 1987 legislative session, Perpich secured state funding for amateur-sports facilities, both to provide more recreational opportunities for Minnesotans and to serve as a tool for tourism and economic-development. These facilities, he said, would bring events drawing athletes and fans who would spend money on food, lodging and other things; they would establish Minnesota as a center for national and Olympic team training and promote amateur sports. Perpich proposed and the Legislature established the Minnesota Amateur Sports Commission to oversee the construction and operation of state-of-the-art amateur-sports facilities around the state.

The jewel of the program was the 250-acre National Sports Center in Blaine which opened in 1990 with 55 soccer fields, a 12,000-seat outdoor stadium, a 250-meter cycling velodrome, an indoor-sports hall, and an arena featuring four ice rinks under one roof. Eleven years later, the commission reported, the impact on the state economy of those facilities was nearly $270 million and more than 11.4 million people had made use of them during that period, either as athletes or fans.[9] The state investment amounted to nearly $70 million, giving a return of almost four-to-one, according to the report. Perpich helped bring other sports prizes to the state including the National Basketball Association franchise awarded to the Minnesota Timberwolves for the 1989-90 season. The grand prize was the 1992 NFL Super Bowl. By 1990 Minnesota had acquired the rights to host some of the top sporting events in the country, the Perpich administration boasted: the U.S. Gymnastics Championships in 1989; WCHA hockey championships and U.S. Olympic Festival, 1990; NCAA Division 1 Hockey Championships; U.S. Diving Championships; U.S. Open Golf Championships; U.S. National Figure Skating Championship in

1991 and International Special Olympics in 1991; NFL Super Bowl XXVI; and NCAA Men's Final Four in Basketball in 1992.

The Legislature had barely adjourned its regular 1987 session when the Dayton Hudson Corporation appealed to lawmakers for help in fighting off a threatened takeover by the Dart Group Corporation of Landover, Maryland. Dayton-Hudson had grown into one of the nation's top retailers since George Draper Dayton opened the original Dayton's store in 1902 in downtown Minneapolis. The five Dayton brothers of the current generation, who held various positions within the corporation, had built post-World War II stores in shopping malls around the state, established the world's first enclosed, climate-controlled shopping mall, and launched the chain of highly successful Target stores that eventually spread throughout the country. The influential family had built up a reservoir of respect and good will, making substantial contributions to cultural institutions in Minneapolis and St. Paul and sitting on boards of business and civic organizations.

The possibility of losing the merchandise giant and Minnesota icon was close to unthinkable. Perpich swiftly called an extraordinary special session June 25, and in just a few hours the Legislature, with little opposition, passed and the governor signed into law a tough bill curbing hostile corporate takeovers. It was a quick response to the crisis facing the huge Minnesota-based retailer with its 34,000 employees and $9.3 billion annual revenues. It was also an opportunity for the DFL governor and Legislature to give themselves a pat on the back as friends of business and to gather ammunition to use against those who charged that they were fostering an unhealthy business climate.

After the session ended, Perpich flew around the state hailing Minnesota's booming economy. In Moorhead he told city officials and reporters the state would end its 1987 fiscal year at the end of the month with tax revenues running $127 million ahead of projections. Faster than Independent-Republicans could carp about bad-business-climate, the Perpich administration cranked out glowing statistics on the creation of new jobs in the state. On his fly-around Perpich said that over the past year 106,000 new jobs had been created statewide and that the state's unemployment rate was the lowest since April 1978—3.8 percent in outstate Minnesota and 3 percent in the Twin

Cities. Finance Commissioner Tom Triplett said that while most states were short on revenue, Minnesota had a surplus which reflected the strength of the state economy. By the time of the next official revenue forecast in November, Triplett predicted the state probably would have built up a $550 million budget reserve, removed an income-tax surcharge, and have money left to pursue property-tax relief.

In a year unusually fraught with drama and crises, Perpich generated further controversy when he declined to attend the grand opening of the World Trade Center in downtown St. Paul because of what he felt was the negative media coverage surrounding the project, and the frequent media criticism of his overseas travels to promote international trade. Yet the trade center was a Perpich brainchild dating back to the 1982 campaign, when he had broached the idea of a "one-stop service center" to bring buyers and sellers together to facilitate the export of Minnesota products. Many doubted the project's utility, and in the end they were proven right. The center never did establish itself as a true hub of world-trade. When the $120 million, thirty-seven-story, reddish-orange granite and glass building opened, only 43 percent of the floor-space was leased and only two of nineteen tenants were open for business. In any case, few of those who had moved in relied on international trade for the bulk of their business.

Former Vice President Walter Mondale, his wife, Joan, George Latimer, and several dozen ambassadors and foreign dignitaries did show up for the opening festivities with thousands of spectators on hand as well. President Reagan sent a taped laudatory message.

Perpich also withdrew as the scheduled host of a Capitol reception and dinner the next evening for the V.I.P.s. The governor said his boycotting of the Trade Center opening had nothing to do with his cooled relationship with St. Paul Mayor Latimer, who had run against him in 1986. Latimer, basking in the glow of what was seen as a boon for downtown St. Paul and given some of the credit for its construction, said Perpich's shunning of the opening was ill-advised.

"The simple fact is, there wouldn't be any World Trade Center if the governor hadn't proposed it. He deserves credit for that, and that's why he should be there."[10]

In a back-handed tribute, a *Minneapolis Star Tribune* editorial said Perpich was a victim of his own success.[11] A towering monument to that success and a symbol of the governor's self-victimization, it said, was the Minnesota World Trade Center, which Perpich had fought hard to get built. "He also helped politicize its governance, and he received criticism in return. So a petulant Perpich refused to take part in last week's celebration of the trade center's opening." The editorial gave Perpich credit for other accomplishments: income and sales tax reforms, improvements in higher education, student's choice in elementary and secondary education, and the Greater Minnesota Corporation. It lauded his skills in attracting business support for some of his projects.

The World Trade Center rocked from one controversy to another in the ensuing years, going back to the Legislature year after year for subsidies, while struggling to attract and retain retail stores, restaurants, and entertainment spots in the lower levels. There were turf battles between the trade-center board and state agencies with trade responsibilities. One explosive issue was a pay raise given Nolan, who was hired in 1986 by the board at a salary of $70,000-a-year. His salary was raised to $78,500 in January, 1988, second only to the governor.

Over the years Rudy Perpich Jr. had become an influential adviser to his father. Tall and dark-haired, he looked very much like his father and shared his zest for politics. Following his graduation summa cum laude from St. Thomas College in St. Paul, Rudy Jr. enrolled at Stanford University Law School, where he earned a law degree. But following graduation, he became ill and was eventually diagnosed with Chronic-Fatigue Syndrome, then a little-known disease.

Rudy Jr. underwent extensive tests at the Mayo Clinic in Rochester and the University of Minnesota Hospitals and began living in the governor's residence. During that time he became increasingly involved in his father's work. A voracious reader, he monitored newspapers and journals, clipping them and writing notes to the governor's staff.[12]

The governor credited his son with being "the brains" behind his 1986 re-election campaign and praised him as an invaluable strategist in spotting trends and opportunities.[13] During the 1986 campaign, it was Rudy Perpich Jr. who had advised his father not to debate Latimer unless the St. Paul mayor released his tax returns. It was he who came up with the idea of a highly publicized bus tour by the governor around St. Paul to point out development projects which the elder Perpich had helped bring to the city. The governor said his son was his closest adviser and "brilliant," but he added, "I make the decisions."

The younger Perpich's influence was evident. GMC President Terry Montgomery said he consulted with Rudy Jr. about twice a week, and said Rudy Jr. had reviewed all of Perpich's major speeches in the past several years and had written some of them.

After Rudy Jr. called the governor's press office a "disorderly operation" in a memo, Gerry Nelson, the veteran journalist who had been Perpich's communications director and senior adviser for nearly five years, was moved to a position outside the governor's office, where he was charged with planning and fundraising for Celebrate Minnesota, a year-long series of events and festivals. The governor's office explained that Nelson wanted to be more involved in "management," but *Politics In Minnesota* questioned whether the new job was indeed a great new opportunity for Nelson or whether he was getting sent to Siberia.[14] "Clearly, dear reader, it's the latter case. There's no way that going from being the Governor's chief press spokesman to chairman of the 1990 Homecoming Dance Perpich plans on throwing can be seen as a promotion," said the newsletter. Editors Wy Spano and D. J. Leary said Nelson had done a good job during his five years of service as the governor's communications director, adding that it was a classic case of shooting the messenger. "Perpich seems to feel that he's getting bad press coverage. Instead of looking inwardly, he blames the intermediary. Gerry Nelson was that intermediary."

The change in the governor's press office also came after the governor's campaign consultant, Raymond Strother of Texas, had told Perpich that the accomplishments of his administration were "the best kept secret in America." Gregory Peterson, 32, who had been vice president for public affairs at Padilla, Speer, Burdick & Beardsley, one of the state's largest public relations firm, was hired to take over. Peterson's job, said chief of staff Terry Montgomery, would be to "orchestrate the communications effort both out of this office and from other departments in order to tell our story as strongly, as effectively, as possible."

Even before the stepped-up effort, Independent-Republicans were criticizing what they saw as inordinate emphasis placed by the

Perpich administration on public relations. State Senator Fritz Knaak of White Bear Lake quipped that the governor's initials were in the wrong order: "Instead of RP they ought to be PR because that is clearly the central emphasis of this administration. The greatest efforts by this administration and its agencies seems to be aimed at convincing the public what a good job they are doing, rather than in getting the job done," and "at the taxpayers expense," Knaak said.

Rudy Jr. worked closely with the governor's new communications director. But when the governor said he was considering putting his son on the state payroll, DFL legislative leaders had doubts. On the other hand, some observers thought the younger Perpich was the right person in the right spot and described him as very intelligent, an excellent writer, and quick-witted. Adding him to the governor's staff would be "a brilliant choice," said Pat Forciea, then the director of Democratic presidential candidate Michael Dukakis's Minnesota campaign. Forciea, who went to St. Thomas College at the same time as Rudy Jr., said, "He has very strong people skills."[15]

In an October 30 letter to the University, Perpich prodded President Kenneth Keller to move the University's Commitment to Focus program along quickly, asserting that a $30 million US West research center had been given to the University of Colorado largely because of the research programs there. Keller had developed the Commitment to Focus, a restructuring of the University system, after a push from Perpich, who wanted it to be a "world class institution." The program called for tougher admission standards, a gradual reduction in undergraduate enrollment, the elimination of some programs that were duplicated at other state institutions, and a concomitant redirection of energies toward research.

At a meeting the previous January, Perpich and Gus Donhowe, Commissioner of Finance, had bluntly warned regents and university officials that if they wanted legislative approval of the governor's recommended 21 percent funding increase, they would have to focus on professional schools and doctoral programs and abandon programs such as general education that were duplicated in state universities and community colleges. In the letter of October 30 Perpich underscored this position and added that the University needed a new lobbyist who "can speak a legislator's language," someone who "can go out and have a beer with these guys and listen to some cowboy music." Keller and Regents Chair David Lebedoff said the problem was inadequate funding by the Legislature, not the lack of strong support for Commitment to Focus.

Rudy for President?

E arly in 1987 Perpich advisers began talking about a Rudy Perpich-for-President campaign. Perpich, who had brushed off such suggestions in the past, didn't tell them to stop. And although he had said he wouldn't run for governor again, Perpich hired national pollster Peter Hart and campaign consultant Raymond Strother, and stepped up his communications and press office operations. Vance Opperman, a Minneapolis lawyer and Perpich's finance chairman, who had been a leading organizer of Eugene McCarthy's 1968 presidential campaign in Minnesota, drafted a campaign plan in hopes of persuading the governor to go for it.[16] Opperman argued that by running for President, Perpich could draw more national attention to the plight of Midwest farmers and the rural crisis. He estimated it would cost $1.5 million for a respectable campaign and said that was doable. Supporters of the idea, including Rudy Perpich's brother George, believed that if the governor ran and launched an energetic "save the farmers" crusade, he would have a good chance of a favorable reception in presidential primaries in neighboring states, particularly in Iowa, where the first test for presidential candidates would come.

Perpich might have been tempted to run and add his name to those of Humphrey and Mondale and other Minnesotans who had made a mark on the national scene. It might have given him a long shot at the vice-presidential spot on the 1988 ticket, an ambassadorship or other appointment by a new Democratic president. He told the *Star Tribune* editorial board in May that being elected president in 1988 wouldn't be as tough as being elected governor was in 1982. "When I started out for governor, that was a much longer shot than what I see now." But he stopped short of acknowledging that he was seriously thinking about a bid for the White House, either as a favorite son or an all-out candidate, saying, "I'm going to wait and see. I like being governor. I

like this job better than anything." He admitted he had gone so far
as to ask a few political allies to hold off making a commitment to
other presidential candidates. And, he said, as he surveyed the field of
Democratic candidates already campaigning: "I know those people. I
can do as good a job as they can."

Senator Doug Johnson told Perpich he'd support him in a
presidential race. As for Perpich's chances, the Cook DFL senator
said, "Who thought [Georgia Governor] Jimmy Carter would ever
be president?" At the urging of his brother George, who encouraged
Rudy to make an exploratory foray, Perpich went to Iowa to speak to
the state Legislature on education. George Perpich said that since Gary
Hart dropped out of the race it was wide open, and Rudy would have
as good a chance as anyone. His brother Tony also encouraged him to
run and thought he would do "very, very well."

In June, Perpich was asked in an interview with *USA Today* if he
were considering running for President, and he replied that he'd "take a
look and see what's happening" in September. "It's a good opportunity
for a Midwesterner; it's a good opportunity for a governor," he said.
At the same time Perpich was dropping hints that he might run again
for governor in 1990, a reversal of his earlier statements, and said his
family's wishes would be the determining factor in a decision as to
his political future. Aides said his family was split; Perpich told one
staff member that his daughter, Mary Sue, wanted him to run for
president, while his wife and son were against it. State and national
leaders of groups opposed to abortion and gun control urged Perpich
to run for president. They considered the Minnesota governor a friend
who would give them an alternative to other Democratic candidates
opposed to their positions. But Perpich's antiabortion and anti-gun
control positions were at odds with the national Democratic Party
platform and would almost certainly have kept him from getting
favorable consideration for the nomination. He failed, too, to attract
favorable attention from the national press.

Meanwhile local cartoonists began lampooning the idea. And
when WCCO-AM Radio conducted an unscientific, call-in poll, 94
percent of the respondents said Perpich should not run for president.
Many DFL activists scoffed at the notion of a Perpich presidential
candidacy—though they had scoffed at him often enough before and

been proven wrong. Yet it was clear that he lacked both the big bucks and the organization usually required to launch an effective campaign, and in any case, there were already seven Democratic candidates in the field.

In September Perpich said he would not run for president. He said he had talked with his family and decided, "I have obligations in Minnesota, and I want to complete the job I started." But he added in a statement released by his office and first published in the *Hibbing Daily Tribune*, "In my heart I feel I could have made a credible run for the presidency, and I could have done so very honorably."

When the Minnesota Twins won the World Series in the fall of 1987, the governor moved to bring Minnesotans together to share the excitement and pride. He declared October 27 Minnesota Twins World Championship Day, ordered state offices closed for part of the day and threw open the Capitol grounds for a huge celebration. It started with a victory parade beginning in downtown Minneapolis, traveling through downtown St. Paul, and ending at the Capitol with a rally attended by tens of thousands of jubilant Twins fans.

Two top financial officials, Finance Commissioner Jay Kiedrowski and John Haynes, Assistant Revenue Commissioner and principal architect of the 1971 "Minnesota Miracle" tax reform, resigned after the legislative session. Perpich credited Donhowe, who had left earlier to become chief operating officer of Fairview Community Hospitals, with probably doing more than any other person to get state finances turned around. "He has brought credibility back to state government finances," said the governor.

Speaker Bob Vanasek, with an eye to the 1988 elections, said House DFLers would chart a more independent course than they had in the past and develop their own priorities for the 1988 session. That course might not necessarily reflect the priorities that the DFL governor set forth, such as a state arts high school or income tax cuts, he said. Steven Dornfeld of the *Pioneer Press* wrote that Vanasek's remarks came at a time when DFLers were talking privately about whether the governor was coming unglued. Dornfeld wrote, "They are concerned about such irrational acts as Perpich's decision to boycott the opening of the World Trade Center, one of the governor's pet projects, or his angry letter to the University of Minnesota Board of Regents about the need to streamline the University." There were doubts, too, said Dornfeld, about the wisdom of the governor's decision to transfer longtime aides Terry Montgomery and Gerry Nelson, who had had some success at "keeping Perpich under control [and] replace them with yes-men and -women and rely increasingly on the political advice of his house-bound son, Rudy Jr."[17]

But while governors generally rely upon their staffs to carry their message to the public and Legislature, Perpich was always confident that he could work his magic best by personal campaigning in the small towns of Minnesota, talking up his tried-and-true themes of creating jobs, making Minnesota the "Brainpower State," and protecting the environment. Throughout his terms as governor, he set a punishing travel schedule for himself with Lola often at his side. David Carr, a free-lance writer, accompanied the governor on the road on a long day of campaigning, with Perpich showing no signs of being tired or frayed as he shook hands and talked and listened to people. "Perpich actually wanted to know what people thought," Carr said. "He was an excellent listener."

Late that night they took off for the next day's campaign events in another part of the state, Lola driving and Carr sitting up front with her, while Perpich catnapped in the back seat. About 3 a.m. Perpich woke up and said he needed pancakes, so they stopped at a Perkins Restaurant. Carr was desperate for sleep, but Perpich was fired up over his stack of cakes, eager to hash over the past day's happenings and plan for the next campaign stops.[18]

By the fall of 1987, Perpich was plummeting in opinion polls, however. He blamed the decline not on poor performance, but on what he said were unfair attacks on him by the Twin Cities press.[19] In an effort to polish his image and build support for his 1988 legislative initiatives, Perpich made several major news announcements outstate and held press conferences in St. Cloud and other cities. He closed the year with informal meetings in northeastern Minnesota at which he lashed out at the Twin Cities press, while refusing requests by the Capitol press for traditional year-end interviews. To counter the charge of unpredictability laid upon him by the news media, Perpich asserted that he had consistently pursued his goals of jobs, education, and environmental protection. If he appeared to have acted impulsively, it was only when jumping at an opportunity to meet those goals.

Chapter 16

The Environmental Governor.
The Gambling Governor.
The Building Governor.

Amid speculation that he was planning to run for an unprecedented fourth term, Rudy Perpich underscored his concern for outstate Minnesota by delivering his 1988 State of the State speech on February 9 at Winona State University in Winona. Billed as the first time a governor went outside the Capitol for that event, the gesture was applauded by small-town newspaper editors.

Members of the Legislature opened the 1988 session in St. Paul at 2 p.m. Later that day constitutional officers, Supreme Court justices, and other dignitaries drove their cars or loaded onto buses to make the 120-mile trek for the governor's 6:30 p.m. speech. Most of the House and Senate Independent-Republicans stayed at the Capitol to watch the speech on television. Perpich said their absence was an offense to the people of rural Minnesota and to a city that was "a shining light," while House Minority Leader William (Bill) Schreiber described the governor's move as "preposterous," an unnecessary expense for taxpayers, and motivated by politics rather than by policy.

Perpich's State of the State speech was widely hailed as the strongest environmental-protection message by a governor since the early 1970s when Governor Wendell Anderson had focused on the same theme.[1] Perpich renewed his call for the creation of a major environmental trust fund and the earmarking of half the proceeds of a proposed state lottery to finance it. He said the other half should go to the Greater Minnesota Corporation, which he called a "rural revival" program to halt rural Minnesota's economic erosion and the exodus of young people to the cities. The environmental trust fund, he said, would provide long-term financing for the preservation and improvement of the state's natural resource attractions including hunting and fishing.

Perpich also proposed a sweeping statewide program to reduce and recycle solid waste, regulate dumping in landfills, and protect ground water, all of which would be paid for with fees on packaging materials that could not be recycled and deposits on beverage containers. "We have a serious garbage crisis in the state, and of course it's getting worse," the governor said. Soft-drink bottlers, longtime foes of mandatory container deposits, lobbied heavily to defeat the fee proposal. A recycling and waste-reduction bill finally passed in a 1989 special session, imposing a 6 percent tax on garbage bills to pay for a county-administered program. The governor signed the "environmental landmark" legislation at the Dakota County Recyclables Collection Center in Burnsville flanked by huge bundles of crushed aluminum cans.

For Perpich, environmental concern was not a new thing. As lieutenant governor, he had accused the DFL Party of having "gone soft" on environmental problems, citing inaction on Reserve dumping into Lake Superior, protection of the BWCA, and iron-mine reclamation.[2] During his first years as governor, he played a leading role in establishing the state's toughest-in-the-nation acid rain standards and expanded the Reinvest in Minnesota program that took marginal farmland out of production to preserve wetlands and wildlife habitat. He championed a law requiring the recycling of waste tires. Perpich, whose desk was always clean, crusaded against litter in the outdoors, promoted river cleanups and screening of dumps and used-car lots, and ordered the beautification of Minnesota Department of Transportation truck stations.

He even wrote to Ciatti's Ristorante on Grand Avenue in St. Paul, urging owners to spruce up the outside of their Italian restaurant. "Why no trees or greenery in front of Ciatti's?" the governor asked. "It reminds me of a garage in Chicago where the St. Valentine's Massacre took place." Dan Danford, president of Ciatti's, promised to support anything that would beautify Grand Avenue. Perpich urged the City of Rochester to plant trees in a median and asked the Metropolitan Airports Commission to put trees along roads leading to the International Airport.

He supported the establishment of state parks at sites of unusual beauty or historical significance, including Tettegouche, Wild River, Grand Portage, Hill Annex, and Mystery Cave. He initiated a massive sewage-treatment program, providing for the separation of combined sanitary-storm sewers in St. Paul, Minneapolis, and South St. Paul, as well as other outstate sewage-treatment plant improvements that would end the release of raw waste into the Mississippi River. The program was financed by a hike in cigarette taxes, which tied in with the governor's plan to have a Smoke-Free Minnesota by 2000.

Environmental activists gave Perpich mixed ratings, however. One of their biggest disappointments was that he agreed to what they felt was the weakening or even gutting of Minnesota's hazardous-waste "Superfund" law. Business lobbyists blamed the 1983 law, the strongest in the nation, for clouding the state business climate, and said it made it nearly impossible for industry to buy environmental-impairment (liability) insurance. The original law gave considerable power to Minnesotans claiming harm from toxic wastes to recover damages from the responsible parties. With Perpich's support, pro-business interests succeeded in amending the law to limit business's liability.[3]

Environmentalists also criticized the governor for not working harder to pass a "no-net-loss" bill to ensure the replacement of any wetlands that were drained or filled. Just before the November, 1990, election he unveiled an environmental program including the wetlands legislation, which he said he would push if he were re-elected. His 1990 Republican opponent, Jon Grunseth, endorsed a moratorium on solid-waste incinerators sought by environmentalists; Perpich did not. Grunseth favored a ban on mining non-ferrous metals in Minnesota; Perpich supported "strictly controlled" mining. In 1986, Perpich had sent letters to twenty-two mineral exploration firms holding mining leases, encouraging them to explore for copper, nickel, and other minerals in Minnesota, a big turn-around from his earlier "Us and Them" antipathy towards iron mining companies. He ordered state agency heads "to recognize the importance of the mining industry to the state's economy and to encourage its expansion, with due concern for the environment." Perpich said, "I would like Minnesota to be known as a reasonable state to deal with, where both environmental protection and mineral development can occur through cooperation of government and industry." Back in 1970, when geologists urged drilling in the Boundary Waters Canoe Area of northern Minnesota to determine the value of its mineral holdings and recommended mining if minerals were found, Perpich fought to block the search.

Perpich also shook up environmentalists when he abolished the Waste Management Board by executive order after chairman Joseph Pavelich, whom he had appointed, was strongly criticized by other board members and legislators for firing staff members.

Following up on his 1988 State of the State message, the governor stumped the state promoting legislation to put a constitutional amendment on the fall ballot for a state-operated lottery with the proceeds dedicated to the research and jobs-development agency and environmental trust fund. The trust fund, a compromise between environmentalists and more conservative sportsmen's groups, was sponsored by two powerful DFL legislators who sometimes were at loggerheads over environmental issues: Representative Willard Munger, a Duluth motel owner, "Mr. Environment" in the House and hero of environmentalists, and Senator Robert Lessard of International Falls, a fishing/hunting/tourist outfitter, a DFL Party maverick and the bane of some environmental activists.

Terry Montgomery, the governor's chief of staff, enlisted a coalition of lobbyists for both the lottery and environmental initiatives to put pressure on legislators who resisted linking the two and threatened a veto otherwise. The trust fund was a popular idea, but Roger Moe, Vanasek, and other legislators rejected Perpich's notion of constitutionally dedicating $1 billion in lottery revenues to the controversial Greater Minnesota Corporation (GMC). The lottery amendment was put on the ballot without the GMC funding, but Perpich did not campaign for it and said he might vote against it. General-election voters overwhelmingly approved the amendment. Voters also approved a separate amendment dedicating 40 percent of the state lottery proceeds to the Environment and Natural Resources Trust fund until the year 2001.

Sometimes called the "gambling governor," Perpich oversaw the greatest expansion of gambling in state history during his years in the governor's office, despite his strong reservations about what he said were its harmful effects on families.[4] In 1978 he had allowed a bill to become law without his signature which expanded charitable gambling by permitting the use of wheels of fortune, tip boards, and raffles licensed by local governments. When he was lieutenant governor, he strongly opposed a pari-mutuel betting bill, saying he doubted the revenue projections made by proponents and saying it would breed "illegal bookies in every town of the state." Perpich said he voted against a constitutional amendment approved by voters in 1982 authorizing pari-mutuel gambling on horse races, but as governor he signed the 1983 pari-mutuel racing enabling act, and Canterbury Downs racing track opened soon afterward. Perpich signed a bill that repealed local licensing and regulation of charitable gambling and transferred that to a state-taxed operation; it set the stage in Minnesota for the largest charitable gaming industry in the U.S., which became a billion dollar-plus business in the late 1980s. He signed compacts authorizing the state's eleven Indian bands to open 17 casinos. Perpich signed the bill creating a state lottery after the amendment passed, and then appointed the state's first lottery director and the first commissioner of gambling. The lottery bill created a new Gaming Department to supervise the lottery, charitable gambling, and horse racing. By 1990 Minnesotans were able to buy scratch-off lottery tickets that paid off instantly, and high-stakes lotto games were also available.

But Perpich was always torn between what he felt was the critical need for state revenues and jobs from gambling and his own reservations about its social desirability. Concerned about the addiction of compulsive gambling, he urged gaming organizations to establish programs to help people overcome the addiction.

Business groups were angry when Perpich vetoed two more workers' compensation reform bills passed in the 1988 legislative session, which would have reduced employer premiums and cut employee benefits. The bipartisan legislation had been passed and sent to the governor with the help of House DFL pro-business "woodticks." One bill passed the DFL-controlled Senate 42 to 25 and the DFL-controlled House by an 81 to 53 margin. An attempt to override the veto, which required a two-thirds vote, failed by three votes in the Senate. Business spokesmen said that despite the governor's longstanding theme of "jobs, jobs, jobs," when it came to the crunch on "important job-creating bills," the governor buckled under to the AFL-CIO.[5] Perpich replied that the proposals cut benefits to injured workers but did not guarantee that the insurance industry would pass along cost reductions to employers. Labor leaders, praising the governor's veto, said the bills went too far in cutting benefits for injured workers. AFL-CIO leaders threatened that DFLers who voted for the bills would not have the union's future support.

Perpich's popularity had been in decline since his 1986 re-election. Sixty percent of the respondents in a Northstar Poll published in the May 26 *Pioneer Press Dispatch* rated Perpich's performance as "fair" or "poor," while only 37 percent gave him "excellent" or "good" marks. Only 19 percent of the respondents in a survey taken earlier by St. Cloud State University's Social Science Research Institute said Perpich deserved to be re-elected in 1990, while 72 percent said they wanted to give a new person a chance in the office. Perpich dismissed the polls, saying they weren't giving a true picture of his popularity. "I've never had a warmer reception than I do now," he insisted. He said he'd decide whether to seek re-election after the 1989 legislative session.

Soon after the unfavorable opinion polls, however, Perpich held several press conferences around the state to celebrate a drop in the Minnesota unemployment rate in May to 3.2 percent, the lowest level in nine years. The state economy was the healthiest it had been in a decade, he said. The wood-products industry he was promoting in northern Minnesota was growing, he boasted, the Twin Cities metropolitan area was thriving, and farmers with state assistance were doing well. Perpich, looking more and more like a candidate for re-election in 1990, took some credit for the good news. "This represents a complete recovery from the conditions of five years ago" when he came into office, the governor said.

The governor launched a monthly "Capital for a Day," one of his most successful ventures in carrying his message to the people of the state. He picked Marshall in southwestern Minnesota for his first. It was an expanded version of a smaller program started by former Governor Quie and was intended to bring state government closer to citizens and to get state officials out of the Capitol to find out what was happening around the state. While Perpich insisted the events were nonpolitical, they had all the hoopla of a campaign blitz and were the kind of feel-good, grass-root politics at which Perpich excelled. He was sure of favorable coverage by the local press and a warm welcome by city officials and citizens, who were glad of a chance to talk with the governor and commissioners about their concerns. Republicans charged that Perpich's monthly "Capital for a Day" programs were nothing more than taxpayer-financed campaign trips.

The Marshall event, with a jam-packed schedule carefully planned by his staff and the local Chamber of Commerce, set the pattern for other trips around the state. Perpich and two planeloads (the governor and lieutenant governor flew on separate planes for security reasons) of staff members and state officials swept into the airport and were met by an ensemble from the high school band and "Welcome Governor Perpich" banners throughout the city. In Marshall, as he did in successive cities, Perpich started with a speech at a breakfast in a school cafeteria for school officials, students, and local dignitaries. Perpich always went back to the kitchen to thank the cooks and perhaps give them a hug—Perpich was a hugger. Then, flanked by the mayor and other area officials and legislators, DFL and Independent-Republican, the governor would visit a factory or an industrial plant, walk along the main street, shake hands, greet shoppers, talk with merchants, lunch with business people, visit senior citizens and community centers, and wind up with a late afternoon reception for local government officials. The word got out that the governor liked carrot cake, and at coffee stops friendly greeters often presented him with one freshly-baked.

Frequently the governor announced an economic-development grant or loan or a state-funded construction project for the city where he was visiting. Throughout the day an aide, dubbed "Polaroid Patty" by the press, took pictures of the governor and everyone he shook hands with and the scores of people at each stop who received some kind of award or certificate from the governor; they were given the instant photo of themselves and Perpich to take home. Gerry Nelson quipped that soon every household in Minnesota would have a picture of the governor stuck on the refrigerator.

Perpich and his entourage used these day-long visits to tout their Minnesota-is-doing-great theme. There would be advertisements in local newspapers beforehand announcing that the governor was coming; afterward there would be ads with a picture of Perpich and a local resident—often a school child—and a thank-you note signed by the Governor. A Capital for a Day cost about $4,000 excluding travel costs, which could double that figure.

Celebrate Minnesota was another successful Perpich idea to "foster a sense of community that will carry our state forward into the international economy of the 1990s." Heavy on boosterism and feel-good rhetoric, it called for community celebrations, sporting events, economic-development efforts, and cleanup and beautification projects and was partially financed with a special $1 million legislative appropriation. The Perpich administration said the year-long celebration was timed to coincide with the Olympic Festival scheduled for 1990, an election year, fueling further speculation that Perpich would run for a fourth term.

In July, 1988, Perpich became chairman of the prestigious Education Commission of the States, a prized post that other governors, Democrat Bill Clinton of Arkansas and Republicans Lamar Alexander of Tennessee and Thomas Kean of New Jersey, had used to stake out national leadership positions in their parties. Perpich had obtained the position with the lobbying help of Ruth Randall, his energetic education commissioner, who had built a nationwide network among educators. It brought him important contacts in national education circles and speaking invitations around the country, mostly to talk about his open-enrollment initiative. But Perpich had already announced that he was not interested in seeking national office, and when he stepped down from the post a year later, no one hailed him as a rising star on the national scene.

When Perpich announced a new Minnesota Family Investment Program, a major human-services reform plan that he said would make Minnesota a national leader in helping people to make the transition from public assistance to work, Senate Minority Leader Duane Benson accused the governor of stealing an old Republican idea. Yet even during his days as a state senator, Perpich had proposed that able-bodied welfare recipients be assigned to work on environmental projects.[6] (The Minnesota Family Investment Program was expanded by Perpich's successor, Arne Carlson, and it became a model for federal welfare reform.)

Perpich wanted to build, and as governor he signed legislation authorizing more than $1.5 billion in new construction. Although conservatives called his capital budgets imprudent, the Legislature passed record building bills in 1987 and 1990, and Perpich got much of what he wanted. While he was governor, the state built or began construction of a new History Center, a Judicial Center housing the Minnesota Supreme Court, the Court of Appeals and related agencies, and an array of Olympic-class sports facilities.

Perpich also pushed for remodeling and renovation of the 80-year-old Cass Gilbert-designed state Capitol and its grounds. During his first term as governor, he had initiated the closing off of a street and landscaping of an eyesore-parking lot west of the Capitol to create the small Leif Ericson park. He now began a major historic restoration project in the governor's office and the start of the restoration of the original Rathskeller decor in the Capitol basement cafeteria, which had been painted over during the anti-German feelings of World War I. He included money in his bonding bills for a new University of Minnesota electrical-engineering and computer-science building, new buildings and improvements at other higher education institutions around the state, a new convention center in Duluth, and a new women's prison in Shakopee. He also promoted the building of the Mall of America in Bloomington and the World Trade Center in St. Paul.

But Rudy Perpich's greatest building vision was never publicly unveiled. Perpich wanted to build a new state-financed convention center in downtown Minneapolis, and he invited world-famous architect I. M. Pei to Minnesota to look at sites. Pei had just completed the Fragrant Hill Hotel in Beijing and had designed other renowned buildings, including the John F. Kennedy Library in Boston. Mike Hatch, commissioner of commerce, was assigned to escort Pei around. First they flew to the Range to look at a possible location on the edge of an iron pit for a new hotel which Perpich had in mind after seeing one in Europe built on the face of a mountain. Although no one spelled it out, Hatch figured out that it was his job to get the idea across to Pei that a commission for the convention center might be the quid pro quo for doing the out-of-the-way hotel. Hatch recalled in an interview years later, "This guy (Pei) was world class, and the idea of a hotel in northeast Minnesota on the Iron Range would not be something he'd be drawn to, not in the least. But of course, what he would be drawn to was doing the Convention Center." Pei was politically astute and got the message. Hatch said, "I didn't have to connect one dot. He already knew right away."[7]

The next morning Hatch and Pei met Perpich for breakfast at the Marriott Hotel in downtown Minneapolis. The governor planned to show Pei around the city. It was a cold and drizzly November 7, the day after the 1984 general election, when Mondale lost his presidential bid and DFLers lost control of the Minnesota House. Hatch remembered, "You talk about a guy [Perpich] in a sour mood. Republicans had won the Minnesota House. He knew there wasn't going to be a convention center because Republicans wouldn't fund it. He liked to build things. All great politicians like to build things. It goes back to Pharaoh, and goddammit [he knew] the Republicans weren't going to let him build. You could tell he was mad." But over breakfast Perpich warmed up to Pei, and he invited Pei to tour the possible sites for a convention center. They walked over to Hennepin Avenue, between Seventh and Ninth Streets, one site under consideration. Pei was enthusiastic about the location, which had plenty of room for a mall and greenway leading up to it. Then the governor led them down to Loring Park and the Walker Art Institute and Guthrie Theater, and described his vision of a large campus for the arts: "Over here is going to be a school for arts. Here's a school for dance. All of the arts are going to be around this park."

Hatch said later, "He's got them all picked out, fine arts, performing arts. He had a vision. It was like a college campus. Every major art you could think of would be going around Loring Park, and Hennepin Avenue, culminating with the Walker, the Guthrie, the statuary garden. I'd never heard any of this. He had it right down, this vision, he was laying it out. He knew which building was going to be in which place. Pei was nodding. I could tell he was impressed."

Finally they walked over to the site of the old Minneapolis Auditorium where a new convention center was eventually built. Pei thought that the location was terrible, saying it was too far removed from the main city and had no space for a great mall leading up to it.

Chapter 17

Zigging and Zagging

Word that the FBI was investigating criminal allegations of fraud and embezzlement involving Midwest Federal Savings and Loan and its chairman, Harold Greenwood Jr., a prominent Perpich supporter, rocked the Twin Cities business community. The investigation came in the wake of Midwest's heavy 1988 losses, and the state's second largest savings and loan was put under federal control. Although Greenwood's difficulties didn't involve Perpich directly, the governor had appointed him to several high-profile positions, including chairman of the Metropolitan Airports Commission. Greenwood denied any wrongdoing in his financial dealings but resigned February 7 from the Airports Commission, and it was disclosed that he had stepped down earlier from his chairmanship of the Greater Minnesota Corporation. He said he didn't want to become a "political football" and needed to concentrate on his legal difficulties.[1]

In his January 4 State of the State speech, Perpich took credit for having led the state from the edge of bankruptcy in 1983 to its current prosperity and low unemployment. Reiterating the job-creating theme that had been at the heart of his vision from the first, he claimed that 340,000 jobs had been created in Minnesota over the previous six years, and he also touted tax reform, sound fiscal management, and a $550 million rainy-day fund (budget reserve) that had improved the business climate, and helped to bring about more than seven new business start-ups or expansions in Minnesota every day.

In his proposed $14.1 billion budget for the next biennium, Governor Perpich laid out his goals for the 1989 legislative session, including "the world's best education system" and statewide testing for elementary and secondary students. With great fanfare and visits to crime-ridden neighborhoods in both Minneapolis and St. Paul, he proclaimed 1989 as the Year of the Cities and called for a $70 million package to fight crime and drug abuse and to fund housing and school programs in both the Twin Cities and Duluth. He got most of what he asked for. When rural legislators grumbled that once again, the metropolitan area was gobbling up most of the pie, Perpich replied that when outstate Minnesota was hit by drought and depression, urban area-legislators had responded to their needs.

He called for more money for property-tax relief for business. But the governor budgeted only a modest increase for elementary and secondary schools, including $40 million for personal computers and other new technologies for students. That led to a clash with DFL legislative leaders, who counted the education lobbies among their most important constituencies. The governor said schools must make more effective use of current funds. He also ruffled academic feathers by recommending only $46 million in new money for the University of Minnesota, which had asked for $198 million more. He said he'd consider increasing the amount if officials showed they were taking care of their management problems. House Speaker Robert Vanasek and Senate Majority Leader Roger Moe said they expected the Legislature to provide more money than Perpich had recommended for property-tax relief, schools, and the University of Minnesota.

For the most part, Perpich, Moe, and Vanasek had tried to project a public image of a united DFL leadership at the helm of state government, but by May, the governor's legislative package was floundering, especially in the House, where DFL-controlled committees had inflicted heavy damage on the Perpich budget.[2] That set off a public quarrel within the Troika. The governor blamed Vanasek, saying the Speaker was young and hadn't kept a tight rein on his 80-member majority caucus. "I just don't think he has control over there," Perpich said.

Vanasek, 40, was a pragmatic conservative from New Prague and one of an emerging new breed of DFL legislators convinced that there were limits to what government could and should do. The activists of the DFL Party still looked much like the liberals of the 1970s, but DFL legislative caucuses were becoming moderate, even conservative, and more independent of the party in the wake of the fiscal crises and forced budget cuts during the early 1980s and the ceaseless demands by supplicants for even more largesse from the state. Vanasek's belief that it was time to focus on efficiently managing current state programs and to curtail new spending seemed to be in tune with the public attitude. Just re-elected to his ninth term, he had been winning huge margins in an only marginally DFL and largely rural district. Furthermore, he had led his majority caucus to victory in the 1988 elections. A low-key, less partisan, but nonetheless effective Speaker, he had never lost a floor vote on a major bill, and, unlike the Senate with its late-night sessions, the House typically finished its floor sessions by 6 p.m.

Majority Leader Ann Wynia, 45, St. Paul, was the first DFL woman to be elected to that post by her caucus, and she was an able teammate for Vanasek. Quiet-spoken, thoughtful, and competent, a political science instructor at North Hennepin Community College, she was a consensus builder like Vanasek and well-respected by Republicans as well as her DFL colleagues. In September, 1989, she resigned to accept appointment by Perpich as Commissioner of Human Services, succeeding Gardebring, who had been appointed to the Court of Appeals by the governor.[3]

Vanasek helped keep the Perpich train on the track. Time and again he worked to get the governor and legislative leaders to come together. So when Perpich took a shot at him, an indignant Vanasek fired back, saying Perpich was trying to blame the Speaker for his own shortcomings. Vanasek said, "I have never seen a year when he has been so disengaged and paid so little attention to his initiatives. He's got a staff that I don't think are getting clear directions or have a plan. But then he comes back the last two weeks of the session and starts blaming others, including me, because his programs aren't being implemented. That isn't my fault. It isn't the Legislature's fault. It's his fault." Vanasek said, "It's vintage Perpich for him to blame others. He's a master politician at grandstanding." In the two years Vanasek had been Speaker he had attempted to shed the DFL's tax-and-spend image, and he said at his weekly press briefing on Monday after the skirmish between the two, "I don't think there's enough money to pay for all those things" that Perpich promised.

Vanasek's conservative agenda and his vow to develop his own priorities for the session made it unlikely that he and the governor would ever quite see eye-to-eye. But later that day, he, Perpich, and Moe made peace at a private meeting in the governor's office and came out smiling and apparently united again. Perpich and Vanasek were carrying foam paddles and joked about their weekend disagreement. It had been a healthy exchange, they maintained, and they predicted a successful conclusion to the session by the next Monday midnight deadline.

The DFL-controlled Legislature passed a major tax-reform bill that included $270 million in property-tax relief, and, saying it was a good bill for homeowners, farmers, business and rental property, they adjourned and went home. Perpich, who had called for more commercial and industrial tax reductions to reduce "highest-in-the-nation" taxes on business property, warned that he might not sign it. On June 2, the deadline for the governor to act on the bill, tension built as legislative leaders waited for Perpich's decision. It was Moe's birthday, and the governor stopped by the Senate majority leader's office for cake but gave no hint of his plans. It was Vanasek's sixteenth wedding anniversary, and he canceled a planned celebration with his wife, Mary, to wait for the governor's decision. Perpich had two messages prepared, one to veto the bill, the other in case he signed it. He went up north to deliver two commencement addresses, one at 7 p.m. at Itasca Community College in Grand Rapids.

Perpich waited until the last minute to announce at an extraordinary midnight press conference in the governor's reception room at the Capitol that he would veto the tax bill. He acknowledged that there was no guarantee that lawmakers would pass a better bill in a special session. "It means all hell breaks loose," he said. "It's going to make a bad summer out of it."

Independent-Republicans and business groups, afraid their property taxes would have increased sharply under the vetoed measure, applauded Perpich's action. "Governor Perpich's veto of the 1989 Omnibus Tax Bill is both statesmanlike and visionary. It is true leadership," the Greater Minneapolis and St. Paul Area Chambers of Commerce proclaimed in press releases. They called for a new tax bill that would be fair and not place what they called an ever-increasing burden of property taxes disproportionately on commercial and industrial properties.

On the other hand, the veto and the unconventional midnight press conference infuriated DFL legislative leaders. Vanasek tried but failed to head off the required formal delivery of Perpich's veto message to the House that night by instructing the sergeant-at-arms to lock the doors to the Chamber. He said the governor's office apparently got Capitol Security to open the doors and allow a courier to place the veto message on the Speaker's desk.[4] Vanasek called the veto "the most irresponsible act I have witnessed in my seventeen years as a state legislator." During the session, when the Legislature was struggling to find money for property-tax relief and education, the governor didn't show up, Vanasek said. Many legislators, including Dee Long, House tax committee chair, had vacation plans and were tired and dismayed at the prospect of a special session to negotiate a new bill.

The next week bitter members of the House Ways and Means Committee harshly criticized the governor. Dee Long said that during the session, "He gave us about as much direction as a compass sitting on top of a magnetic field. Every time you look, the needle is pointing in a different direction." She said the governor's veto had created chaos for schools and local governments facing budget deadlines and not knowing how much state aid they would get or what taxing limits would be. Senate Tax Chairman Doug Johnson, Perpich's good friend, was also angry at the veto. "Afterward he [Perpich] told me that was one of the stupidest things he ever did," Johnson disclosed later.[5] Perpich didn't think the final product passed in a special session that fall was worth vetoing the bill, said Johnson.

Although there was a substantial pot of money for the "buydown" necessary to overhaul the complex, inequitable property-tax system without hiking taxes, the governor and the DFL-controlled Legislature failed to achieve another "Minnesota Miracle" like the landmark 1971 tax reform of former Governor Wendell Anderson. Perpich and the lawmakers were unable to curb huge state subsidies to local governments and property-tax relief targeted disproportionately toward homeowners and renters; critics said the system fueled more uncontrolled spending and higher property-tax levies by school districts and city and county governments which maintained a powerful lobbying presence at the Capitol. "Some people are beginning to talk about our fiscal system as though it had been a wonderful puppy that no one thought would grow into a very large dog, who's now eating all the family's food, and we can't get him out of the house," said Curtis Johnson, Citizens League executive director.

For the third time, in a replay of the 1988 session, Perpich vetoed a bipartisan workers-compensation reform bill sought by business

221

groups and called for a study of the issue and recommendations for the 1990 Legislature. That veto chilled the warm feelings the business community felt after the governor's tax bill veto.

Perpich, who once spent a day in a wheelchair to better understand and dramatize the difficulties of the disabled and had pushed for handicapped-accessible buildings since he first took office, signed another bill that put Minnesota in the forefront of initiatives for the disabled. The legislation, spearheaded by Human Rights Commissioner Stephen Cooper and Michael Ehrlichmann, chairman of the Minnesota State Council on Disabilities, provided handicapped Minnesotans with more legal tools to help them move about in the business world. The new law, which Cooper called a "giant step," broadened the definition of who was disabled and required businesses open to the public to make "reasonable accommodations" for the disabled. Later Perpich appointed Ehrlichmann, who was confined to a wheelchair, chairman of the Metropolitan Transit Commission. He was believed to be the first handicapped person to head a major state agency.[6]

When his wife became a leading advocate of a school for the arts, the project became a priority for the governor, too. Legislators were cool to the proposed arts high school, however, and public school representatives said that the money—estimated at $31 million—should go for art instruction for all students. Terry Montgomery, Perpich's chief of staff, marshaled Perpich friends like Gene Merriam, powerful Senate finance committee chair, to sponsor the bill, and influential lobbyists like former House Speaker Sieben and Tom Kelm to work for it, and the legislation passed. In the 1990 session Senator Randolph (Randy) Peterson of Wyoming, chairman of the Education Committee funding division, shepherded through a $4.25 million appropriation for the purchase of a thirty-three-acre campus in Golden Valley for the Lola and Rudy Perpich Minnesota Center for Arts Education. On December 4, just before Perpich left office, he appointed Peterson to the Court of Appeals.

Another Lola Perpich project was wildflower planting along Minnesota highways. The governor and his wife traveled to Texas to the LBJ Ranch to consult Ladybird Johnson, widow of former President Lyndon Johnson, who had made highway beautification her priority in the White House and had initiated a similar program in Texas. Leonard Levine, Commissioner of Transportation, expedited the wildflower program on Minnesota roads.

In July, 1989, both Perpiches were awarded honorary doctor's degrees from the College of St. Thomas—Lola in humane letters and Rudy in law. "As a valued adviser in the administrations of your husband, Governor Rudy Perpich, you have had a significant and lasting impact on the citizens of Minnesota," said the college in making the award to Lola Perpich, citing her efforts for a state high school for the arts in particular. "Above all else, you have placed in prominence for all Minnesotans to observe the example of a loving, caring, tightly knit family. Your devotion to your children Mary Sue and Rudy, and to traditional family values...has earned our admiration and brought you honor."

Perpich was rushing to catch a plane on May 24 on his way to New Orleans along with other Minnesotans to make a pitch to host the 1992 Super Bowl, when he lost his lucky purple tie in the Minneapolis-St. Paul International Airport. He called it his "Latimer tie" because he wore it when he defeated St. Paul Mayor Latimer in his 1986 reelection campaign. Fortunately, the governor had another lucky purple tie along which he wore to the NFL meeting. It must have worked. Minnesota, which had been the underdog in the intense competition for the site, was awarded the 1992 Super Bowl prize. "Nobody gave us a snowball's chance in hell," said Vikings general manager Mike Lynn, who lobbied hard behind the scenes in Minnesota's behalf. Latimer gave much of the credit for capturing the event to Perpich. The governor had been working since 1984 to snare the Super Bowl for Minnesota and had tapped Marilyn Carlson Nelson to head a task force to make Minnesota's case to the National Football League. Perpich was the only governor to show up to help his home state make a bid, but he himself attributed the success in large part to the efforts of the energetic daughter of billionaire entrepreneur Curt Carlson, who later succeeded her father as head of Carlson Companies. The governor had also recruited Nelson to chair a Midsummer Music Festival, "New Sweden '88," in Bloomington, a commemoration of the 350th anniversary of Swedish settlement in the U.S. She and Minnesota

Twins owner Carl Pohlad co-hosted a $5,000-a-couple fundraiser for the Perpich campaign.

In the summer of 1989 a Legislative Auditor's report said that financial controls in the office of Governor Rudy Perpich were weak, particularly in regard to the travel expenses of the governor and his wife. The auditors found unsatisfactory vouchers for Lola Perpich's trip reimbursements, including one for a New York trip reading: "Represented the State of Minnesota in an official capacity while assisting the governor at meetings with bonding companies Goldman Sachs & Moody's regarding Minnesota credit rating." Another said "To attend the Minnesota Vikings and the New Orleans Saints face-off in the National Football Conference playoffs. Mrs. Perpich represented the State of Minnesota in an official capacity." The auditor's report said travel at state expense by Lola Perpich needed clearer justification and was valid only when the state received a benefit. State checks were signed for personal expenses by a receptionist, according to the report, without previous review and approval. That person probably would not question payments to superiors, and ineligible payment might occur, the report said. The auditor reported that an unidentified person ran up $1,354 in long distance calls on a state telephone at the governor's mansion for "personal benefit." Perpich had his own private telephone at the mansion, and his staff was instructed to use it for long distance calls. The governor reimbursed the state for the cost.

Chief of Staff Lynn Anderson wrote in response to the auditor's report that documentation procedures had been improved, and that many shortcomings had been corrected. Dan Loritz, deputy chief of staff, said nothing in the report was improper, and said the governor and his wife "have acted as a team," and "Mrs. Perpich plays a key state role with the governor."

Early in 1989 Perpich appointed his longtime friend Peter Popovich to be Chief Justice of the Minnesota Supreme Court, succeeding retiring Chief Justice Douglas Amdahl. Perpich named another longtime friend, D. D. (Don) Wozniak, a St. Paul lawyer and former legislator, as Chief Justice of the Appeals Court, succeeding Popovich. But when Perpich told his old friend Sandy Keith that he was going to appoint him to the state Supreme Court to fill the vacancy left by elevating Popovich, Keith wasn't enthusiastic.

Over the years, Sandy Keith had been an ever-loyal Perpich supporter and an influential member of his kitchen cabinet. He had solicited many thousands of dollars for Perpich's campaign coffers from the well-to-do Republicans of Rochester and southern Minnesota. Perpich owed him. And George Perpich said of Keith, "Sandy has a relationship with Rudy that is unusual for someone outside the family. Rudy has a lot of 'yes men' around him, but Sandy isn't one of them. He tells Rudy the unvarnished truth as he sees it, even if it's unpleasant. That's the mark of a true friend."

Keith had previously turned down several Perpich appointments, and he was not pleased with this one either, because he and Popovich simply did not get along. In fact, they had been on opposite sides of almost every political fight in their careers. Perpich assured Keith that Popovich would soon reach the mandatory retirement age of seventy and would be leaving. "You can get along a year-and-a-half," the governor told Keith and promised, "Then you will be chief." Later Perpich called the reluctant Keith at home around midnight, but Keith wasn't in, and the governor talked with Keith's wife, Marion, and told her the announcement would be made the next morning.

The next year, Popovich, who loved his job, considered contesting the mandatory retirement law. But after consulting with Chief Deputy Attorney General John Tunheim, he decided it would be unseemly for a judge, especially the chief justice, to be involved in such litigation. However, Popovich favored fellow justice Lawrence Yetka (also from northeastern Minnesota) to be chief, not Keith. Don Wozniak, chief judge of the Minnesota Court of Appeals, was also against the Keith appointment, and they tried to dissuade Perpich from choosing him. "None of us ever trusted Keith. We didn't want him to be appointed chief judge because he had no loyalty," said Wozniak, who had also sided with Rolvaag in the 1966 election. [7]

Nonetheless, Perpich announced on July 6, 1990, that Keith would be the next Chief Justice. When Keith got the certificate of appointment, he filed it immediately with the secretary of state before Perpich could be persuaded to change his mind, although Keith would not be sworn in until Popovich left on November 30.

Popovich, during his brief tenure as Chief Justice, oversaw the completion of the Judicial Center, part of it a new building and part of it the remodeled old Minnesota Historical Society building across the street from the Capitol.

Perpich was faced with a bigger problem that fall than trying to get his old friends to work together. When Boise Cascade Corporation announced a $535-million paper-mill expansion in International Falls, it looked like a major success for the governor. Minnesota had offered special tax benefits to Boise Cascade under a Minnesota law relating to economic development in high-unemployment counties. But when Boise contracted with BE&K, an Alabama construction firm employing mostly nonunion labor, to build the new facility in International Falls, angry union members protested, and during the summer of 1989, demonstrations escalated into a wildcat strike by building-trades workers.

Perpich was soon being besieged by both management and labor unions to intervene. He didn't want a repeat of the 1986 Hormel strike, which had drawn stinging criticism from labor union members, but he had worked hard for years to gain the trust of the business community and put to rest claims that Minnesota was anti-business.

Perpich chastised Boise for its "deplorable" tactics and suggested that the state might revoke the $16-million sales tax break Boise had coming. "I cannot imagine why a chief executive officer of a company would choose to take such actions against a state that has shown the spirit of cooperation and offered such extensive assistance," Perpich wrote. He also ordered state agencies to check state laws and permits affecting Boise's operations. The Minnesota Business Partnership protested that Perpich's actions were heavily slanted against the company.[8]

When Boise officials warned of impending violence in early September and asked the governor to send the Guard to protect the community, Perpich decided against it. On Saturday, September 9, a mob attacked the company's International Falls housing complex. The fenced camp was nearly destroyed and mobile homes were demolished by at least 100 union sympathizers, mostly out-of-towners, and there was a roving demonstration of 400 to 500 people.[9]

Perpich defended his decision not to activate the Guard, saying he could not have done that on the basis of rumors. "We did all we could in this particular case," said the governor, who credited the "threat" of sending in the National Guard with helping disperse the rioters. Perpich had received a call for assistance at 8:16 a.m. Saturday from Koochiching County Sheriff William Elliott, who told him that "the town was burning" and said up to 3,000 people were involved, although the State Patrol later estimated that figure at about 400. Perpich said he assured the sheriff, "We are going to give you all the help we can."

The governor received five calls from Ted Kennedy, head of BE&K, the general contractor for the expansion project, asking Perpich to send the National Guard and telling him of the destruction. The governor sent an emergency team headed by Mark Shields, superintendent of the Bureau of Criminal Apprehension, and Lieutenant Colonel Ron Deppa of the Minnesota Department of Military Affairs, to International Falls to assess the situation, standard practice in considering whether to send out the Guard. Meanwhile, he ordered 275 Guardsmen to be assembled. But by 12:30 p.m., when the emergency team arrived in International Falls, the three-hour riot was over, and Perpich decided not to send the Guard. Shields reported there was "no imminent danger" and said local law enforcement officials had the situation "well in hand."

The riot resulted in an estimated $1.3 million in property damage, and five security guards were hurt. Twenty-nine arrests were made, mainly by eight agents of the Bureau of Criminal Apprehension who filmed the rioters while they were investigating the situation along with representatives of the U.S. Bureau of Alcohol, Tobacco and Firearms, the FBI, and the state fire marshal's offices. Later in the day, Andrew Drysdale, chief spokesman for Boise, agreed that the situation was quiet for the time being, but said Perpich made "a grave mistake" in not sending the Guard. Boise had "solid information, not rumors" of the impending violence which it had shared with the state, he said. On the basis of that information, the company had vacated its main housing camp for workers by Saturday, and local law-enforcement officials had brought in reinforcements from surrounding areas, he said. "The sheriff clearly got to the point where he couldn't handle the situation. They were completely outnumbered. I don't know what he was waiting for."

Perpich said he would not have hesitated to send in the Guard had it been warranted: "I have said from the beginning I will enforce the law in a fair and evenhanded manner for all the parties in the situation," he said. The governor promised Boise CEO John Fery in a Saturday-afternoon telephone call that "this kind of thing would not happen again."

The expansion was completed despite recurring vandalism, and in December, 1990, gigantic new machinery began producing paper at the showcase plant. But the no-win, politically damaging labor battle tempered any satisfaction Perpich might have felt about the development plum. The war of public words with Boise executives and the governor's blaming the company for failing to resolve the dispute before violence erupted did not endear Perpich to business leaders.

There was a happier time. The governor's daughter, Mary Sue, married Edward Bifulk on September 16 at the Basilica of St. Mary in Minneapolis. Eight hundred guests were invited. Mary Sue, employed by A.M. Myers and Associates, Minneapolis, which marketed annuities to financial institutions, and Bifulk, a sales representative for Kencotronics of St. Paul, a manufacturer of industrial control equipment, had met in college seven years earlier. They were both twenty-nine. A private reception and buffet dinner for about 300 was held after the ceremony at the governor's mansion. Mark Dayton hosted a black-tie reception for the couple at Woodhill Country Club in Wayzata the night before the wedding.

Although many old friends attended the wedding, some observers felt that Rudy was fraternizing more and more with business leaders, and even questioned whether he was still the open, folksy governor he had been in the early years. Steven Dornfeld, looking back at those years, wrote in *Law & Politics* that Perpich's inner circle was growing smaller and smaller and that the governor was cutting off contacts with old political friends. "To the extent he made new friends, they were titans of business and industry like Curt Carlson, Carl Pohlad, Robert Maxwell and Richard Burke—not the kind of folks you bump into on the bocce ball court or in small town cafes." Dornfeld wrote that "somewhere along the way Rudy Perpich seemed to forget who he was—and lost touch with traits and values that made him such an engaging, effective and memorable political leader."[10]

There were continuing signs that Perpich was getting ready to run for a fourth term. In June the governor held a $250-per-person fundraiser at the Minneapolis Club, facetiously billed as his thirty-ninth birthday party.

Sandy Keith advised Perpich, who had been in office for ten years and was already the state's longest-serving governor, not to run again in 1990. "I wanted him to go out on top. He had done so much for women, for the judiciary, the school systems. It was just the most perfect time for him to walk out of that office. He was in his early sixties. He still had time to have whatever job he wanted, to make some money, [and he] had a pension. All my life in politics I have sensed too often my friends didn't know when to quit. He was having trouble with the press. The economy wasn't perfect again. We were going into a slowdown. That always affects you. It's a hard job. It takes a lot out of you. He had aged a lot."

Elmer L. Andersen also tried to discourage him from running. The former Republican governor, noting that "paranoia is the occupational disease of politicians," thought Perpich looked tired and was becoming supersensitive about criticism. "He cares deeply about Minnesota. On balance I think he's done a great deal to leaven out the thinking of our people, which I think is one of the major jobs of governor, to make them internationally conscious…he's done really a good deal for the people of Minnesota," said Andersen. But he added, "I'm beginning to have a feeling that the people are getting a little tired of Governor Perpich, and that he's kind of wearing out, and that for his own record, his own good, it might be he should feel he's done about all he's going to be able to do. No one ever does all they would like to do."

Andersen wrote U.S. Senator Durenberger, suggesting that the Republican senator ask President-elect George Bush to give Perpich some kind of appointment, perhaps an ambassadorship to Yugoslavia, Czechoslavaka, or Austria. This would remove the DFL governor from the political scene and give Republicans a better shot at the governor's office. Durenberger said he would not assist such an effort and said it would be perceived by Minnesotans as buying Perpich out of state office.[11] A State Department source in the Bush administration said there was no intention of appointing Perpich, of Croatian descent, to a Yugoslavian ambassadorship, given the tensions between the Serbian majority and Croatian minority there.

Perpich shrugged off a Northstar Poll published by the *Pioneer Press* August 13, showing that only 31 percent of Minnesota adults wanted him to run for re-election. On August 19, in a straw ballot taken at a meeting of the party's state central committee in Winona, DFL Party leaders agreed, by more than a 3-to-1 margin, that he should not run again. Newspaper editorials urged Perpich to retire.

Representative Paul Ogren of Aitkin got sixty DFL House members to sign a petition urging Governor Perpich to run for another term, but some said Ogren gave them the misleading impression that Senate Majority Leader Moe would not run, which irritated Moe supporters. In retaliation, when the House-passed tax bill arrived in the Senate, Doug Johnson, tax committee chair, deleted aid for a hospital in Ogren's district.

Tony and George encouraged their brother to run again.

Perpich himself appeared to be convinced Minnesotans wouldn't tire of him as long as the state was in good shape. "The question isn't 'How long have you been here?' The way I gauge it is, 'How well are you doing?'" he said. The key question in the 1990 gubernatorial campaign, said Perpich, would be, "Are you better off today than you were seven years ago?" He was confident most voters would answer "Yes."

Rudy blamed the press for his declining popularity. The governor was outraged by one especially harsh *Star Tribune* editorial headed "King Rudy's royal sideshow," which said "The real puzzle about Governor Rudy Perpich isn't what he plans to do with the rest of his life, but what's gone wrong with his head. Perpich has either grown extraordinarily self-absorbed or the horrid shoe-polish brown tint that's been applied to his hair also has affected his brain." The editorial observed that governors become extremely important figures in the life of a state, adding that the best ones remind themselves that the importance attaches to the office and not to them personally. "Perpich has apparently forgotten that."[12]

Perpich chose a site at the headwaters of the Mississippi River in Itasca State Park to announce on Sunday, October 9, that he *would* run again. Several dozen reporters and photographers from the Twin Cities traveled the 225 miles to the north-central Minnesota site. Though there was some grumbling and puzzlement over the remote location, in his speech the governor portrayed the picturesque setting as symbolic of his governorship. "The basic themes of my administration have always been three: jobs, education, and the environment," he said. "Yet certainty does not mean stagnation. Like the Mississippi, my administration is self-renewing, ever-fresh, ever-vigorous, and always at the service of the people of Minnesota. I hope you will allow me to continue in your service as governor of our great state." He seemed in good spirits, but he was not the excited, bubbly Perpich of the early years, spilling over with innovative ideas and enthusiasm.

It was noted that Marlene Johnson, his lieutenant governor for eight years, was not at his side, although the Perpich campaign said she would be his lieutenant governor choice again. Johnson had made no secret of the fact that she wanted to be governor and intended to run if he stepped down. She was increasingly frustrated when the governor kept her in suspense about his future plans amidst rumors that he was considering switching running mates this time, but she put aside her personal ambitions and promised to campaign hard for the DFL ticket and another term as lieutenant governor.

The next day the *Star Tribune* and KSTP-TV reported the results of a not-so-encouraging Minnesota Poll showing Minnesotans were evenly split on a fourth term for Perpich. Slightly more than half of those surveyed approved of his job performance, while 42 percent disapproved of it.

But Independent-Republicans were increasingly confident that they could unseat Perpich, and by the end of 1989, five IR candidates were preparing to run against him: State Auditor Arne Carlson, St. Paul businessman Jon Grunseth, Minneapolis businessman David Printy, State Representative John Burger of Long Lake, and Doug Kelley, Durenberger's former chief of staff.

There were also several fellow DFLers nipping at his heels. The pack of potential candidates included Mike Hatch, Robert Vanasek, Roger Moe, John Derus, Harry Sieben, and, if Perpich changed his mind and didn't run again, Marlene Johnson.

Roger Moe in particular badly wanted to be governor. He had worked hard in the Legislature and stood aside for others over the years, including Spannaus in 1982, dutifully waiting his turn. At the end of the year Moe was agonizing over whether to run against Perpich, who had been his friend and political ally over the years.

"It will be extremely difficult for Governor Perpich to win in the November election," Moe said when he announced an exploratory campaign for governor on October 13, 1989, a few days after Perpich announced he would run again. "They [voters] think ten years is long enough, that we don't elect governors for life, at least not in Minnesota."[13] Perpich's response to Moe and other naysayers was that, "I have heard that [can't do it] many times back when I was trying to get impacted teeth out [as a dentist]."

In the end Moe decided not to run, fearing that a divisive primary election would weaken the party's chances for success.

Meanwhile, DFLers were optimistic about defeating U.S. Senator Boschwitz, who, they felt, had few accomplishments to point to after six years in office and had voted against the interests of the people of Minnesota on numerous occasions. Four would-be challengers were already in the race: Agriculture Commissioner Jim Nichols, U.S. Attorney Tom Berg, state Representative Todd Otis, and Carleton College Professor Paul Wellstone.

When the Legislature finally adjourned, it found that it had emptied the state purse for the next two years by spending nearly $14 billion for the 1989-91 budget, an eighteen percent increase over the current budget. State Finance Commissioner Tom Triplett announced that the state faced a $161 million revenue shortfall over the next 19 months. Triplett played down the shortfall, pointing out that it amounted to about one percent of the state budget. It was early enough in the budget period that the problem could be fixed with minor spending cuts or dipping into the "rainy day fund," though Perpich disliked that prospect. A tax increase would be a last resort, and the governor was not anticipating any increases in major taxes, Triplett said. The finance commissioner also disclosed that Data Resources Inc., the state economic consultant, felt that the Minnesota economy was cooling down and had projected a 40 percent chance of a recession before the end of 1992.

Independent-Republicans criticized the state's top three DFL leaders, Perpich, Moe and Vanasek, all absent from the Capitol, for not taking the shortfall and the bad economic news seriously enough to return. And they also railed at spending and tax increases. During the 1980s the state's two-year budget had climbed from $7.2 billion to $14 billion as state government grew under DFL control. The sales tax had increased from four percent to six percent and extended to more items. Fees for everything from state-park admissions to motor vehicle, boat, hunting and fishing licenses had increased sharply as lawmakers searched for more dollars to fund state programs.

Triplett, a 42-year-old lawyer from Clinton, Iowa, had held various senior positions in the Perpich administration, going back to 1977. Perpich called him "one of the brightest and most hard-working people in state government." He was methodical, soft-spoken, somewhat reserved, and he was considered an adviser who often took the freewheeling governor's ideas and ran with them. But Perpich was skeptical of the complex revenue-forecasting process based on economic data from an eastern consultant and always believed that revenue forecasts by the Department of Finance understated future revenues. Triplett was sometimes at odds with the ever-optimistic Perpich over whether more money could be squeezed out for the governor's budget.

Perpich had his own method of estimating future revenue; he happily counted construction cranes which were proliferating around the metropolitan area and came up with his own figures, which he claimed were more accurate than those of the financial experts. Once he wrote his forecast on a slip of paper and put it in a sealed envelope, giving it to a reporter with instructions not to open it until the end of the biennium, a year later, when the actual revenue collections were known. Sure enough, when the envelope was opened, to Perpich's glee, his figure was right on the mark, while the official forecast from the Finance Department was notably different.

In late 1989 Triplett disagreed with Perpich's decision to run again and resigned as Commissioner of Finance. "I urged him to become a senior statesman, to leave office voluntarily with his enormous legacy behind him." But Perpich said his reforms were not yet cemented into place. Triplett said the governor thought, "Things were too vulnerable; one more term was needed to position the state for the challenge of the next century." Triplett later became executive director of the Minnesota Business Partnership, a leading critic of state government spending under the Perpich administration.

Chapter 18

Dark Days. Harold Greenwood
Terry Montgomery. Mikhail Gorbachev. Mike Hatch.

The new year did not start off well for Governor Perpich. On January 16, 1989, *Newsweek* magazine published an unflattering article headlined "Minnesota's Governor Goofy," in which it was suggested that Minnesotans were becoming impatient with the "eccentricities" that once made the governor beloved. It was one of the lowest points of Perpich's political career, and the label haunted him throughout the campaign and afterward.

Looking around for the source, Perpich first maintained that the article had been planted by media consultant Roger Ailes, who was then working for Independent-Republican gubernatorial candidate Doug Kelley.[1] Kelley denied the accusation. Later Perpich blamed outspoken Senate Independent-Republican Minority Leader Benson for the epithet.[2] Perpich also accused Jack Coffman, a reporter for the *Pioneer Press* and stringer for *Newsweek*, of providing the nickname. The *Newsweek* Chicago bureau reporter who wrote the article, John

McCormick, denied that anyone from Minnesota had fed him the story, saying it was prompted by articles about Perpich in the St. Paul and Minneapolis newspapers.

Close on the heels of that article, Rudy Jr., in a letter to the *Pioneer Press*, accused the newspaper of trying to prove he was mentally ill, in an attempt to damage his father's chances for re-election. The letter accused the newspaper of trying to imply that the illness from which he suffered affected his mental health. The *Pioneer Press* had not published such an article,[3] although a reporter for the paper had made phone calls to friends and associates throughout the country inquiring pointedly about the mental health of the governor's son.

That same week, less than two months before the precinct caucuses and the start of the selection of delegates to the DFL Party endorsing convention, Perpich's campaign manager, Michael Sieben, resigned, citing the pressures of his law practice. Although he denied that he was dissatisfied, the *Star Tribune* reported that people close to the Perpich campaign said Sieben and others had been increasingly frustrated at being shut out of campaign decisions by the governor and his son.[4]

On January 21, Mike Hatch, Perpich's former commissioner of commerce, announced that he would challenge his ex-boss in the gubernatorial race.

On January 28, a *Pioneer Press*/WCCO poll reported Perpich's approval rating at an all-time low with only 36 percent of those surveyed giving the governor favorable marks for his performance while 62 percent gave him unfavorable marks. Sixty-one percent felt he should step aside. On the other hand, he still led all the other candidates, both Independent-Republicans and DFLers, by a wide margin in voter support; no one else was catching fire.

On March 30 the Greater Minnesota Corporation announced a $130,000 out-of-court settlement with a 22-year-old Norwegian exchange student who had applied for an internship at the corporation and accused GMC President Terry Montgomery, Perpich's former chief of staff, of making sexual advances. Later, three other women who worked for Montgomery filed sexual harassment suits. The agency paid a total of $262,000 to settle all claims out of court and sued Montgomery, who denied the allegations but eventually agreed to pay $125,000. A subsequent legislative auditor's report of agency money spent by

Montgomery and others for expensive dinners and entertainment gave the governor's political opponents more campaign fodder.

On June 26, Harold Greenwood Jr., former chairman of Midwest Federal Savings and Loan, and three other former executives of the company, were charged with fraud and conspiracy in financial losses sustained by the failed thrift. A jury found Greenwood and the three, including his daughter, Susan Greenwood Olson, guilty of racketeering and fraud. Greenwood was sentenced to forty-six months in prison and the others to shorter terms.

Perpich held press conferences around the state disassociating himself from the once-powerful business leader.[5] He observed that the regulation of savings and loans was a federal not a state responsibility, and that he had made no attempt to intervene with federal regulators on Greenwood's behalf. Political opponents countered that the appointments of Greenwood and Terry Montgomery were part of a larger pattern of poor judgment and cronyism in the Perpich administration.

The bad news continued. A legislative auditor's report harshly criticizing the state education system put Perpich, who had cast Minnesota as the brainpower state, on the defensive, prompting him to put $22 million more for education into his proposed budget for the next biennium. Much of the money was marked for computers in classrooms and fiber-optic telecommunications in higher education institutions. Meanwhile, the Minnesota Taxpayers Association reported that the state had returned to the top ten high-ranking states in taxes per capita, invalidating Perpich's claim that Minnesota was now competitive with other states in all major taxes except business property taxes.

The governor delivered a fifteen-minute State of the State message at Bloomington's Thomas Jefferson Senior High School, calling for building a drug-free environment in Minnesota. He hired David Carr, a free-lance writer and recovering cocaine addict, to help write the speech. Busloads of students from around the state were brought in to hear the speech and stand up afterward to take pledges to abstain from chemical abuse, which was Rudy Jr.'s idea. It made great TV spots that evening.

When the governor invited Soviet President Mikhail Gorbachev to visit Minnesota, it made headlines because the idea seemed so farfetched. Gorbachev and his wife, Raisa, accepted, however, and the surprised media corps scrambled for front row seats. With the Cold War at an end, Gorbachev had seized upon the invitation as an opportunity to come to America's heartland and ask U. S. industrialists to help rebuild his economically floundering nation.[6] His seven-hour, whirlwind visit on June 3 was a historic event in the state and a major coup for Perpich. It spotlighted Minnesota as a center for international trade and capped Perpich's tireless quest to put the state on the world map.

Perpich asked *Star Tribune* publisher Roger Parkinson to head the planning for Gorbachev's visit. There was national and international coverage of the event, and local TV and radio stations broadcast live coverage of the entire seven hours. Although it was a cold, drizzly day, thousands of thrilled Minnesotans lined the motorcade route to catch a glimpse of the charismatic, man-of-the-people-style Russian president and his wife.

The guest list for the luncheon at the Governor's Residence included Dwayne Andreas, chairman of Archer Daniels Midland Company, and British publishing magnate Robert Maxwell, a native of Czechoslovakia who had business interests in Eastern Europe. Maxwell had just launched a newspaper, the *European*, promoted as Europe's first national newspaper. When Minnesota's two Republican U.S. senators, Boschwitz and Durenberger, showed up at the governor's residence without an invitation, they were turned away. Joseph Reed, chief of protocol for the U.S. State Department, who traveled to St. Paul with the Gorbachevs, chided the Minnesota governor and said he had "behaved very badly" in not involving the two senators. A little-noticed name on the guest list was then-unknown Condolezza Rice, a consultant to the State Department, later U.S. Secretary of State.[7]

Food writers gushed over the luncheon menu. The first course was a sautéed square of pecan-breaded Rainy Lake walleye topped with a dice of poached baby artichoke hearts, tomatoes and olives, the *Pioneer Press* reported. Veal medallions garnished with Minnesota morel mushrooms surrounded a ring of polenta heaped with wild rice, corn, and roasted red peppers. Sweet biscuits with summer berries were served for dessert, topped with whipped sour and sweet creams and caramel sauce. For the toasts, there was 1987 Blanc de Noirs for everyone except the non-drinking governor, who saluted

Gorbachev with ginger ale. Nine waiters and waitresses attired in uniforms designed by Guthrie Theater costumers, with their hair and nails done by Rocco Altobelli, served the eighteen guests in the dining room, and a similar team tended tables for more than thirty others in the adjacent solarium. The cost of the meal was underwritten by General Mills and Pillsbury, and it was prepared by Nathan Cardarelle, Governor's Residence chef, and his assistant, Kenneth Grogg, with assistance from Tim Anderson, executive chef of Goodfellow's Restaurant.[8]

After the luncheon President Gorbachev, Maxwell, and Perpich went out on the patio where freezing reporters and photographers were waiting and announced an agreement for a new Gorbachev Maxwell Institute of Technology in the Twin Cities, which they said would focus on communications and the environment. They envisioned scientists from around the world working there for the benefit of all humanity. Maxwell was to contribute up to $50 million to the center over the next five years, starting with $8 million to be put into escrow that year. Perpich would have one year to come up with matching funds from private sources for each increment with a final goal of a $100 million fund to build the institute. Maxwell reportedly got the first donation for the matching funds at a private dinner the Saturday night before Gorbachev's arrival, at which he persuaded Andreas in a five-minute conversation to give $1 million. Maxwell spoke to about forty guests at the dinner, hosted by Whitney MacMillan, chief executive officer of Cargill Incorporated.

Perpich said the new research center would not conflict with the Greater Minnesota Corporation, which focused on applied research and was financed by state lottery revenues. The Gorbachev Maxwell Institute was to be financed by the private sector. He was confident the institute would have strong support regardless of what happened in his or Gorbachev's political futures.

It was Rudy Perpich Jr. who had come up with the idea of asking Maxwell, believed to be a billionaire, to finance a new research center in Minnesota, the governor said later.[9] His son had read that Maxwell intended to give away his fortune for the benefit of humanity before he died. So the governor and Lola quietly flew to London on September 5, 1989, to ask Maxwell for $200 million for the research center. Perpich reported that Maxwell said, "How about $50 million?" and told the Minnesota governor to raise $50 million himself and then come back. Time went on, and Perpich heard nothing definite from Maxwell. When Perpich learned that Soviet President Gorbachev would be coming to Minnesota, he called Maxwell and invited him to the luncheon.

The marvelously successful Gorbachev visit gave Perpich a big boost going to the state DFL convention a week later. The Governor, whose antiabortion position put him at odds with his challenger, Mike Hatch, and a strong majority of convention delegates, wanted a prominent abortion-rights, "pro choice" person to nominate him to overcome that handicap. He asked Secretary of State Joan Growe to do it, and she did. "I liked and respected him," she said. "I didn't agree with him on that [abortion] issue, but I also knew he wasn't going to carry on, or [belabor] that issue."[10]

Her action outraged militant abortion-rights delegates, and they railed both at Growe herself and at Elaine Voss, deputy secretary of state and Growe's close friend. Voss said, "I have never been so horribly and viciously attacked. I remember being skinned alive at that convention."[11] Growe recalled, "They were screaming at us. Rudy said he 'didn't mean you should have to take all of this.' But there was no question in my mind when he asked me. I didn't hesitate to say 'yes.' He was the incumbent governor. I thought he had done a decent job.'"

Hatch, in a speech to the convention delegates, said the people of Minnesota were saying, "'Fourteen years is too long for anyone to be governor.' They want change. They are weary of world-class race tracks and trade centers. They're tired of one-shot miracles like Saturn and Endotronics." But Perpich led in the hard-fought balloting and reached the required sixty percent of the votes for endorsement on the fourth ballot. After his victory, the jubilant governor told the delegates, "You've worked hard. I have worked hard, and Minnesota has worked hard. Together, we have made this a state to be proud of." That would be the theme of his campaign.

Before resigning as commissioner of commerce, Hatch had said he would not run for governor if Perpich sought re-election and said he was sensitive to any appearance of disloyalty.[12] "I owe the governor. He has been very good to me," Hatch declared. "He trusts me enough that if he were to run, I would support him." When Hatch changed his mind and said he would run against Perpich in the primary, the governor felt that Hatch, a member of his cabinet for seven years, had betrayed him.

Hatch launched his primary challenge by accusing the governor of abusing his power and called for a constitutional amendment limiting the terms of governors and state legislators. The former state DFL chair attempted to make anti-incumbency an issue that he could use against Perpich in the primary and later against Arne Carlson, who had been in various public offices for twenty-five years. He charged the governor with unethical conduct and lumped Perpich and Durenberger in the same category. "Look at the stories on mansions, press conferences in St. Paul, limos, corporate jets, book deals, condo deals, and sexual harassment," Hatch said in speeches throughout the campaign.

For the most part, Perpich ignored Hatch's jabs. The governor said he would resume his foreign travels if he were re-elected, and concentrate over the next four years on winning a chunk of the world market for Minnesota products. That would be the only way for the state to create new jobs, he said. "If you are going to have the next ten years as good in job creation as we had in the last eight, you have to obviously look at opportunities in foreign markets, especially in East Europe," the governor said. "We have to get out and sell our product, be it agricultural, natural resources, high tech, even services." European countries were looking for U.S. know-how in a variety of services, from police agencies to chemical-dependency programs, he said. He wanted to establish more Minnesota trade offices abroad and be more active in Canada, he said.

Independent-Republicans endorsed Jon Grunseth of Afton, 44, vice president of public affairs at Ecolab Inc. of St. Paul, over three major competitors: David Printy, 42, a Minneapolis businessman and former commissioner of economic development under Gov. Al Quie; Doug Kelley, a 43-year-old Bloomington lawyer; and State Auditor Arne Carlson, 55. Grunseth, sandy-haired, good-looking, genial, with a booming voice, had run unsuccessfully for Congress in the Sixth District in 1974 and 1976, and had worked in Washington as chief of staff for Congressman Larry Pressler, a South Dakota Republican. He hauled out the familiar themes, criticizing Perpich for "flip-flops" and "lack of judgment" and called for putting the brakes on state taxes and spending. Grunseth said the DFL governor had broken a 1986 promise not to raise taxes and had changed his mind on issues such as the Greater Minnesota Corporation and World Trade Center.

Perpich lashed out more at the news media than at his challengers, complaining bitterly that reporters had not been fair to him and his family. At an emotional news conference in June, the governor, angry, rambling, tearful at one point, said his accomplishments and those of his administration had not been reported fairly and that he and his family were scrutinized more closely than other officeholders.[13] The governor was particularly irate with the media for focusing on his appointments of two men, Harold Greenwood and Terry Montgomery, who were later disgraced, to high-level positions "without regard to thousands of other superb appointees." He said the news media had failed to put things in perspective and complained about press comments on his hair color, his clothes, the state-owned car he used, and his family's lifestyle at the Governor's Residence. Perpich's eyes brimmed with tears when he recalled a WCCO-TV news report referring to his son, Rudy Jr., as a recluse. "Where the hell [else] in the United States would they print that?" the Governor asked. "You think anywhere else in the United States they would print that about a governor's son?"

Relations were strained between Perpich and Lieutenant Governor Marlene Johnson, who was angry at her increasingly diminished role in the campaign. At one point she talked with the governor privately, offering suggestions as to how she could be more helpful. Johnson said Perpich assured her they would start using the lieutenant governor in campaign ads, but it didn't happen. She crisscrossed the state, running her own campaign, raising money, visiting senior-citizen centers, technical colleges, small-town radio stations, and union meetings as well as attending ceremonial events in her official position. Now married to a Swedish businessman, Peter Frankel, who commuted to the U.S. frequently, she was a trailblazer for women in the second-in-command job. In 1990, most of the major candidates for governor in Minnesota chose women to be their running mates.

In a July, 1991, interview with *Star Tribune* columnist Doug Grow, Perpich said a decision was made to reduce Johnson's visibility because of fears of an attack against her by the Grunseth campaign. "We were told that the Grunseth campaign was going to come after her," Perpich said. He told Grow he had been told by a campaign consultant, whom the column did not identify, that Johnson had sent the consultant a letter saying she was quitting the campaign. Johnson denied that she threatened to quit the ticket, and said, "I don't know how he got that idea."

On September 11, Perpich and Johnson with 55 percent of the total handily defeated Mike Hatch and his lieutenant-governor candidate, former state Senator Emily Anne Staples, who had 42 percent. On election night Johnson stood on the podium with the Perpiches but was not introduced nor asked to speak.

Hatch later commented, "I screwed up big time. I should never have run against him. It was the wrong thing to do. It was absolutely the wrong thing to do, and I have no explanations. It's something I regret having done, wish I had never done it. It was the most stupid thing in the world."[14] Until Perpich made his announcement at Lake Itasca, Hatch thought Perpich was not going to run again. On numerous occasions he had talked with Perpich, he said, and Perpich would compliment him on his "Draft Mike Hatch" campaign brochures and posters. "I was the biggest fool in the state. You've got to be really stupid to think he wasn't going to run at that point." After the election, Hatch apologized to Perpich many times. "He was marvelous to me afterwards," Hatch said. He also made peace with Lola Perpich and Rudy Jr. "She's so gracious to me, I always feel like shit." Hatch's wife Patricia had grown up in Keewatin and knew the Simic family.

In the Independent-Republican primary, Grunseth and his running mate, Sharon Clark, a Madison farmer, won with an intensive and well organized get-out-the-vote effort in the final days. They pulled 169,451 votes, 49 percent, overwhelming Carlson and Joanell Dyrstad, mayor of Red Wing, who had 108,446 votes, 32 percent. Kelley and his running mate, Jean Harris, the African-American mayor of Eden Prairie, had 57,872 votes, 17 percent. The Grunseth camp was jubilant, heading into the general election campaign on a roll and confident that Perpich was highly vulnerable.

Chapter 19

Grunseth Quits. Arne Carlson Wins.
Rudy's Out.

S tate Auditor Arne Carlson, 55, was the second of three sons of poor Swedish immigrants and grew up in the Bronx. His father was a janitor, and his mother was a waitress. His life story read like a modern day Horatio Alger saga. Awarded scholarships to the prestigious Choate prep school in Connecticut and later to Williams College in Massachusetts, Carlson came to Minnesota to get away from the East and to do graduate study in history at the University of Minnesota.

He worked on Hubert Humphrey's 1960 campaign for president but later switched to the Republican Party. Carlson spent much of his working life in public office, first as a Minneapolis City Council member, 1965-67, and then running for mayor in 1967 and nearly defeating DFL Mayor Arthur Naftalin. He was a member of the Legislature representing the Lake Calhoun area of Minneapolis from 1971 to 1979. In 1978 he was endorsed for state auditor by the Independent-Republican Party and, amazingly, by the AFL-CIO. He upset DFL incumbent Robert Mattson to win the election. He was reelected auditor in 1982 and 1986.

Ambitious, sometimes charming, sometimes short-fused and sharp-tongued, Carlson was a fiery stump speaker and was recognized, too, for his thoughtful approach to problems. He ran for governor briefly in 1986 but dropped out of the contest for Independent-Republican endorsement, saying he was too moderate for the hard-line conservatives who dominated the party, although they, in turn, were out of step with mainstream voters.

When Carlson, an abortion-rights supporter, challenged party-endorsed, anti-abortion Jon Grunseth in the 1990 primary, he was trounced by his well-organized, well-financed opponent. When Carlson spoke at a Republican post-primary luncheon about his defeat, his wife, Susan, sat at a nearby table and sobbed.

The final month of the general election campaign was bizarre and ugly, unlike anything ever seen before in the land of "Minnesota Nice." Carlson, bitter over what he thought were Grunseth's misrepresentations of his record, met with Perpich and suggested how to attack the Republican nominee, according to Grunseth campaign spokesmen.[1] Members of Carlson's campaign staff delivered research on Grunseth. Perpich, in an interview with the *Star Tribune* in July, 1991, said that prior to the election Carlson had given the DFL campaign information about Grunseth and talked to Perpich personally on one occasion about how to prepare for his challenger. Carlson also frequently leaked information about Grunseth to former state DFL chair Ruth Stanoch, the wife of Perpich campaign manager John Stanoch, Perpich told the *Star Tribune*. But Carlson vehemently denied that he was "feeding information" to Perpich and Stanoch after the primary, calling the allegations "absurd" and "absolute nonsense." In fact, Carlson said, after Grunseth apologized for "distortions" in his primary campaign, Carlson was "actively campaigning" for him.[2]

Meanwhile, Perpich had grown increasingly inaccessible. His inner circle of advisers seemed to have shrunk to his wife and son, wrote Bill Salisbury in the *Pioneer Press*.[3] Wary of reporters who he thought seemed intent on undermining his campaign, he was reluctant to disclose his schedule and frequently drove around the state campaigning with Lola, stopping unexpectedly in coffee shops and on Main Streets. He also refused to appear before the Citizens Jury, a respected good-government group evaluating candidates, which gave Carlson a top rating.

Going into the last month of the campaign, Perpich allies were stepping up negative attacks against Grunseth, trying to paint him as delinquent in paying his property taxes—a charge that misfired, being based on partly erroneous information—and bringing his child-support disputes with his ex-wife into the campaign. With polls showing the race tightening, Perpich flew around the state on October 8, holding press conferences at which he handed out Grunseth's 1983-85 divorce papers. The governor said the public documents showed a pattern of harassment and intimidation by Grunseth against his ex-wife and three daughters through the withholding of court-ordered payments.[4]

Grunseth had since remarried and had another daughter. Perpich's personal attack on Grunseth's character and his attempt to cast doubt on Grunseth's family values and contrast them with his own solid family background seemed strangely out-of-character. Grunseth accused Perpich of smear tactics, and his spokesman said Grunseth had disputed the terms of the divorce but eventually fulfilled his financial obligations.

Grunseth's daughter Nina appeared in a TV ad calling the governor's actions "the dirtiest politics Minnesota has ever seen" and demanded that Perpich apologize. Mike Hatch, who had agreed to endorse Perpich after the primary, withdrew his support, saying Perpich was dragging in the whole Grunseth family and, "You just don't do that to someone's family."

On October 15 and on October 22 the *Star Tribune* published accusations that Grunseth had swum nude with teen-age girls and had tried to pull down the bathing-suit strap of one of them during a pool party at his home in Hastings, in July of 1981, where he then lived with his first wife. Grunseth said the charges were lies. They came from women at the party, including two who were advised by DFL attorney Robert Tennessen, a Perpich supporter and former state senator from Minneapolis. Grunseth took a polygraph test that he said exonerated him, while acknowledging that as recently as the early 1980s he was living his "wild years" of drinking and womanizing.[5] In an interview with the *Pioneer Press,* Grunseth said, "I think it's fair to say that there was a period in my life, through the late '70s and early '80s when I was very much a warm-blooded American male."

Grunseth campaign spokesmen were quick to explain that he had cleaned up his personal life after meeting Vicki Tigwell, a nationally respected Republican fundraiser, in 1983; they were married the following year.

When Grunseth became a candidate for governor, Vicki interrupted her vigorous campaigning for her husband only briefly to give birth to their first child, Maryann, on Aug. 30, 1989. She worked in the campaign headquarters with baby and cradle at her side and drove around the state with Maryann in a car seat.

On October 22, 1990, the day of the disclosure of improper behavior allegations against Grunseth, Arne Carlson announced that he would conduct a write-in campaign, a seemingly hopeless endeavor, making it a three-way race. His campaign began distributing thousands of Carlson-Dyrstad ballot stickers.

With pressure mounting from many Independent-Republican leaders, including Senator Boschwitz, former Governor Elmer L. Andersen, and legislative leaders, to drop out for the sake of the party, Grunseth scheduled a news conference on Thursday evening, October 26, supposedly to announce his withdrawal. He called Tracy farmer Cal Ludeman and asked the 1986 Independent-Republican gubernatorial candidate to seek party endorsement to replace him and head off Carlson, his arch-rival. Ludeman agreed, shaved off his beard, and chartered a plane to fly to the Twin Cities, planning to announce his candidacy after Grunseth withdrew.

Grunseth then kept reporters and a crowd of supporters waiting for several hours at Bloomington's Holiday Inn International as he agonized over his decision and consulted with major contributors to his campaign who were outraged that he would consider quitting. His wife, Vicki, joined them in urging Grunseth to stay the course. Finally, flanked by his wife and daughter and running-mate Sharon Clark and her family, he appeared before the crowd, ripped up a prepared withdrawal speech, and said he would stay in the race. The crowd cheered.

The already fractious Independent-Republican Party was badly split over the fracas. Grunseth supporters were angry at Boschwitz for "trying to play God," and vowed to work to defeat him in November.

The following night, a one-and-one-half-hour debate among the three candidates turned nasty. The governor and Grunseth accused each other of mud-slinging. Grunseth, shaking his finger at the governor, accused him of masterminding the nude-swimming charges but offered no evidence to support his claim. Perpich vehemently denied he had anything to do with the charges. (If there was such a "mastermind," that person or persons were never identified in the campaign or after.) Carlson also joined in the angry exchange, complaining that during the primary campaign the Grunseth campaign had repeatedly sent out inaccurate materials, including a false charge that Carlson had sponsored a bill to reduce the penalty for murder. Carlson and Grunseth attacked Perpich's handling of state finances, contending that government taxation and spending were out of control and predicting major fiscal problems ahead. The two Independent-Republican candidates disputed the governor's claims that the revenue outlook was excellent and that the Minnesota economy was doing well.

Two days later, on Sunday, October 28, Grunseth was hit with another bombshell when both the *Star Tribune* and the *Pioneer Press* published allegations by 32-year-old Tamara Taylor that Grunseth had had an extramarital affair with her beginning in 1980 and continuing during both of his marriages. Taylor, a sales representative for a telephone equipment manufacturer, said that as recently as the previous year, 1989, they had had sex in a Washington, D.C., hotel. Grunseth acknowledged an affair but said it had ended "a long time ago." Grunseth, who was married for the second time in 1984, told the *Star Tribune*, "I have what I consider an excellent marriage. I have a wife who's demonstrated incredible strength, and I'm very happy with that."

At 5 p.m. that Sunday afternoon, Grunseth announced his withdrawal from the race for governor. Grunseth's running mate Sharon Clark did not withdraw and maintained that she was still the lawful candidate for lieutenant governor.

Newsweek reporting on the bizarre chain of events, cited a bumper sticker that the magazine said reflected the mood of voters: "Vote No For Governor."

The fourteen-member executive committee of the state Independent-Republican Party hastily called a closed-door meeting on

Tuesday, and afterward reported that it had unanimously concluded that it had no authority to select a replacement for Grunseth. That paved the way for Carlson's name on the ballot by default as the official Independent-Republican candidate for governor. Under state law, the committee said, after the withdrawal of the party's nominee, the Independent-Republican spot on the ballot went to Carlson by virtue of his second-place finish in the September 11 primary. Despite reservations and even abhorrence on the part of some, the conservative-dominated committee was convinced that the state auditor was their only chance to unseat Perpich. The committee reported that it also had adopted a resolution, again by a unanimous vote, supporting Arne Carlson for governor, and said it had no control over who should be in the lieutenant governor slot.

That thrust Secretary of State Joan Growe into the middle of the controversy, for she had the responsibility of certifying candidates on the ballots and having the ballots printed. Growe decided that Carlson's running mate, Joanell Dyrstad, Red Wing mayor, should be on the ticket with him, based on the 1972 constitutional amendment which required candidates for governor and lieutenant governor to run as a team.

With the encouragement of conservative Republicans who thought Dyrstad was too liberal, Clark asked the Supreme Court to overturn Growe's decision. Her attorney, Mark Briol, argued that while Jon Grunseth had quit the race, his running mate, Clark, had not dropped out, and her candidacy was not affected by his withdrawal. She had been half of the winning primary team and should be on the ballot with Carlson, he contended. John Tunheim, chief deputy attorney general, arguing for Growe's decision, said Grunseth and Clark were a team and could not be separated. The DFL Party joined the fray, filing a "friend of the court" brief written by its attorney Alan Weinblatt arguing that Growe had no authority to place Carlson's name on the ballot.

On November 1, five days before the election, the Minnesota Supreme Court ruled five-to-two that the name of Dyrstad should be on the ballot with Carlson, affirming Growe's decision. Associate Justice Rosalie Wahl, who wrote the opinion, Associate Justices Esther Tomljanovich, Alan Page, Jeanne Coyne, and Sandy Keith voted in the majority. Keith, who was attending a legal seminar in St. Petersburg, Florida , participated in all the deliberations, in telephone conference calls with other members of the court and by fax machine. It was a tough decision to make, but Wahl and the court majority believed the law was clear. Wahl said, "We couldn't have ruled any other way." She never thought the ruling would be crucial in the election outcome. "If I had, it wouldn't have made any difference," she said.[6]

Chief Justice Peter Popovich and Associate Justice Lawrence Yetka dissented. Popovich wrote an angry minority opinion, arguing that the Independent-Republican Party, not the court, should decide the IR ticket, and saying state law allowed a party executive committee to nominate a new governor-lieutenant governor ticket even though the committee had said it did not have that authority. Popovich wrote, "Avoiding its duty and requiring the court to settle the political differences within that party is disrespectful of the role of the judiciary and a misuse of the judicial process." Candidates for both governor and lieutenant governor are required for a party's ticket, and logically two withdrawals are required to nullify that ticket, he said. "Accordingly, the attempted withdrawal by Grunseth was invalid, and logically, Grunseth and Clark remain the IR nominees," he wrote.

Popovich said later that Perpich was deeply disappointed that Keith wasn't in St. Paul to participate in person. He told the *Star Tribune* that in the governor's view, if Keith had been present and had sided with Popovich, personal dynamics among the justices might have changed the legal outcome.[7] Others speculated that had the matter been returned to the Independent-Republican Party, conservative leaders might have blocked Carlson from replacing Grunseth on the ballot, forcing Carlson to run a difficult write-in campaign. Wozniak, then chief of the Minnesota Court of Appeals, said Keith was disloyal to Perpich. "He didn't have to" clear the way for putting Carlson's name on the ballot, Wozniak said, "There was no reason to put Arne on the ballot. He had just got beat [in the primary.]"[8]

On the day that the Supreme Court handed down its ruling, Perpich and Peter Hutchinson, state finance commissioner, held a joint news conference to release the state financial report. It showed that the state took in $27 million more in tax receipts than expected during October. "Minnesota's economy is doing exceptionally well," said the governor. The state had $620 million in reserve, more than any other state, he said, dismissing Carlson's warning that the state was facing a deficit.

The Secretary of State's office hurriedly prepared and ordered the printing of special paper ballots to record the voting for governor and lieutenant governor to be distributed to county auditors and polling places before Tuesday's election. Both the *Star Tribune*/KSTP Minnesota Poll and the *Pioneer Press*/WCCO Northstar Poll published on Sunday, two days before the election, showed the race between Perpich and Carlson dead even, with many undecided voters.

The last-minute campaigning was fierce. President Bush, who had come to Minnesota September 27 to campaign for Grunseth, was now making a final campaign swing around the country on Air Force One. He stopped in Rochester on November 2 and gave a vigorous endorsement to Arne Carlson. Minnesota Citizens Concerned for Life, the state's largest anti-abortion group, which had endorsed Grunseth, attacked Carlson and endorsed Perpich, who had declared that he opposed abortion but had attempted to keep the issue low-key during the campaign. The National Rifle Association supported Perpich, saying Carlson had a record of voting for handgun restrictions when he was in the Legislature. But Carlson's pro-abortion-rights stand, and other perceived liberal positions, brought him the support of other powerful organizations and prominent DFL feminist leaders, including former state Senator Emily Anne Staples. Staples, who had been DFL gubernatorial candidate Mike Hatch's running mate in the primary, said she was backing Carlson because he supported "the access to privacy for a woman making a choice." The Abortion Rights Council and the Minnesota Women's Political Caucus also backed Carlson.

The *Pioneer Press* endorsed Carlson, saying the state auditor, with his unexcelled understanding of state finances, and his promise to trim state spending and avoid tax increases, was better equipped to bring needed change to the state. At the same time the newspaper praised Perpich for his initiatives in education, for connecting Minnesota to the world economy, and other advances, though it could not resist dispensing another shower of comic-book epithets, describing the governor as frequently "flaky, fickle and even fluky."

Conversely, the *Star Tribune* gave Perpich a glowing endorsement, saying "Rudy Perpich has been an extraordinarily positive force for Minnesota." The endorsement lavishly praising the DFL governor came after Robert White, editorial page editor, over-ruled a majority vote of the editorial board favoring the endorsement of Carlson.[9]

On the Sunday before the election, Carlson was upbeat, saying, "If we win this election it will be the biggest political story in the United States."

Late Tuesday night, as returns were coming in and Carlson was building an insurmountable lead, Perpich realized that he was losing. He attempted to conceal his disappointment, telling reporters that losing would mean a "nice easy life," whereas winning would have meant "four more years of you guys doing a number on me."

Carlson was elected governor with 895,988 votes, 51 percent of the vote. He carried the metropolitan area, benefiting from extremely heavy voting in the suburbs, but lost in the rest of the state. Perpich had 836,218 votes, 47 percent. Once again Minnesota voters split their ticket, with liberal DFLer Paul Wellstone unseating Rudy Boschwitz for the U.S. Senate. Wellstone, who had run humorous ads on a very slim budget and campaigned around the state in a dilapidated green bus, won with 911,999 votes, a bare 50 percent, while the two-term Republican senator had 864,375 votes, 48 percent. DFL challenger Collin Peterson defeated Arlan Stangeland after it was disclosed that the Republican congressman had made more than 400 questionable long-distance phone calls at public expense, involving a woman who lived in the Washington, D. C. area. (Stangeland insisted that the calls, which included calls at all hours to the woman's home, were business related and that he was not romantically involved with her.)

At a Capitol press conference the morning after the election, Perpich announced that he had no regrets. He was through with politics, he said; he and his family were looking forward to returning to private life, and he'd "hit the street now and look for a job."

"I'm not bitter. I'm not unhappy. The fact that I lost is a blessing for my family," he said.

An Election Day survey by the *Pioneer Press* found that abortion was an important factor in the election and that most voters opposed government restrictions on abortions or felt abortions should be legal under some circumstances. Men split evenly between the two candidates, but women favored Carlson by a 59-41 percent margin. "Women elected Carlson," said Nancy Zingale, a professor of political science at the University of St. Thomas. "And they elected him on the choice issue."

Perpich may have been hurt, too, by Grunseth's unproven allegations that the governor was behind the reports of sexual improprieties by his Independent-Republican opponent. Perpich advisers also thought the governor had made a mistake when he distributed Grunseth's divorce records early in October. "Both Rudy Perpich and Rudy Boschwitz waged the most negative campaigns of their careers, featuring personal attacks or questionable allegations," wrote Dane Smith in the *Star Tribune*. "Most Minnesotans had never seen this side of two candidates who had always seemed to embody friendliness and decency."

On the weekend before the election, with Boschwitz sliding in the polls, Jewish supporters, with Boschwitz' knowledge, mailed a letter on "People for Boschwitz" stationery that included Boschwitz' trademark, a little smiley face. It was addressed "To Our Friends in the Minnesota Jewish Community." The letter, which set off a firestorm on the eve of the election, read, "Paul Wellstone has no connection whatsoever with the Jewish community or our communal life. His children were brought up as non-Jews," implying condemnation of Wellstone's inter-faith marriage to Sheilah Wellstone, a Baptist. (Their children were raised in both faiths, the Wellstones said.) The letter linked Wellstone with Louis Farrakhan, Islamic leader accused of being anti-Semitic, while referring to Boschwitz as "The Rabbi of the Senate." After the election, Boschwitz, the only incumbent senator defeated in the nation, issued a written apology for the letter disparaging the Jewishness of Paul Wellstone and injecting religion into the campaign.

Grunseth, who chose not to accept public financing or abide by campaign-spending limits, spent a record $2.27 million in his ill-fated campaign and wound up $231,941 in debt. Perpich reported spending $2.24 million in his unsuccessful bid for a fourth term with $613,338 coming from public-financing. Carlson spent considerably less, $1.52 million. A group of well-heeled Twin Cities businessmen guaranteed $191,000 in bank loans to finance his campaign when he re-entered the race in late October. Large campaign contributors included Wheelock Whitney, who gave $34,800. Much of Perpich's money came from organized labor, with which he had worked closely throughout his time in office. Perpich's largest individual contribution was from Mark Dayton who gave him $30,000, half of that on October 30 just before the election, when the Perpich campaign reportedly was strapped for cash. Dayton was elected state auditor on November 6.

It was unclear just when Perpich learned that Justice Sandy Keith was out of the state when the Supreme Court considered the question of which lieutenant governor candidate should be on the Independent-Republican ballot. Jack Fena said he got a call from Rudy Perpich just after the election, inviting him to come to the Governor's Residence. Fena took his two daughters, Susan and Mary Anne, and brought along bottles of his homemade wine. The conversation got around to the Supreme Court ruling, and Fena mentioned that the court hadn't convened but had arrived at its decision by a round robin. Perpich asked, "What do you mean?" Fena explained that the justices talked with each other on the telephone because Keith was in Florida. Perpich was so upset, Fena recalled, that he wasn't able to tell him that conference calls are not an uncommon practice for courts.[10]

Keith and others later disputed Fena's version of the events, however. Keith went to see Perpich on the Wednesday after the election to express his condolences. They talked. "It was sad. I was crying. He was crying. We had been through a lot together."[11]

According to Keith, the angry telephone call from Perpich had come the next day. During the call the governor expressed the belief that the ballot decision had defeated him and that Keith was the key vote in influencing the decision. He was devastated by the fact that Keith hadn't actually been present.

"I told him that's nonsense," Keith added, "that he had to have an election. I felt the decision was sound, as did Rosalie Wahl [who wrote the opinion]. I said I felt terrible." Although members of the court were not supposed to talk about their private deliberations, Keith said, "He knew. I think what happened, Popovich told him, broke the confidence. He [Perpich] said that cost him the election. Popovich wrote a big dissent and had a press conference which I thought inappropriate for the Chief Justice."[12]

Keith told the *Star Tribune* that Perpich wanted to discuss the decision when he phoned on Thursday, and Keith said he couldn't discuss decisions.[13] Keith said he felt Perpich was blaming him and other friends for his election defeat. "It upset me...He obviously felt this had something to do with his election [defeat]." Keith said he had enormous respect and love for Perpich and was saddened by his charges.

His falling out with his longtime friend was a painful thing for Keith, and for years he carried a copy of the decision showing that he had participated fully, ready to pull it out of his briefcase for verification any time the subject came up. He never had the chance to show it to Perpich, however. Keith and Perpich, who had been friends for thirty years, never spoke face-to-face again.

Perpich and Keith had fought shoulder-to-shoulder through many political battles, through great victories and heartbreaking defeats. Perpich considered Keith to be among his closest friends, almost a member of the family, and he had bestowed the highest honor it was in his power to give, naming Keith chief justice of the Minnesota Supreme Court. But for Perpich, loyalty to family and friends was the highest ethic, and he considered Keith's action to be a personal betrayal.

Perpich did not attend Keith's swearing-in as chief justice November 30. In a brief speech at the ceremony Keith referred to Perpich as "the closest political friend I've ever had" and praised him for his appointment of women and minorities to the bench. Keith was the eighteenth chief justice of the court, and one of only a few Minnesotans to serve in all three branches of state government.

As time wore on, Perpich began to make other complaints—for example, about the wording that had been used by phone-bank volunteers for the Wellstone campaign—and he was still bitter the next summer when *Star Tribune* columnist Doug Grow traveled to Zagreb, Croatia, to interview him. He said, "Look what we did for Wellstone on the Range. We worked damn hard for him—I even rode on that damn bus with him. If it hadn't been for that damned phone bank, I'd be governor right now."

In the interview with Grow, Perpich also lashed out once again at the media, as well as friends and allies who he felt had brought about his defeat. He talked of running for governor again in 1994. His greatest obstacle in the 1990 campaign was the media, he said. "If the press had been fair, I'd still be governor," Perpich told Grow. "I'd have won by a landslide."

Furthermore, Perpich told Grow, he'd still be governor if Secretary of State Joan Growe had ordered the state to print all new ballots rather than ordering supplemental ballots for the governor's race. "A lot of people were confused," he said. Growe was stunned when she read that Perpich blamed her, too, for his defeat. "I didn't know he was angry with me until I read it in the paper when he was angry with everyone else. I never had any confrontation with him, anything that was unpleasant." She campaigned with the governor on the last weekend before the election. "We worked hard. We were on very good terms." Nothing was said at the time about her part in the ballot battle. "I remember on one of the flying campaigns, we were all gossiping [with reporters on the plane] about what the papers hadn't dared print about Grunseth." Growe did not recall ever talking with Perpich again. On Election Day Rudy Jr. called the secretary of state and thanked her for everything she had done to help his father and help the ticket.

Perpich also faulted Boschwitz, blaming the infamous letter suggesting Wellstone was not a good Jew for stirring up anti-incumbent sentiment throughout Minnesota. "If Boschwitz hadn't sent that letter, Perpich said, "I'd still be governor, and he would still be senator."

The *Star Tribune* took Perpich to task in an editorial for blaming everyone else for his defeat when he should have blamed himself. "Why does the former governor continue to show his worst side—one that obscures, even devalues his many accomplishments?" It said. "Many of us were sorry when Perpich lost. Now we are even sorrier that he's gone beyond eccentricity to blaming everyone but himself."

The governor refused to talk to Twin Cities reporters after he was defeated. In December Perpich, while in Europe, told an Austrian radio reporter that he planned to return to Europe to represent Minnesota companies in international trade when he left office. Vienna was his first choice for a base, he told Martin Rauchbauer of Radio Austria International; and he went on to say that the three years he had spent there as a sales representative for Control Data Corp. were "probably the best three years of my life," according to a report of the interview published in the *Pioneer Press*. Perpich, who once said he owed everything to the education he received in Minnesota public schools, was also quoted in the article as calling Austria "the best country in the world." The remark set off a furor, though Perpich insisted that he had been misquoted. The director of the Austrian radio station later sent Perpich a letter of apology for "such a flagrant violation of elementary journalistic ethics." Professor Paul Lendvai, director of Radio Austria International, wrote that the reporter "admitted that he had been guilty of serious misconduct."

There was bad news for Governor-elect Arne Carlson. On November 28 the Finance Department projected a $197 million shortfall for the budget period ending June 30, 1991, which the new Republican governor and the DFL-controlled Legislature would have to fix right away with budget cuts, tax increases, tapping the budget reserve, or a combination of the three. Also, finance officials said, there would be a $1.21 billion shortfall in the next two-year budget cycle unless taxing and spending changes were made.[14]

During the transition Perpich fired off caustic letters to Carlson, taking the Republican Governor-elect to task for asking state agency heads to recommend ten-percent cuts in their budgets for the next six months. It was unfair to make across-the-board cuts, Perpich scolded. Such cuts could cripple important state services, penalize departments with lean budgets, and cause little harm to department budgets that had grown at a rate faster than state spending as a whole. Perpich also criticized Carlson's management of his own budget during his twelve years as state auditor. He maintained in his letters, as he had during the election campaign, that his administration had brought fiscal stability to Minnesota and that the state led the nation in economic growth and job creation. He blamed the budget shortfall on a national recession and higher-than-anticipated use of nursing homes, and said Carlson was misleading Minnesotans about the extent of state economic problems.

Carlson said Perpich's commissioners were cooperating in trying to help solve the budget crisis but said he was unable to get the governor to meet with him. The governor-elect said he tried to reach Perpich by phone and was told the governor had a dental appointment. On January 7, three hours after taking the oath of office, Carlson ordered a freeze on hiring and state travel. At least twenty-eight other governors were also struggling with similar budget woes at the time, and some were forced to lay off state employees.[15]

Meanwhile Perpich had resumed his foreign travels. In November he flew to London to meet British publisher Robert Maxwell and discuss the proposed Gorbachev Maxwell Institute of Technology, for which the British publishing magnate had pledged $50 million. In December he traveled to Yugoslavia with Monsignor Terrence Murphy, president of the University of St. Thomas, to explore the possibility of starting a business-school program at a college in Kumrovec, a small city north of Zagreb.

On Friday, January 4, his final working day in office, Perpich made history again, appointing Sandra Gardebring to the Minnesota Supreme Court, thus giving the court a four-to-three female majority, the nation's first. He also appointed six other lower-court judges; one was his campaign manager, John Stanoch, whom he made a Hennepin District judge. Carlson considered challenging some of those last-minute appointments but in the end let them stand.

Rudy and Lola Perpich held an open house on Saturday, just before they moved out of the governor's residence, and thousands lined up outside to say goodbye. "People loved him. I don't think he knew that people really loved him," Mike Hatch said.

Perpich's friends were saddened to see him leave on such a sour note. Despite all the good things he had accomplished, people remembered those final days, said Robert Vanasek. "If he had just gone around the state and thanked everybody for giving him that opportunity to serve, he would have gone out on such a high note. His legacy deserved much better."[16] The *Pioneer Press* said Perpich's "quirky behavior" in his final months as governor overshadowed his accomplishments in ten years as governor.

But Perpich had difficulty dealing with failure. Robert Aronson, Perpich's communications director during his early years as lieutenant governor and governor, said, "He could not come out, say, 'We made a mistake." He would find some [other] reason, say, 'Somebody [else] screwed up.' "

At the end of 1990, the Gorbachev Maxwell Institute of Technology proposal was stalled.[17] Although Maxwell and Gorbachev had signed documents when the Russian president was in St. Paul in June, the plan hadn't progressed since then, the *Pioneer Press* reported. The institute hadn't been incorporated, had no board of directors, hadn't raised any money or established a bank account, hadn't received the $1 million promised by Dwayne Andreas, chairman of Archer Daniels Midland, and had no staff or office space. In August, 1991, the *Star Tribune* reported that Maxwell had provided funds to open an office in downtown Minneapolis with a one-person staff, Mary Sue Bifulk, Perpich's daughter. Perpich said the Soviet leader and Maxwell had talked twice in the past two months and discussed the project. Bifulk was expected to contact business leaders and other potential donors to see if there was interest in the project. But when Soviet President Mikhail Gorbachev was ousted that month, the former governor said it was a setback for the institute.

In other post-election news, Grunseth, his reputation badly damaged, reportedly tried to return to the six-figure salary position he had held at Ecolab; he was fired and was unable to find another job. The bank began foreclosure proceedings on his Afton, Minnesota, hilltop home, and he disappeared from the public scene. Nine years later WCCO-TV found Grunseth living on remote and small Bruny Island, off the coast of Australia, accessible only by boat. The station reported that Grunseth and his wife, Vicki, had moved to Tasmania, where they built a successful telecommunications company, selling it later for about $10 million. He and Vicki, who had stood by him in his darkest hours, were divorced, the station reported. She had moved back to Minnesota with their two young children.[18]

Chapter 20

One or Two Portraits?
Zagreb and Paris. Cancer Strikes.
Will Rudy Try For a Comeback?

It was not likely that he would run for office again, Perpich told the *Hibbing Daily Tribune* in February, in his first Minnesota interview since leaving office. "I don't think so, but you can never say never," said the former governor. "I feel like I worked hard, as hard as I could. I did the best I could do, and I feel good about it from a historical sense. I made my mark. But they voted me out, and that's that."

He planned to leave soon, he said, for Europe, to begin working as a consultant to countries formerly under Communist governments, several of which had invited him to help them carry out privatization plans. He had met with the prime minister of Bulgaria and had contacted officials in Yugoslavia, Czechoslovakia, Hungary, and Poland. He said he would lead a team of experts who would help nations make contacts with U.S. companies. His son, Rudy Jr., would be on the team.

Shortly after Perpich left office, State Auditor Mark Dayton accused the former governor of taking unfair advantage of loopholes in state pension law.[1] At a meeting of the board of the Public Employees Retirement Association (PERA), Dayton, a board member, tried unsuccessfully to eliminate $18,000 of Perpich's $56,000 annual pension, money he received for his three years on the Hibbing School board and eight years as a state senator. Perpich had left the original pension system covering those years and joined another one, and had taken out $2,102 he had paid into the system. Just before he left office as governor, 18 years later, he put that money back into the system, plus about $4,000 in interest, thus qualifying for a $17,879 annual pension for his eight years of service in the Senate, in addition to $38,123 he received from his years as governor and lieutenant governor. (Perpich's salary as governor when he left office was $103,860.) No one on the

PERA board seconded Dayton's motion to deny the $17,879 part of Perpich's pension. The board disallowed an additional $2,332.08 pension claim by Perpich for service on the Hibbing school board after the PERA staff said school records showed Perpich had only two years of paid service on the school board. But in 1994, after Rudy Jr., found a PERA letter in the Hibbing School District files indicating pension contributions were made on Perpich's behalf for at least three-and-a-half years, the PERA board reluctantly approved the extra money. Board member Dick Stafford called it an "abuse of the system." Rudy Jr. said, "This case is not about money. It's a simple matter of justice." If the PERA board could arbitrarily take away money due his father, he said, it could do the same to any other retired public employee. He said the extra payment would be donated to charity.

Rudy Jr. said that Dayton was pressing the issue for personal reasons, because Governor Perpich had once refused to give him an appointment he wanted, an allegation Dayton said was "nonsense." Dayton, a longtime Perpich friend and supporter, said, "I regret the damage that I expect this will do to our friendship. But this is what I had to do. This is what I was elected to do."

When Perpich left office, he insisted that since he was the only governor to serve nonconsecutive terms, he should have a second official portrait hung in the state capitol in addition to the one done after his first term in 1976-79, showing him with an open-pit iron mine in the background. Furthermore, he said, his wife Lola should be in the new portrait because she was truly a partner and had worked hard with him for the people of Minnesota. During his final days in office he contracted with an Evanston, Illinois, portrait studio for a $6,000 portrait which also included Lola, painted from a photograph taken by a photographer flown in from Sacramento, California, at state expense. He asked that the new 36- by 48-inch painting of him standing beside his sitting wife be displayed beside the first portrait on the ground floor of the Capitol. But the Capitol Area Architectural and Planning Board, which has jurisdiction over the art displayed in the Capitol, said one portrait per governor was enough, and that it would not be appropriate to have a wife in an official portrait. The board guidelines specified that portraits must be of "museum quality," referring to an oil painting and of a single subject. The board recommended that the new portrait be given a prominent place in the Minnesota History Center near the Capitol.

An angry Perpich called Minnesota Public Radio to complain about the board action, arguing that if former Governor Quie could have his horse in his portrait, he should be allowed to have his wife with him. In April Perpich rented a billboard on University Avenue near the Capitol showing a picture of the banned painting of himself and Lola, with the message, "They won't let us in the Capitol so—Hi from here, Lola & Rudy." The former governor also distributed buttons around the Capitol bearing a picture of a horse and the caption, "Mr. Ed Says Let Lola In," a reference to the talking horse of the TV series. But despite Perpich's attempt to enlist public sympathy for his request, the Capitol caretakers did not yield.

After Perpich's death, Secretary of State Joan Growe published the controversial picture of Lola and Rudy in the 1997-98 Legislative Manual, the official state book on government and elections, and received a thank-you note from Lola Perpich. State Representative Tom Rukavina of Virginia, a longtime friend of Perpich, sponsored a bill passed by the 1997 Legislature appropriating $20,000 to finance a new official portrait of Perpich and his wife. But Governor Carlson used a line-item veto to nullify it. In 1998 Rukavina got through another bill, ordering the state to hang a painting of Perpich and his wife in the capitol building, financed this time with private funding, and Carlson signed the legislation authorizing the new portrait. Twin Cities artist Mark Balma was commissioned by the Perpich family to paint a "museum quality" portrait, the first official governor's portrait that included a spouse. Mark Dayton contributed $25,000 toward the cost.

In April Rudy, Lola, and their son, after a long Hawaiian vacation, moved to Zagreb, the capital of Croatia, a Yugoslav republic and the homeland of Rudy's father, Anton. Perpich's ability to speak fluent Croatian stood him in good stead as a foreign-affairs and economic adviser for the government; he also did consulting for Robert Maxwell and other business interests. The younger Perpich told *Star Tribune* reporter Carol Byrne in May that they had set up Perpich International, representing American companies, and had clients in insurance and currency printing. The elder Rudy, who couldn't speak English when he started school, was named to the board of Berlitz International Inc. by Maxwell, the chairman and CEO of the language institute. The former governor was offered the position of foreign minister by Croatian President Franjo Trudjman whom he met in the fall of 1990, when a Croatian delegation came to the Twin Cities, but he turned it down, fearing he would lose his U.S. citizenship.

The Perpiches settled comfortably into their new life. Every morning a government limousine-driver picked Perpich up and drove him to his office at the Interior Ministry, where he worked on getting foreign investments in Croatia. The government first offered them the old East German embassy as living quarters, but the Perpiches had had enough of mansions, and they asked for something smaller, and an apartment was found for them.

Minnesota and the golden horses (the Quadriga on the Capitol dome) were behind him. Rudy Perpich talked with Byrne about his years as governor: "Nobody worked harder than we did for Minnesota, but the last year was miserable. The press made it that way."

That summer, however, Perpich was thinking about running again for governor in three years. In July he told Doug Grow of the *Star Tribune* that he was keeping his options open for a possible comeback try in 1994. In a September 18, 1991, broadcast interview with Karen Boros of Minnesota Public Radio in London, where the Perpiches were on business for Croatia, Perpich said he was considering a possible run for governor as an independent, abandoning the DFL Party after three decades. Perpich said he would specifically campaign in 1994 against the *Pioneer Press*, and said, "They are bullies. They lie. They twist. They don't tell the truth."

Civil strife was escalating in the Republic of Croatia, which had announced its intention to withdraw from the seventy-two-year-old Yugoslavia federation. Serbs wanted to withdraw the region they dominated from the rest of Croatia, and violent skirmishes had broken out between Serbs and Croats. The Perpiches told Boros they were lucky to have left war-torn Zagreb just three hours before the city was shelled. Rudy said he had driven his family back recently from the Adriatic coast at speeds of up to 95 miles an hour to avoid sniper fire. He criticized the U.S. government for not aiding Croatia in its fight for independence.

The former governor came back to Minnesota on September 23, 1991, for several weeks, spending most of the time at his lake home near Gilbert or on the North Shore. He planned to travel the state early the next month to visit coffee shops and talk about "Minnesota's decline under Arne Carlson." He mailed fundraising letters to past supporters, asking for contributions to pay for the tour and to "replenish my campaign fund, which is as empty as Arne's brain trust."

On November 5, 1991, Robert Maxwell vanished from his luxury yacht while cruising off the Canary Islands. His body was recovered after an extensive air and sea search. Rudy Perpich, speaking by phone from his home in Zagreb, Yugoslavia, that evening, told Aron Kahn of the *Pioneer Press* that he was crushed by the news. He had had a call that afternoon, the former governor said, from Maxwell's son, Kevin, who said his 68-year-old father was missing. The Perpiches had been doing some consulting work for Maxwell and had been in regular contact with him. Perpich and Rudy Jr. had eaten breakfast with Maxwell in London a week-and-a-half earlier. Perpich said he and Lola had been working that day and the day before on a Maxwell plan to buy fifty-two magazines and three newspapers in central Europe. "It's very difficult. He was one of my best friends," Perpich said.

After Maxwell's death it was revealed that his vast publishing empire was in financial distress, and it collapsed. When market conditions turned adverse, he could not sustain his empire in spite of apparent massive theft from pension and other funds.

With the death of Robert Maxwell, Rudy Perpich's dream of creating the Gorbachev Maxwell Institute, a major private research center in the Twin Cities, evaporated. Perpich said that if he had stayed as governor, the institute would have been put together, but, "When you lose your office, you're like a toothless tiger."

Early in January, 1992, Rudy called his brother Joe and told him he had colon cancer.[2] Rudy had been traveling and while in San Diego on a business trip, had felt weak and lightheaded and had had some bleeding. He went to a doctor at the Scripps Clinic in San Diego for a checkup and was stunned when he was told the diagnosis. On January 7, Joe called Tony and George to tell them Rudy was in the hospital with cancer. He underwent surgery at the Scripps Clinic, and a large part of his colon was removed, but he had enough remaining so that he did not need to have a colostomy. Determined that no one outside his immediate family should find out, he arranged his subsequent medical treatment out of Minnesota at Mount Sinai Hospital and also Memorial Sloan-Kettering Cancer Center in New York. His doctors and the Blue Cross Blue Shield employees in Minnesota who processed his insurance claims kept his illness confidential. His cancer was apparently in remission.

One of Perpich's greatest triumphs was playing a leading role in bringing Super Bowl XXVI to Minnesota. He had lobbied hard to win the coveted prize, and worked to put together a nearly $10 million bid offer to the NFL including a $750,000 state subsidy for the game and exemption of the state's usual 10 percent tax on tickets. In 1989, when the NFL chose Minnesota as the site of the 1992 game, over Detroit, Indianapolis, and Seattle, Perpich said the state now would be seen as an international sports center. "This is the Sugar Super Daddy of them all. You can't buy the advertising that the Super Bowl brings. More important to me is the fact that we're getting the recognition. We are in the big leagues. We're going to feel better about ourselves." There was national publicity, focusing on Minnesota's freezing winter weather. The January 20 issue of *Sports Illustrated* featured an article about Minnesota's favorable sports climate, saying, "These days you can't win a major sports championship without making a trek to Minnesota." It was a bonanza for hotels and downtown retailers who expected to make about $6 million in extra trade that weekend from 77,400 potential customers attending the $150- per-ticket game.

Friends urged Perpich to come to the game on January 26, 1992, between the Washington Redskins and Buffalo Bills, but the former governor was a no-show. A news story reported that he and his wife Lola were "vacationing" in San Diego.

In mid-1993, the Perpiches returned from Paris, where they had moved when the Balkan conflict worsened, and rented a lakeside home in Wayzata. The *Pioneer Press* reported that family friends said the 65-year-old Perpich planned to launch a campaign for governor in 1994.[3] Perpich, a lifelong DFLer, told friends that he would skip the endorsing convention and the primary election and run in the general election as a political independent if he thought he could win, the newspaper reported. Rudy and Lola also wanted to be close to their first grandchild, Madyson Bifulk, the daughter of the Perpiches' daughter, Mary Sue, and her husband, Edward. The *Star Tribune* reported that the former governor said he would operate his international consulting business in Minnesota for at least three months.

As the 1994 gubernatorial election approached, Perpich was the wild card. Would he try for a comeback? The politically shrewd Perpich kept everybody guessing as to whether or not he would run, a strategy he thoroughly enjoyed. Mike Hatch, running again for governor and seeking party endorsement, was calling DFL convention delegates and saying, "Perpich is still the 800-pound gorilla."

Early in 1994, after chemotherapy and other determined efforts to conquer his disease, Rudy was supposedly cancer-free, said Joe. "What I knew was that he was apparently free, but this was a tough disease, and you're not really certain whether it would come back or not." Rudy and Joe had long discussions about whether Rudy should run for governor again, and Joe told Rudy to think hard about whether or not he really wanted to do it.

DFLers considered Carlson highly vulnerable in his re-election bid, and the field of challengers was crowded. The Republican Party, dominated by followers of social conservative Allen Quist, was hostile to the moderate GOP governor. A divisive Republican primary was almost a certainty.

Perpich's supporters thought he could win in a three-way race, particularly against a liberal DFL candidate such as Paul Ogren, a former House Tax Committee chair who was eyeing the race; they also thought Perpich could win against Carlson.[4] Perpich would be a formidable contender also in a multi-candidate DFL primary where the vote would be split several ways; he would be helped by his northeastern Minnesota base, and his support from anti-abortionists and anti-gun control groups. On the down side, Perpich would be sixty-six by the time of the election, and baby boomers, who did not know the former governor very well, made up a large portion of the voters. At the same time, he had burned a lot of bridges when leaving office, lashing out bitterly at those he blamed for his defeat, including many former friends and allies. Key DFL factions—feminists and Paul Wellstone's powerful political machine, the Wellstone Alliance—were not behind him. Even if old labor leader friends backed him, union members were more independent and no longer falling in line behind labor bosses. The Teamsters supported Carlson.

On January 31, 1994, Perpich, upbeat and brimming with ideas about what he'd like to do as governor again, appeared on Barbara Carlson's KSTP-AM radio talk show, and said he was "setting the stage for a campaign." But he said he wouldn't make up his mind until after the Legislature adjourned in late April or early May. He was accompanied by his son, who frequently jumped in and answered questions from listeners. Rudy Perpich said that if he were elected, his son could have "whatever position he wants to play" in his administration. Nick, (as Rudy Jr. was calling himself at this time) quickly added, "It wouldn't be an official position." Lola Perpich seemed less enthusiastic about doing battle again. "You see your wife getting up at six in the morning, working long hours, getting the Governor's Mansion in St. Paul to the point where people feel comfortable and even comment on how good it is," he said. "You never get a thank-you from anyone. Lola's not out there looking for any headlines, OK? Just leave her alone and let her do her business."[5]

State Senator Doug Johnson was considering running for governor and had formed an exploratory group headed by cochairs Gary Cerkvenik and Pat Forciea. Johnson, who opposed abortion, would be unlikely to win party endorsement and would be going for the primary. But he said it would be difficult for both him and Perpich to run because they would be seeking many of the same votes from rural and northeastern Minnesota, and the anti-abortion and the labor vote, particularly in the Twin Cities area.

In addition to Mike Hatch, DFLer Mike Freeman, a Hennepin County attorney, former senator from Richfield, and son of former Governor Orville Freeman, was positioning himself for the race. Roger Moe, the senate majority leader, was a possible candidate. Tony Bouza, Perpich's former gaming commissioner and former Minneapolis police chief, was running. Paul Ogren took himself out of the race, saying it would be too difficult for his wife, Sandra Gardebring, who had to maintain political neutrality because of her position as Minnesota Supreme Court associate justice. It could have been awkward, too, for Gardebring to have a conflict between her husband and the former governor who had done so much for her.

That spring Perpich called Robert Vanasek and asked the former House Speaker to meet him in the coffee shop of the downtown Minneapolis Hilton Hotel.[6] Vanasek, no longer in the Legislature, had just taken a job as vice president of public affairs at Metropolitan State University. When they met, Perpich laid out a strategy of how he could win in the primary and in the general election. He asked Vanasek to be his running mate. Perpich said if he were elected, he envisioned being Minnesota's salesman and selling Minnesota to the world. He told Vanasek: "I don't care what the media says, this time, I'm going out. I'm going to go traveling, be selling the state, selling industries. I need somebody back home to run the state. I know you can do it." Vanasek thought about it and told Perpich that although he didn't disagree with the strategy, he had just taken a new job and needed a pay check. He couldn't afford to take six months off to campaign and said "no." Perpich also told Vanasek that if he were re-elected governor, he might not finish out his four-year term. He wanted someone like Vanasek as lieutenant governor who would be able to take over.

It never occurred to Vanasek that Perpich might have a health problem. The former governor looked great and said nothing about being ill. Vanasek thought Perpich might be alluding to a possible appointment in the Clinton administration or an ambassadorship.

In April , Rudy and Rudy Jr. gave an interview with Bill Salisbury of the *Pioneer Press*.[7] They outlined an economic-development plan for Minneapolis and St. Paul that the former governor said would be part of his platform if he ran for a fourth term that fall. They envisioned a gambling casino and a convention, entertainment, and hotel "megaplex" that would be the economic salvation of the central cities. It would be as large as the Mall of America and would be an international tourist attraction, providing thousands of jobs for inner-city residents and millions of dollars in tax revenues for the cities.

Perpich said he had asked St. Paul Mayor Norm Coleman and Minneapolis Mayor Sharon Sayles Belton to meet with him to discuss the idea. If they weren't interested, he said, he would urge Bloomington officials to build the megaplex next to the Mall of America. One way to get around the state constitutional prohibition of gambling, he said, would be to have the casino operate under an American Indian tribe's legal authority. However, the Minnesota Indian Gaming Association was on record in opposition to any expansion of gambling in the state. If Indians did not agree to his plan, Perpich said, he'd propose a state constitutional amendment on the 1996 ballot to legalize casino gambling. While opinion polls had shown most Minnesotans opposed expansion of gambling, Perpich said he believed he could "hit the road and sell it" if he were governor.

Perpich planned to travel the state testing his political strength and said he would make a decision whether to run for a fourth term after the DFL and Independent-Republican conventions in June. "I don't know if the conditions are right, and I don't know if I want to run. I'm doing well [in business.] Life is easier, and I'm happy doing what I'm doing." But he said he believed he could win the election and that "all the signs are right."

Both parties endorsed candidates who were more extremist than centrist at their state conventions in June: Republicans chose social conservative Allen Quist of St. Peter over incumbent Governor Arne Carlson. DFLers picked liberal state Senator John Marty of Roseville, reportedly with the help of anti-abortion delegates who thought Marty would be the easier candidate to defeat in a primary. Perpich supporters believed the way was clear for the former governor to offer himself as a safe, middle-of-the-road candidate.

Perpich kept everyone, even his brothers and close friends, guessing as to what he might do. That summer while Rudy Perpich was tantalizing everyone with the question of whether or not he would run for governor, he and Lola met a small group including Tom Vecchi for breakfast at the Quality Inn in Duluth. Vecchi had gone around, at Perpich's request, asking for $35 donations to pay the former governor's expenses for a campaign exploratory trip up north. Perpich wanted their advice about running again and wanted to find out what kind of support he might have. "It sure sounded like he wanted to run, and [was] serious," Vecchi said. But Vecchi thought Perpich had lost some of his shine. "He was very agitated, but we didn't know about his cancer," Vecchi said. "Now when you think back on it, we know he was facing this terrible dilemma." Perpich looked okay physically, Vecchi said, although he and Lola were down emotionally, Vecchi thought, because of unfavorable news stories.

Among the naysayers was the *Red Wing Republican Eagle*, which said the day before Perpich's expected announcement that Perpich was past his prime and had worn out his welcome. "His unpredictable behavior has continued since he left office. He alienated friends and foes....We're also tired of Perpich's ideas," said the Red Wing newspaper, citing a Perpich proposal during a recent visit there to put the Legislature on a 24-hour call whenever a business opportunity knocked which could use state assistance. "Minnesota needs less government—not more," said the newspaper.[8]

Gornick and other Iron Range supporters produced thousands of "Perpich '94" buttons, bumper stickers, caps, and T-shirts. They also hung a 24-foot banner on a storefront in Perpich's hometown of Hibbing reading "Rudy Perpich '94—Good for the Range, Great for Minnesota."

Early in July, on a campaign exploratory trip in northeastern Minnesota, Perpich said that if he became a candidate, he would not run as an independent. "I don't want to be a spoiler in any way for the DFL candidate who wins the primary," he said, explaining why he had changed his mind. He also kept everyone guessing about his political plans when he began showing up in TV commercials in Duluth and the Twin Cities for Schneiderman's Furniture, a Duluth-based company. The commercials, which inexplicably had more to do with Perpich than furniture, showed a couple of grumpy old men, a theme taken from a currently popular movie, talking politics. In one ad, one of the men said, "There's already six candidates running for governor." Then Perpich walked in and said, "Do you think there's room for one more?"

On Tuesday, July 19, 1994, the final day to file as a candidate in the fall election, Perpich appeared on WCCO radio's early morning Boone and Erickson show and unexpectedly announced at 6:55 a.m., almost at the end of the hour-long program, that he would not run for a fourth term that fall. He said he planned to run in 1998 when he would be seventy years old. Perpich said Minnesotans were not yet ready for his brand of "innovative leadership." He had traveled the state and while people were friendly, he said, his ideas had received "a lukewarm response." Rudy Jr. had prepared a couple of other funny commercials for the start of the race, but when the senior Perpich called his campaign fundraiser, he learned there wasn't enough money to cover the costs. On Saturday, Rudy, Lola, and their son and daughter had gathered around the table and decided he should not run.

It was a let-down for Perpich supporters. The election campaign would not be very exciting without the colorful Iron Ranger.

Doug Johnson had been absolutely sure Perpich was going to run and believed he could win. So he was not surprised when Perpich phoned him and told him to come down to the cities because he wanted him to be his lieutenant governor candidate. That would have been an unconventional choice—both the governor and lieutenant governor candidates from northeastern Minnesota—although Perpich now was a Twin Cities suburban resident. Early on the morning of July 19, Johnson drove to St. Paul. He was sitting in his car outside the Sheraton Midway Hotel where he was to meet Perpich for breakfast, and he heard Perpich's announcement on the radio. Lynn Anderson, Perpich's former chief of staff, drove up and told him, "Rudy wanted you to know he's not going to run." Johnson was stunned. After his WCCO bombshell, Perpich and Lola came to the hotel, where they urged Johnson to run himself. Johnson didn't know why Perpich changed his mind. "He looked fine. He looked great. He said he would help me raise money for my campaign." But Doug said no to running for governor.[9] Ron Gornick believed Perpich could have been elected in 1994 and was disappointed when he heard the former governor say that he would not run "I think then he knew he was very, very ill," Gornick said.

Republican David Jennings thought if Perpich had run he would have lost and been embarrassed. "I think his time was over, and it was hard for him to accept that. That was probably a very hard [decision] for him to come to, but he was very smart. He was an extraordinarily smart politician. One of the sad things for politicians is when they can't accept the fact that when their time has passed, it's passed," said Jennings, the former House speaker who had made the decision to bow out of politics himself eight years earlier.[10]

Joe didn't know which way his brother would go until Rudy made the announcement. Joe was relieved at his brother's decision but didn't think that Rudy's fear of his cancer recurring was the only reason he decided not to run. Rudy was very thorough and had tested the waters for a lot of things including campaign financing, and there was also the fact that he was doing well in his work as consultant to software manufacturer CWC Inc. in Mankato and others in Europe and Asia.[11]

Perhaps Rudy Perpich felt that the "golden years" of the 1970s and 1980s, when he was lieutenant governor and governor, were over, and the days were gone when the public favored government programs to help people and spur business development. He also deplored the dominance of single-interest groups in politics. "People no longer support someone because they think he or she is the best candidate, people vote for [party endorsement for] the candidate they believe their candidate can beat in the primary," he said. And maybe Perpich did not have the heart for a campaign where opponents would surely paint him once again as a "quirky" governor. He thought "the Twin Cities media was treating Arne Carlson with kid gloves. I feel I would have been battered by the Twin Cities media."

Late that summer Perpich's cancer recurred, said Joe. Rudy kept working up to the end, hiding his illness from almost everyone.

Arne Carlson handily defeated Allen Quist in the September primary, and the Independent-Republican state central committee then endorsed Carlson for the general election. John Marty won the DFL primary.

That fall Perpich campaigned for Ann Wynia of St. Paul, the Democratic nominee for the U.S. Senate who had formerly served as Minnesota House majority leader and also as Perpich's Commissioner of Human Services. He said he had no regrets about not running. He intended to stay active in Minnesota politics and continue his consulting work. Perpich called himself a "moderate Democrat" and reiterated that he had not ruled out the possibility of seeking the governorship in 1998. "I'm going to come out about things I think are important in Minnesota; property taxes will be the first thing," he said. "And then I'll have to see how everything goes. There are many factors involved. But this will give me time to get a base together and raise money, and four years from now I'll be in a better position than I am now."

George Perpich ran for state auditor but lost to former state Senator Don Moe in the DFL Primary. Moe had 119,100 votes to Perpich's 83,542 votes. It was the last hurrah for the Brothers Perpich. In the general election, Moe, the brother of Senate Majority Leader Roger Moe, lost to Republican Judith Dutcher, thirty-one-year-old daughter of former University of Minnesota basketball coach Jim Dutcher.

Arne Carlson won a landslide victory over John Marty and was re-elected with 1,094,165 votes to Marty's 589,344. It was the worst defeat for a DFL gubernatorial candidate in the party's fifty-year history, giving the Republican governor a mandate for another four years and putting to rest claims that he had won office by a fluke in 1990. Republican Rod Grams, a former TV anchorman, was elected to the U.S. Senate, carrying the Eighth District narrowly despite Rudy Perpich's efforts for Ann Wynia on the Iron Range and upsetting the conventional wisdom that northeastern Minnesota was an impregnable Democratic stronghold.

Chapter 21

The Bugles Blow

That last year Rudy Perpich made farewell visits to many of his old friends, but none knew he was ill. Those who saw Perpich during the summer thought he looked fine, normal, maybe a little thinner. They didn't know of his secret battle with cancer. Many thought he was ready to run again to regain his old office as governor. Rudy Perpich, an optimist throughout his life, died the way he had lived, maintaining a positive front and determined to win his final and biggest battle. Tony Perpich said, "In the Legislature if you are in the Democratic or Republican Party, when it ends, you declare a victory, say you did a nice job, you did this or blocked that. You're not going home and say 'We got beat.' Maybe it was that. I can't tell you how optimistic he was. Everything was good. No matter what."

George Perpich said Rudy handled his illness with class. "Rudy believed there should be a public person and a private person, that we'd lost some civility by telling everything, baring the full facts on TV." More than anything, said George, Rudy Perpich didn't want people wasting time worrying about him or feeling sorry for him. "He just wasn't going to go into coffee shops and be discussing his colon cancer. He was going to be talking about his initiatives on education, welfare reform, how jobs would be created."[1]

The last public images of Rudy Perpich were of a vital, seemingly healthy man ready to run another time and take back the governor's office. Perpich had watched Hubert H. Humphrey dying and looking terribly frail, with the press reporting every agonizing phase of his fight with cancer, from his surgery in the final weeks of his 1976 U.S. Senate campaign up to his death January 13, 1978. Perpich was a proud man, and that was not the way he wanted to be remembered. He left the stage keeping his sickness private even from his closest friends, wanting to be remembered as he once was—energetic, upbeat and dignified.

In February 1995 Gornick had prostate-cancer surgery at University Hospital in Minneapolis. He didn't think Rudy Perpich knew he was there, but one day he got a big plant from the former governor. That evening Perpich popped into his room, all dressed up, to find out how he was doing. "We talked just about everything, the election, about how he was more than positive he was going to run [again.] He said, 'We're doing things different this time. We've got to concentrate a lot on the Twin Cities. We're going to do it again. You're going to be part of it." Gornick, like other close friends, did not know Perpich had cancer until his death. When Gornick asked about Perpich's health, Perpich said absolutely, he was in good health. They talked for two hours and told stories and laughed until they cried, and Perpich never let on. "He had to have known then [about the cancer.] That was February. He died in September.'" Gornick thought, "He looked okay, maybe a little thinner. That guy was running one hundred fifty miles-an-hour. He was in Europe today, somewhere else tomorrow, back and forth. I couldn't keep track of him."

The last time Gornick saw Rudy was that summer, when Rudy and his father stopped by Gornick's house in Chisholm. "His dad said to me [out of Rudy's hearing], 'You know Rudy don't look so good. He's got some kind of marks on his stomach and shoulder.' He must have told his dad; maybe his dad couldn't quite understand."

Perpich had asked Gornick to reserve rooms for the Gornicks and Perpiches late that summer at a resort on the North Shore. Gornick did so, and he kept calling Rudy, leaving messages on the answering machine, telling him he had rooms reserved and to let him know if it was okay. Rudy didn't return the calls. "He got the messages, [and] said, 'Lola, don't tell Gornick.' What a guy. He was dying, going back and forth to [doctors in] New York, San Diego, Houston, I don't know how many different doctors."

That summer Perpich called Don Wozniak and his wife, Angie, and invited them to have dinner with him and his wife at a new restaurant in Wayzata. "We dropped out there, had a lot of fun. He looked pretty good. I told him that. No one had any idea he was sick," Wozniak recalled.[2]

Near the end of July, Rudy came to see Frank Ongaro and his wife, Kay, in their home on Howard Street in Hibbing. He said nothing to the Ongaros about his illness. Ongaro thought Perpich looked jaundiced but didn't think much about it.

In late August, Ron and Valerie Jerich got a call from Perpich, during which he told them how much he loved them and valued their friendship. "I thought that was kind of funny," Jerich said later.

Bruce Orwall, a former *Pioneer Press* reporter who had covered Rudy Perpich when he was governor, saw him that summer in a bookstore in downtown Minneapolis. When Orwall went up to the former governor and said, "Hi, Rudy," Perpich said, "No." Orwall, thinking Perpich didn't remember him, introduced himself, and again, Perpich said, "No," as if denying he was Rudy Perpich and walked away. Orwall was taken aback, even hurt, thinking perhaps the former governor still was angry with him and didn't want to acknowledge him. While he thought Perpich looked older, he didn't look terribly ill. Later, when he heard of Rudy Perpich's death, Orwall believed Perpich then was trying to avoid having his illness known.

Joe was especially close to Rudy during his four-year battle with colon cancer. Carol Sulzberger, Joe's mother-in-law, was diagnosed with cancer shortly after Rudy was stricken, and Joe, the medical doctor, was an informal and close adviser for both. Like Rudy, Carol didn't want people, even many in her family, to know. Like Rudy, she wanted to keep up appearances, going to parties and dinners as long as she looked normal. Both Rudy and Carol underwent very tough chemotherapy treatments at Mount Sinai Hospital and Rudy at Memorial Sloan-Kettering Cancer Center as well, and Joe would visit them. In August, 1995, Joe and his wife, Cathy, and their children, Sarah and David, were in Southampton visiting Arthur and Carol Sulzberger. One morning, after Carol had had an especially bad night, Joe left to go to New York City to visit Rudy. He had been in his brother's room in the Waldorf Hotel about fifteen minutes when he got a call that Carol had died. Rudy was very upset about her death. "He was always looking for people who beat it [cancer]," Joe said.

On September 16, Joe helped bring the very ill Rudy back to Minnesota on the private plane of Richard Burke, a Perpich friend and millionaire businessman and spent the last weekend with him. When he got home, Rudy, ravaged from the chemotherapy, put on a robe and sat in a chair. The brothers watched the Miss America pageant together. "I see him standing, sitting, my oldest brother. I knew what he must have felt like," recalled Joe. Joe said goodbye to Rudy on Sunday and returned to New York, saying he'd be back. Although Rudy put up an argument, Joe arranged for doctors and nurses for him, which he didn't want because it meant telling someone else about his condition. "He didn't want people to see him in a debilitated condition." But Joe knew Lola and the children couldn't continue caring for Rudy on their own.

"He was telling me at the very end, 'I have almost licked this. I know I am down on the ropes, but let's see what happens this week, if this is just the chemotherapy wiping me out.'" The New York doctors were taking many people off the chemotherapy who couldn't endure the excruciating treatment. Perpich stood it to the end and was looking for new treatment methods. "He was saying 'Call that doctor in Duke I told you about.' I knew his condition. I knew what it took for him to sit there in that chair to the end, in great pain," said Joe.

On the evening of September 20, Frank Ongaro got a phone call from George and Tony, who told him Rudy was in a coma at his home in Minnetonka. They wanted Frank to hear it from them rather than from the media. He said he and Kay would drive to the Twin Cities the next morning to see Rudy. Early the next day the Ongaros started out and were driving into Forest Lake when they heard on the radio the announcement of Rudy's death. It was over. Rudy Perpich had died at his home in Minnetonka at 12:05 p.m. with family members at his bedside. He was sixty-seven years old.

Gornick was in Valentini's Restaurant in Chisholm when someone walked in and said he had just heard on the radio that Perpich had died. He was stunned at the news.

Ongaro said, "It was a tough one" for Perpich's close friends. He recalled Perpich's fastidiousness. "Hard to believe, especially with Rudy. He was so fussy about anything he ate, fussy about having the right things, as far as healthwise. I don't think he ever ate without washing his hands thoroughly, that comes from dentistry. I never thought of all people…" It was difficult for Ongaro to talk about his lifelong friend, even several years later.

Later Ongaro frequently drove Anton Perpich to visit his wife Mary in the Leisure Hills nursing home, and the grieving Anton would talk about Rudy's death and lament, "Why should he die before I die?" Ongaro wasn't sure whether or not Mary Perpich in her declining health understood that her oldest son had died.

Governor Carlson ordered state flags to be flown at half-mast. The family declined to have Perpich's body lie in state in the Capitol rotunda, a traditional honor for prominent Minnesota officeholders. It spared Lola Perpich, who would have felt compelled to stay with the coffin throughout any public display. The funeral was held September 25 in the Basilica of St. Mary in Minneapolis. Between 1,500 and 1,800 people gathered to say goodbye at the nearly two-hour mass. His family was there, including his ninety-five-year-old father Anton, but not his mother Mary. His three younger brothers, Tony, George and Joe, were pallbearers. There was live coverage of the service on all Twin Cities television stations. Friends and former political foes, now mostly silver-haired, were there to pay their last respects and honor the former governor, the son of an immigrant miner. Governor Carlson, former Governors Wendell Anderson and Al Quie, and former U.S. Senator David Durenberger were there. Judges, former cabinet members, legislators and elected officials, both DFL and Republican, attended. Sandy Keith, Chief Justice of the Minnesota Supreme Court, and Warren Spannaus, state attorney general, were there, along with Minneapolis Mayor Sharon Sayles Belton and St. Paul Mayor Norman Coleman. There were grieving friends from Hibbing and Chisholm and other misty-eyed mourners from the Iron Range and ordinary people whose lives Rudy had touched.

"Rudy Perpich was an original, from beginning to end," Perpich's brother, Joe, said in his eulogy. William Janklow, back in office as governor of South Dakota, serving a non-consecutive term as Perpich had, delivered one of the eulogies. "I speak for all the people of South Dakota and I speak for all the people of America when I say to [the family], thanks for sharing Rudy [with us]."

The Rev. Dennis Dease, president of the University of St. Thomas, officiated at the service and called Perpich "a can-do, make-it-happen kind of person whose vision was as big as his heart." He said, "Rudy Perpich was a good governor, probably even a great one. But what really counts is that he was a good human being." After the service the motorcade drove up Hennepin Avenue to a private service at Lakewood Cemetery, where other prominent Minnesotans, including former Vice President Hubert H. Humphrey and former Governors John S. Pillsbury, John Lind and Floyd Olson were buried. The Perpich family and friends went to a luncheon at Burke's home in Medina.

Rudy Perpich had dominated the state's political horizon throughout much of the 1970s and 1980s and had made a difference in state politics and policies for a quarter of a century. There was an outpouring of affection and recounting of fond memories of the former governor, who had obtained almost 100 percent name recognition in Minnesota, matching that of Hubert Humphrey. Everyone had affectionate, funny stories to tell about Minnesota's self-styled Number One Salesman.

Governor Carlson paid tribute to his predecessor: "He will long be remembered for his remarkable energy, creativity, and deep personal commitment to moving Minnesota forward. He brought a unique blend of the unconventional and the innovative to the Governor's office."

Roger Moe predicted that Perpich's "quirky" image would wear off, and in the long run he would be given high marks. "I think he will be remembered in terms of his public contributions, as a governor who wasn't afraid to try things. He wasn't afraid to float an idea. He wasn't afraid to dream big dreams. When many of his dreams seemed like fantasies, they turned out to be dreams that came true," said Moe. Was he a great governor? "I don't think you can say that yet. He certainly was a very good governor. He made some important and lasting contributions. We'll have to kind of weigh that out over a period of time."[3]

Sandy Keith called Perpich one of two or three great governors in recent history and credited him with being the first politician to see the global economy coming and to understand that Minnesota had to compete with all the world. "I think he was so far ahead of his time with women in public life, the necessity of bringing women into the executive, legislature, judicial process. He was the first one who understood we are going to have to be retraining people, that you're never going to be sitting at one job all your lifetime but going to a whole series of jobs in industrial society. He could articulate that one better than anybody. The whole rethinking of education—he was the first one to challenge the traditional methods we had used in the state since Governor Orville Freeman." But, said Keith, "To go out in a huff like he did. It was not easy for his friends like me, his saying I betrayed him. God almighty, I killed myself getting him elected. I would do it again. I never enjoyed anything more. I have no regrets. He was just a fascinating person." Keith chuckled fondly as he recalled Perpich dying his hair: "I couldn't believe it. His hair was gray the same color as mine. All of a sudden he shows up, and he's stunning black again. That Grecian formula really works."

Congressman David Minge of the Second District, said that without the leadership of Governor Perpich, Minnesota would have been a step behind instead of a leap ahead of the pack in world trade. "Before most of us even heard the phrase 'global economy,' Governor Perpich was advocating for all Minnesotans and Minnesota companies on the international level."

Sandra Gardebring remembered, "He used the term 'world class' a lot. He wanted Minnesota to be world class. He thought about Minnesota in the context of the larger world scene. He wanted to make Minnesota visible on the world stage."

His long-time friend Thomas Vecchi said: "He had a lot of way-out sort of ideas, but look at how many of the things really did materialize. He did have some really good ideas, ahead of everything. We would all chuckle and get a big kick out of it. Then he would do it."

Former Governor Wendell Anderson recalled when Rudy Perpich became governor in 1976: "The whispers were 'Could an Iron Ranger do the job as governor?' It was unthinkable; we never had an Iron Ranger as Governor of the State of Minnesota. That prejudice is gone forever. Whether your name is Perpich or Vukelich or Mayasich or Fugina or Begich, your name does not disqualify you from running as a serious candidate for statewide office."[4]

Ron Dicklich, former state senator from Hibbing, said, "He made us [Iron Rangers] proud of who we were, where we were from, and why we were here. He made us not be ashamed to ask for the best."

As governor, Perpich did a lot for the Iron Range, but he was not just an Iron Range governor, said Doug Johnson. While Perpich worked tirelessly to restore the economic health of depressed northeastern Minnesota, he was out front with initiatives for all of Minnesota, Johnson said, listing the Torture Victims Center, Arts School, Mall of America, the Metrodome, Final Four basketball, the Super Bowl, open enrollment, and post-secondary education options. "My region of the state, where we had the depressed taconite industry, without Rudy Perpich things would be a lot worse off up here because he went nationwide searching for new companies to bring to the Iron Range. He worked to get expansion of the wood-products industry, stabilize the taconite industry."

Duane Benson, executive director of the Minnesota Business Partnership and a harsh critic of Perpich during his years as senate minority leader, remembered Perpich as "a pretty damn good governor, until those final years. He had his heart in the right place. Whatever else you can fault him for, I don't think early on or up until the last two, three years you could ever doubt he had the greater good in mind... [It was] jobs, jobs, jobs. He was willing to try just about anything, chopsticks, anything, you name it, he tried it." Perpich thoroughly enjoyed the political game and people, "the coffee shop, the collegiality, the 'one of us.'"

Senator Allan Spear predicted, "I think he's going to be up there among the really significant governors, for one thing because he served longer than any other; he left his mark on such a long period of time and had such a strong personality."

Pioneer Press columnist Bill Salisbury, who had followed Perpich closely throughout his political career, wrote: "Critics faulted him for neglecting Minnesota's more basic needs, such as more competitive taxes [rates], a more favorable business climate, and fiscal stability in state government. But with [Soviet President Mikhail] Gorbachev's help, Perpich put Minnesota on the world map, and he prodded Minnesotans to take a broader look at their world."

Mike Hatch called the former governor "one of the most brilliant people I've ever met and probably one of the finest politicians I've ever met. He worked too hard. He had an unbelievable drive; that was his success, and that was his failure. Absolutely, he will be remembered as a great governor."[5]

Pioneer Press columnist Nick Coleman, son of the late Nicholas Coleman, former state senator and one of Perpich's closest friends, had written many sharply-worded columns lampooning "Governor for life" Rudy Perpich. But after Perpich's death, Coleman wrote, "Make no mistake. A great governor was buried Monday." Coleman called Perpich a towering figure, adding, "Yes, his flaws were as large as the Hull-Rust-Mahoning open-pit mine…But for ten years, Rudy bestrode Minnesota. No one else could have done that. It takes a mighty large figure to bestride Minnesota." Coleman wrote sadly, "We will not see his likes again."

Lori Sturdevant, of the *Star Tribune's* editorial page, lauded him as an ever-energetic, creative, idea-a-minute governor. "Perpich was not one to delegate authority, then sit back. He was out in front of the parade at every step. He was the idea factory, whose personal output rivaled that of any of his commissioners. He was the pacesetter, working eighteen-hours days, as prone to start a meeting at 10 p.m. as 10 a.m. He was the cheerleader, projecting optimism and spirit of fun, wherever he went. Soon Minnesota was cheering too." But, Sturdevant added, "He couldn't sustain for a full two terms the intensity of focus and energy he lavished on Minnesota in his third, fourth and fifth years as governor. …The laser beam didn't dim so much as it skittered off in unproductive, self-defeating directions."

The *Star Tribune* said in an editorial that Perpich left a legacy of achievement and service to the state unmatched in modern times. "He occasionally clouded his considerable accomplishments by being a sore loser and a grudge bearer, but those failings are fading, while the things he achieved stand taller with time's passing…Perpich had foibles and idiosyncrasies that Minnesotans will also remember, sometimes with considerable disfavor." But, said the *Star Tribune*, Perpich made Minnesota a better place to be educated, to work, and to own a business. "He has made it a more caring place to be poor, to be handicapped, to be a member of a minority. His kind of caring isn't so popular any more." Saying the state wouldn't soon see another governor like Perpich, the newspaper predicted, "His record will stand the scrutiny of time—and, we think, stand it well."

A *Pioneer Press* editorial said, "Personally Perpich touched people in a way few politicians ever do. Perhaps it was his broken syntax, his unassuming style, the twinkle in his eyes, his periodic disappearances to explore new ideas or drop in on cafes and coffee shops around the state to hear what was on the minds of his constituents. For most of his career, the former Hibbing dentist was a hard guy not to like."

Asked to list his achievements as governor, Perpich said in a radio interview just before leaving office that his most important contribution was to "internationalize" Minnesota's thinking. Until the early 1980s, when he took office, he said, Minnesota had little interest in the rest of the world and looked merely at the market in the U. S. and Canada. "I awakened a sleeping giant," Perpich said, "and now the businesses [in Minnesota]…are worldwide." He listed other accomplishments such as helping to build an education system "considered probably the best in the country" and a "top-rated environmental protection programs." He was satisfied that "I did a pretty good job—we really worked hard. I think some day people will look back and say, 'Best governor ever.'"

Notes

Notes for Chapter 1

1. Eulogy for Anton Russ Perpich, Oct. 17, 1996, Joseph Perpich.

2. *Minneapolis Star*, May 1, 1975, Jim Klobuchar.

3. Eulogy for Anton Russ Perpich, Oct. 17, 1996, notes from Joseph Perpich. Many of the details of personal life contained in the following narrative are based on personal interviews with Tony Perpich, Frank Ongaro, Sr., Thomas Vechhi, and *Star-Tribune* articles by Lori Sturdevant, May 18, 1986, and January 4, 1983.

4. For an interesting description of that era of shifting real estate, see *The Town That Moved*, by Mary Jane Finsand, Dell Publishing, 1983. Eighty-six houses were moved, along with the furnishings they contained, and many of the residents also came along for the ride. The initial moving was done by attaching large chains and ropes to steam-powered cranes from the mines; the chains were wrapped over and under the building, and the crane swung it over and lowered it onto the log roller. Ropes and straps were wrapped around the building, then attached to horses who slowly pulled the building down the street. As soon as the back log rolled out from under a building, people grabbed it, strapped it to a horse, pulled it up to the front and slid it underneath again.

5. Eulogy for Anton Russ Perpich, Oct. 17, 1996; eulogy for Mary Perpich, June 25, 1997, Joseph Perpich.

6. Boarding houses, often run by miners' wives, were a major part of life in the early 1900s. The boarders shared beds, and men on different shifts shared the same bed. Ann Glumac, president of the Iron Mining Association of Minnesota, told about her grandparents' boarding house, and the time when one miner wouldn't get up when someone else needed the bed. Glumac's grandfather, trying to rouse the sleepy miner, twisted the man's leg so hard he broke it.

7. When Rudy Perpich first became governor and would disappear from his office without announcing where he was going, his Communications Director Robert Aronson said sometimes the governor was visiting his mother when she was having one of her

"bad spells," grieving over her daughter's tragic accident. In 1985, when two young people were severely burned while working at a Minnesota resort, Governor Perpich, harking back to the memory of his sister's tragic death, wrote very personal and sympathetic letters to the families, according to Ann Glumac, then working in the governor's communications office.

8. Joseph Perpich, Oct. 17, 1996, eulogy for Anton Perpich.

9. *Pioneer Press*, Nov. 3, 1994, Larry Millett.

10. *Star Tribune*, May 18, 1986.

11. *Star Tribune*, May 18, 1986, Lori Sturdevant.

12. Tony Perpich, interview May 19, 1998.

13. Eulogy for Mary Perpich by Joseph Perpich, June 25, 1997.

14. Tony Perpich, interview May 19, 1998.

15. An Old World pastry made from dough hand-rolled very thin, then layered with walnuts, honey, cream, butter, and vanilla, and then rolled up like a spiral or jelly roll, shaped like a loaf, and baked very slowly for a long time. Pronounced "paw-tee-tzah" with stress on "tee."

16. *Minneapolis Star*, May 1, 1975, Jim Klobuchar.

17. *Mesabi Daily News*, Feb. 23, 1997, Angie Riebe.

18. *Pioneer Press*, July 4, 1982.

19. *Washington Post*, reprinted in *Minneapolis Star*, Aug. 1, 1978, Bill Peterson.

20. Nov. 1, 1990, Peg Meier.

Notes for Chapter 2

1. Details about Perpich's early life were drawns from the following sources: *Star Tribune*, May 18, 1986, Lori Sturdevant; *Mesabi Daily News*, Feb. 23, 1997; Frank Ongaro, Sr., interview, June 9, 1998; Eulogy for Mary Perpich by Joseph Perpich, June 2, 1997.

2 Perpich told this story to Ann Glumac when she worked in the governor's communications office.

3 Simich is the English spelling. In Croatian it is Simic with a tilde, ~, over the c, but when immigrant youngsters went to school on the Range, teachers found names using the tilde difficult to write, and changed the spellings. For details concerning Lola's family see *Star*

Tribune, Jim Klobuchar, Sept. 24, 1994; *Minneapolis Tribune,* April 24, 1977, Robert T. Smith.

4. *Pioneer Press,* Jan. 30, 1977, Eleanor Ostman.

5. *Pioneer Press,* July 4, 1982,

6. *Star Tribune,* Aug. 7, 1989.

7. Thomas Vecchi, interview, June 8, 1998.

8. State archives notebooks, Minnesota History Center, District No. 701 records, when Rudy Perpich served on Hibbing School Board.

Notes: Chapter 3

1. *Minneapolis Star,* Sept. 18, 1969, Ted Smebakken

2. In the summer of 1958 Joe Perpich attended Boys State, a program sponsored by the American Legion to acquaint boys with government operation. He was an editor of the newspaper for the program and interviewed Senator Donald Wright of Minneapolis, the crusty curmudgeon who was chairman of the Senate Tax Committee. When Joe asked about the chances for a bonding bill for the community college in Hibbing, Wright's answer was a flat no, and as Joe Perpich put it, "In those days when Wright spoke, the Senate listened." A new wave of legislators including the Perpich brothers changed that climate.

3. Legislative candidates ran without party designation then and were listed on a nonpartisan ballot.

4. *Minneapolis Star,* Aug. 17, 1980, Patrick Marx.

5. *Minneapolis Star,* May 14, 1963.

6. Candidates for lieutenant governor ran independently from governor candidates until 1974. After party designation for legislators took effect in 1974, Liberals changed their name to DFLers, and Conservatives changed to Republicans.

7. *Star Tribune,* Jan. 4, 1983, Lori Sturdevant.

8. *Star Tribune,* Nov. 6, 1986.

9. In 1966, C. Donald Peterson was elected to the state supreme court where he remained until he retired in 1986.

10. *Pioneer Press,* June 26, 1988.

11. *Minneapolis Star,* Nov. 15, 1968, Jim Shoop.

12. *Minneapolis Tribune,* Feb. 3, 1968.

13. Jack Fena, interview, May 9, 1999.

14. *Minneapolis Tribune,* Aug. 6, 1970.

15. *Star Tribune,* Dec. 22, 1991.

16. *Minneapolis Star,* Apr. 29, 1980, Jim Shoop and author.

17. *The Minneapolis Star,* Aug. 17, 1980.

18. *Minneapolis Tribune,* April 10, 1983, Al McConagha.

19. *Minneapolis Tribune,* Sept. 24, 1964.

20. For details about this chapter in Minnesota's history see *Political Upheaval,* Alpha Smaby, Dillon Press, 1987.

21. Douglas Johnson, interview, Nov. 20, 1999.

Notes to Chapter 4

1. *Minneapolis Star,* Feb. 24, 1969.

2. *Gilbert Herald,* April 24, 1969.

3. *Mesabi Daily News,* June 25, 1969.

4. *Minneapolis Star,* Aug. 6, 1970.

5. *Associated Press,* 7-30-69. *Minneapolis Tribune,* July 30, Bernie Shellum.

6. *Minneapolis Star,* July 30, 1969.

7. *Mesabi Daily News,* June 25, 1969.

8. *Minneapolis Tribune,* Aug. 15, 1969, Shellum.

9. *Minneapolis Tribune,* June 29, 1970, Shellum.

10. *Minneapolis Tribune,* June 29, 1970, Shellum.

11. Doug Johnson, interview, Nov. 20, 1998.

12. A. M. (Sandy) Keith, interview, Nov. 16, 1998

13. *Minneapolis Star,* Oct. 29, 1970.

14. Senator Allan Spear, interview, May 24, 1999.

15. *Minneapolis Star,* Nov. 5, 1970.

16. For details about Perpich's first days in office, see *Pioneer Press,* Jan. 21, 1971, Robert O'Keefe; *Pioneer Press,* Feb. 11, 1971, Robert Whereatt; *Minneapolis Star,* Feb. 7, 1971; *Minneapolis Star,* Feb. 11, 1971.

17. *Minneapolis Star,* June 18, 1976.

18. *Twin Cities Reader,* Feb. 2-8, 1994, Adam Platt.

19. *Pioneer Press,* Sept. 25, 1995, Bill Salisbury.

20. Keith, interview, Nov. 16, 1998.

21. *Minneapolis Tribune*, June 24, 1971.

22. *St. Cloud Daily Times*, June 17, 1975, *United Press International; Minneapolis Tribune*, May 10, 1974.

23. For details about Perpich's proposals see *Pioneer Press*, Dec. 12, 1970, Associated Press; *Minneapolis Tribune*, Feb. 11, 1972; *Minneapolis Star*, Dec. 4, 1974; *Minneapolis Tribune*, May 10, 1974; *Minneapolis Star,* June 16, 1975, Barbara Flanagan; *The Herald*, Duluth, Aug. 20, 1974, Einar Karlstrand; *Minneapolis Star*, May 1, 1975; *Pioneer Press*, Feb. 11, 1972.

24. Andrew Kozak, interview, Apr. 30, 1999; Jack Fena, interview, May 9, 1999.

Notes to Chapter 5

1. For details see *Associated Press*, Oct. 14, 1971; *Minneapolis Star*, May 18, 1979; *Minneapolis Tribune*, Apr. 25, 1971, Frank Wright; *Minneapolis Tribune*, May 17, 1972.

2. Senator Allan Spear, interview, May 24, 1999.

3. *Minneapolis Tribune*, Feb. 15, 1972.

4. *Minneapolis Tribune*, June 15, 1972, Bernie Shellum.

5. Press release, Senators Nicholas Coleman and George Conzemius, March 29, 1974.

6. *Minneapolis Star*, May 18, 1979.

7. *Minneapolis Star*, March 6, 1981.

8. Statement by Lieutenant Governor Perpich, Feb. 13, 1974.

9. *Minneapolis Tribune*, Sept. 12, 1974. Shellum reported that Rudy Perpich originally planned to run for Congress in 1976, anticipating Blatnik's retirement. The timetable was upset when Blatnik announced he would retire at the end of his term in 1974 on the advice of his physicians.

10. Joan Growe, (interview, Nov. 23, 1998) remembered being impressed at seeing the Perpich brothers'wives coordinating the delegate vote count and floor operations at the convention.

11. *Minneapolis Tribune*, Feb.26, 1974, Jack Coffman.

12. *Minneapolis Tribune*, Sept. 11, 1974, Shellum. Minneapolis Star, Sept. 12, 1974, Gordon Slovut.

13. *Minneapolis Star*, Oct. 21, 1974, Associated Press.

14. *Star Tribune*, Nov. 30, 1986, author and Phelps.

15. Robert Aronson, interview, May 19, 1998.

16. *Minneapolis Star*, March 27, 1975; *Minneapolis Star*, May 2, 1975, Jim Shoop.

Notes to Chapter 6

1. Interview, July, 1976, author.

2. *Pioneer Press*, Aug. 13, 1993, Steven Dornfeld.

3. Rudy Perpich, interview, summer, 1976, notes, Jim Shoop, author.

4. *Minneapolis Star*, Oct. 12, 1976.

5. *Pioneer Press*, March 22, 1992, Bruce Orwall.

6. *Minneapolis Star*, Nov. 10, 1976, author.

7. Gail Murray was the first woman judge in northeastern Minnesota, appointed in 1974 by Governor Wendell Anderson at the recommendation of Lieutenant Governor Rudy Perpich.. She had met Perpich in 1968 when she was active in the anti-Vietnam war movement, and was a delegate to the 1968 state DFL convention.

8. *St. Paul Dispatch*, Dec. 29, 1978, Gary Dawson.

9. *St. Paul Dispatch*, Dec. 19, 1976, Dawson.

Notes to Chapter 7

1. *Minneapolis Star*, Nov. 26, 1976, David Early.

2. *Minneapolis Star*, March 11, 1977. author; *Minneapolis Star*, March 17, 1977. Blair Charnley and author; *Minneapolis Tribune*, March 18, 1977, Dornfeld.

3. *Minneapolis Star*, Nov. 22, 1976; *Minneapolis Star*, Dec. 6, 1976.

4. This is the account given Terry Montgomery by Gerry Christenson, commissioner of finance for Governor Rudy Perpich and Governor Wendell Anderson. Montgomery was not clear whether his name came first from Anderson or Kelm. The first indication Montgomery had that he was under consideration was when he got a telephone call from Kelm sounding him out about the job.

5. *Minneapolis Star*, Jan. 12, 1977.

6. For a detailed account see *Powerline*, Barry M. Casper and Paul David Wellstone, 1981, the University of Massachusetts Press.

7. *Session Weekly*, Feb. 2, 1996; *Minneapolis Star*, Feb., 1972, Dec., 1972.

8. See *Uncovering The Dome*, Amy Klobuchar, 1982, Waveland Press Inc.

9. Ronald Gornick, interview, June 9, 1998.

10. *Minneapolis Star*, March 7, 1977.

11. *Minneapolis Star*, April 24, 1974, taken from transcript of hearings on project

12. *Pioneer Press*, Dec. 31, 1997, Associated Press.

13. *Minneapolis Tribune*, April 9, 1977, Dean Rebuffoni.

14. *Pioneer Press*, Dec. 31, 1997, Associated Press.

15. *St. Paul Dispatch*, Jan. 8, 1971, Boxmeyer.

16. *Minneapolis Star*, Nov. 25, 1975, Terry Wolkerstorfer.

17. *Minneapolis Tribune*, June 3, 1977, Steve Brandt.

18. *Star Tribune*, Dec. 29, 1999.

19. *Rosalie Wahl*, interview, Nov. 11, 1999.

20. Koryne Horbal, interview, November, 1999.

21. Rosalie Wahl, interview, March 8, 2000.

22. Star Tribune, Dec. 29, 1999.

23. Gloria Griffin, interview, April 18, 1999.

Notes for Chapter 8

1 Robert (Bob) Aronson, interview, May 19, 1998.

2 *Minneapolis Star*, March 14, 1978.

3 D. D. (Don) Wozniak, interview, January, 1999, said his fellow St. Paulite, Coleman, was "very angry" over Muriel's appointment. "He thought he should have been appointed."

4 Deborah Howell, interview, March 4, 2000. Howell said she was with Coleman at Perpich's lake cabin shortly before Humphrey's death and heard the governor tell the senate majority leader he would appoint him to the expected vacancy.

5. Howell, interview, July, 1998. Howell was Twiggy-like thin, chic, and extremely bright. An audacious reporter, she once got removed

by the State Patrol when she and fellow reporter Finlay Lewis lay on the floor trying to hear from under the closed door what was being said in a legislative committee meeting. Later she became city editor of the *Minneapolis Star*, then a top editor of the *Pioneer Press*, and eventually Washington Bureau chief for Newhouse News Service.)

6. *Minneapolis Tribune*, April 16, 1978.

7. *Minneapolis Star*, Sept. 14, 1977, Robert Ostmann Jr.; *Associated Press*, April 10, 1978.

8. Harris of Edina was a social studies professor at the University of Minnesota and a behind-the-scenes power in the DFL Party for the past 20 years. He knew how to run a statewide campaign. He had been state campaign chairman for Eugene McCarthy's presidential campaign in 1968 and later was state chairman for George McGovern's presidential bid in 1972.

9. *Minneapolis Star*, Aug. 7, 1978, author.

10. *Minneapolis Tribune*, Sept. 30, 1978.

11. A. M. (Sandy) Keith, interview, Nov. 16, 1998.

12. *Minneapolis Star*, Nov. 2, 1979, author.

13. *Minneapolis Star*, Oct. 23, 1978. Leading supporters of Fraser formed a Democrats for Durenberger movement. When President Carter came to Minneapolis for a DFL rally at the Minneapolis Auditorium attended by about 6,000 people, hundreds of anti-Short demonstrators booed and waved red "Stop Short" cards when Short was introduced and when the President referred to Short as Minnesota's next senator. Short's wife and daughters watched in shock and tears from offstage, a testament to the pain and toll a political campaign imposes on families.

14. *Pioneer Press*, Jan. 1, 1990.

15. see *Pioneer Press*, Nov. 6, 1982, Gerry Nelson, Associated Press; *Minneapolis Star*, Dec. 1, 1978, Patrick Marx; *Minneapolis Tribune*, Dec. 2, 1978, David Phelps.

Notes for Chapter 9

1. *Hibbing Daily Tribune*, Feb. 8, 1991.

2. *Star Tribune*, July 11, 1979.

3. Connie Perpich, interview, April 30, 1999.

4. *Star Tribune*, Sept. 26, 1981, Patrick Marx.

5. Joseph Perpich, letter, March 8, 2000.

6. *Pioneer Press*, May 28, 1981, Bill Salisbury.

7. *Pioneer Press*, May 28, 1981.

8. *Mpls St Paul*, Jan., 1979, Lynda McDonnell.

9. Press release, Spannaus Volunteer Committee, Nov. 5, 1981.

10. A. M. (Sandy) Keith, interview, Nov. 16, 1998.

11. *Star Tribune*, Oct. 27, 1981.

12. *Pioneer Press*, Jan. 26, 1982, Steven Dornfeld.

13. *Pioneer Press*, Jan. 26, 1982, Jeffrey Kummer.

14. *Pioneer Press*, April 1, 1982, Salisbury.

15. *Ibid*

Notes for Chapter 10

1. *Mesabi Daily News*, United Press International, April 22, 1982.

2. Emily Staples Tuttle, interview, May 5, 1999.

3. In 1990 Staples was Mike Hatch's lieutenant governor candidate in his unsuccessful challenge of Perpich in the DFL gubernatorial primary. She was elected to the Hennepin County Board in 1992 and did not run for a second term.

4. Joan Growe, interview, Nov. 23, 1998.

5. *Star Tribune*, June 5, 1982, Sturdevant and author.

6. *City Pages*, June 11, 1988, Mary Mussell.

7. *Star Tribune*, June 8, 1982, Sturdevant and author.

8. Eldon Brustuen, interview, March 17, 2000. Brustuen thought Governor Jesse Ventura swept through to victory in much the same way in 1998, winning the votes of many who felt shut out by the political parties.

9. *Pioneer Press*, Sept. 16, 1982.

10. *Minneapolis Star*, Nov. 20, 1980.

11. *Minnetonka Herald*, Aug. 1, 1968.

12. *Star Tribune*, June 17, 1982.

13. *Star Tribune*, June 25, 1991; Jan. 24, 1992; *Pioneer Press*, Jan. 24, 1992.

14. *Pioneer Press*, Jan. 24, 1992.

15. *Star Tribune*, Nov. 4, 1982.

Note for Chapter 11

1. Gerry Nelson resigned as Capitol bureau chief for the Associated Press to become a senior staff member in the governor's office.

2. Marlene Johnson, e-mail, March 23, 2000.

3. *Star Tribune*, Oct. 12, 1983, author

4. *Pioneer Press*, Feb. 13, 1998, Salisbury.

5. *Star Tribune*, Feb. 27, 1993, Gregor W. Pinney. The schools were established, but in 1993 the Legislative Auditor said those and two other engineering schools established at public universities in that period were too expensive and hadn't produced nearly as many graduates as projected. The auditor recommended consolidating or closing some, acknowledging, however, that would be a politically sensitive and unlikely action.

6. *Pioneer Press*, March 15, 1983.

7. *Pioneer Press*, May 25, 1986.

8. *Minnesota Business*, September, 1984, George Perpich, Guest Editorial.

9. Press release, George Perpich and Associates, Nov. 11, 1983.

10. *Star Tribune*, June 14, 1983, author.

11. *Star Tribune*, Oct. 9, 1983.

12. James (Jim) Nichols, interview, Feb. 29, 2000.

13. The full group were Tom Triplett, policy adviser; Gus Donhowe, commissioner of finance; Sally Martin, assistant to the governor; Paul Tschida, commissioner of public safety; Sandra Hale, commissioner of administration; Leonard Levine, commissioner of welfare; Jon Wefald, president of Southwest State University; Sandra Gardebring, executive director, Pollution Control Agency; David Lebedoff, Minneapolis lawyer and adviser to former Governor and U.S. Senator Wendell Anderson; Sun Won Son, economist; John Brandl, DFL senator, University of Minnesota economics professor; Ed Dirkswager, former deputy finance commissioner; Duane Scribner, staff assistant to Governor Wendell Anderson.

14. Michael O'Donnell, special adviser to the governor and executive secretary to the cabinet; Gerry Nelson, communications

director; Keith Ford, the governor's chief legislative lobbyist; Ray Bohn, commissioner of labor and industry; Marlene Johnson, lieutenant governor; Tom Kelm, former chief of staff for Governor Wendell Anderson; Mike Hatch, commissioner of commerce; Gerald Christenson, former commissioner of finance; Doug Johnson, Senate tax committee chair; Paul Ridgeway, DFL activist; Dayton, commissioner of energy and economic development.

15. A. M. (Sandy) Keith, interview, Nov. 16, 1998.

16. D. D. Wozniak, interview, March 18, 1999.

17. *Law & Politics*, January, 1998.

18. *Star Tribune*, Oct. 23, 1983, David Peterson.

19. Allan Spear, interview, May 24, 1999.

20. *Pioneer Press*, Dec. 11, 1993; *Star Tribune*, Nov. 1, 1994; *Star Tribune*, April 2, 1994.

21. *Star Tribune*, Sept. 11, 1987, David Peterson. In 1987 the $90,000-a-year Stockholm office was quietly shut down. It did not generate the expected business.

22. *Pioneer Press*, Jan. 1, 1984. Salisbury.

23. Press release, Governor's office, April 13, 1984.

24. *Pioneer Press*, March 4, 1984, Dave Beal.

25. Press release, Rep. David Jennings, House minority leader, April 27, 1984.

26. The Center had not been built at the time of Perpich's death in 1995, and Gov. Jesse Ventura vetoed legislation funding it in 1999.

27. *Star Tribune*, July 28, 1984, Sturdevant.

28. *TIME*, June 11, 1984.

29. *CITYBUSINESS*, June 4-15. In 1990, his last year in office, Perpich boasted that *Fortune* and *Money* magazines had ranked the Twin Cities the past year as one of the top ten places to do business in the country, and in 1990 the Corporation for Enterprise Development, an analyst of state business climates, ranked the Minnesota business climate seventh in the nation overall.

30. *Star Tribune*, Sept. 12, 1984, author.

Notes for Chapter 12

1. *Star Tribune*, Jan. 22, 1985, Lori Sturdevant.

2. *Star Tribune*, March 17, 1986.

3. *Pioneer Press*, April 20, 1986, Jack Coffman.

4. *Star Tribune*, May 10, 1985, Sturdevant.

5. *Star Tribune*, Gregor W. Pinney, June 21, 1985.

6. *Fargo Forum*, March 12, 1985, Associated Press.

7. During the years their father was in the state Senate and lieutenant governor's office, Rudy Jr. and Mary Sue changed schools more than a dozen times, moving back and forth from Hibbing to rented housing in the Twin Cities. During their father's tenure at Control Data, they switched colleges three times so they could be with their parents, accompanying then first to New York, then to Austria, and finally back to Minnesota, where both graduated from the College of St. Thomas.

7. For reactions to the school choice initiative, see *Star Tribune*, June 22, 1985, author; *Pioneer Press*, Dec. 6, 1993, Bill Salisbury; *Pioneer Press*, April 28, 1985, Steven Thomma; *Star Tribune*, April 15, 1985, Sturdevant.

8. David Jennings, interview, March 15, 1999

9. *Star Tribune*, April 13, 1985, Joe Kimball and Randy Furst.

10. Perpich speech to Economic Summit meeting, Minneapolis, June 19, 1987.

11. *Star Tribune*, Nov. 29, 1985, Joe Rigert.

12. *Pioneer Press*, Sept. 6, 1984, David Shaffer.

13. Elk River Star, July 30, 1985.

14. *Star Tribune*, Feb. 18, 1986; *Star Tribune*, July 28, 1985, commentary, Leonard Inskip.

15. David Jennings, interview, March 15, 1999.

16. *Pioneer Press*, Sept. 17, 1985, Salisbury; *Star Tribune*, Sept. 13, 1985; Press release, Fred Norton, Oct. 8, 1985.

17. *Pioneer Press*, Dec. 29, 1999.

18. *Star Tribune*, Oct. 29, 1985; *Pioneer Press*, Oct. 29, 1985.

19. In 1989, Governor Perpich and Robert Carothers, chancellor of the Minnesota State University system, announced that Minnesota would open a university campus in Akita, Japan, and become one of the first states in the nation to establish a college branch outside the U.S. But 10 years later the campus, 400 miles north of Tokyo, was struggling with escalating costs and a low enrollment of about 300

students, far short of the 900 originally projected, according to a
state audit. In 1999 the board of the Minnesota State Colleges and
Universities voted to phase out the Akita campus by 2003.

20 *Star Tribune*, Nov. 30, 1985.

Notes for Chapter 13

1. For details on this episode see *No Retreat, No Surrender*, Dave
Hage and Paul Klauda, William Morrow & Co., New York, 1989;
Hard-Pressed in the Heartland, Peter Rachleff, South End Press, 1993;
Professor Wellstone Goes to Washington, Dennis J. McGrath and Dane
Smith, University of Minnesota Press, 1995.

2. Roberta Heine, assistant in Governor Perpich's communications
office, interview, July 15, 1998.

3. *Grand Forks Herald*, Feb. 9, 1986, Liz Fedor.

4. see *Pioneer Press*, April 1, 1985, Louis Porter II and Dorothy
Lewis; *Pioneer Press*, Jan. 16, 1985, Jack Coffman. Perpich said he
would support a farm foreclosure moratorium if it were agreed to
by major banking groups and lasted no longer than 120 days. He
also called for an end to bans on corporate and outside ownership of
Minnesota farmland to free up needed capital for agriculture.

5. *Star Tribune*, March 3, 1985, Lori Surdevant.

6. *Star Tribune*, Feb. 18, 1988; *Pioneer Press*, Feb. 19, 1986,
Steven Thomma.

7. Michael Hatch, interview, Dec. 11, 1999.

8. *Pioneer Press*, Feb. 16, 1986, Salisbury and Steven Dornfeld;
Pioneer Press, Feb. 9, 1986, Kohl.

9. *Star Tribune*, Oct. 30, 1985.

10. *Pioneer Press*, Feb. 9, 1986, Kohl.

11. *Pioneer Press,* Jan. 6, 1999, Dave Beal.

Notes for Chapter 14

1. Press release, Leon Oistad.

2. Michael Hatch, interview, Dec. 11, 1999.

3. Later she married attorney John Stanoch, who became Perpich's
campaign manager in 1990 and was appointed a Hennepin District

judge by Perpich on his last day in office.

4. *Star Tribune*, June 14, 1986, Sturdevant.

5. *Pioneer Press*, Sept. 3, 1986.

6. *Pioneer Press*, Sept. 10, 1986.

7. Matt Sjoberg, loan officer, Iron Range Resources and Rehabilitation, interview, March 31, 2000; John Nickila, who was in charge of production at the Lakewood factory, interview, April 3, 2000; *Star Tribune*, Sept. 10, 1989, Donald Woutat.

8. *Wall Street Journal*, July 18, 1989.

9. *Pioneer Press*, Nov. 6, 1988.

10. *Star Tribune*, Nov. 27, 1986, author and Dane Smith.

Notes for Chapter 15

1. *Star Tribune*, Jan. 15, 1987.

2. *Star Tribune*, June 15, 1989. author.

3. *Pioneer Press*, Oct. 1, 1995.

4. *Star Tribune*, Jan. 9, 1999.

5. *Star Tribune*, March 21, 1987, Robert Whereatt and Gregor W. Pinney.

6. *Star Tribune*, March 17, 1987, author.

7. *Star Tribune*, Nov. 3, 1990.

8. *Star Tribune*, March 21, 1987. Whereatt and Pinney.

9. *Star Tribune*, March 2, 1999.

10. *Star Tribune*, Aug. 29, 1987, Richard Meryhew and Joe Kimball; *Pioneer Press*, Aug. 30, 1987, Tony Blass.

11. *Star Tribune,* Sept. 16, 1987.

12. *Star Tribune*, Sept. 16. Randy Furst.

13. *Pioneer Press*, Sept. 20, 1987. Bill Salisbury.

14. *Politics In Minnesota*, Oct. 9, 1987, Wy Spano and D. J. Leary.

15. *Star Tribune*, Sept. 16, 1987, Furst.

16. *Scripps Howard*, Jan. 15, 1987.

17. Robert Aronson, Perpich's communications director during his lieutenant governor days and first term as governor, said, in an interview, May 19, 1998 "Rudy got rid of all resistance. He never liked resistance. I know that in working with Rudy, if you were going

to resist him, you had to be able to do it in such a diplomatic way that you almost had to make him think it was his idea. You just didn't go to him and say, 'Bullshit, that isn't going to work. [Senator] Nick Coleman could do that, but toward the end, he and Perpich didn't get along at all."

18. David Carr, interview, April 27, 2000.

19. *Star Tribune*, Dec. 28, 1987.

Notes for Chapter 16

1. *Star Tribune*, Feb. 10, 1988, Dean Rebuffoni.

2. *Minneapolis Star,* Nov. 5, 1975, Associated Press.

3. *Pioneer Press*, Nelson French, Sierra Club, North Star Chapter, July 1, 1985; *Pioneer Press*, Aug. 29, 1985, Jack Coffman.

4. *Pioneer Press*, April 23, 1990, Gary Dawson.

5. Press release, Jobs for Minnesota, coalition of Minnesota Business Partnership, Chambers of Commerce and other business associations, April 20, 1988.

6. *Pioneer Press*, May 19, 1976; Minneapolis Star, Minneapolis Tribune, Feb. 16, 1963.

7. Michael Hatch, interview, Dec. 11, 1999.

Notes for Chapter 17

1. *Pioneer Press*, June 3, 1989, Bill Salisbury. *Star Tribune*, June 27, 1989, author.

2. *Star Tribune*, May 14, 1989, author.

3. In 1997 Wynia was named president of the college. She also was a University of Minnesota regent before resigning to run for the U.S. Senate in 1994.

4. Robert Vanasek, interview, April 30, 1999.

5. Doug Johnson, interview, Nov. 20, 1998.

6. When he was lieutenant governor, Perpich made a month-long tour of every institution for the handicapped in the state. He and his brother George, chairman of the Senate Welfare and Corrections Committee, collaborated on proposed legislation to develop new programs, including community-based facilities which would allow

handicapped persons to live in their own neighborhoods. *Minneapolis Tribune*, Jan. 22, 1975.

7 D. D. (Don) Wozniak, interview, March 18, 1999.

8 *Pioneer Press*, Aug. 31, 1989, Bruce Orwall.

9 *Star Tribune*, Sept. 11, 1989, David Hage, author; *Star Tribune*, Sept. 15, 1989, Larry Oakes.

10 *Law & Politics*, Nov. 1995, Steven Dornfeld

11 *Star Tribune*, July 26, 1989, Robert Whereatt.

12 *Star Tribune*, Oct. 6, 1989.

13 Roger Moe, interview, Jan. 20, 1999.

Notes for Chapter 18

1. Robert Aronson, communications director on Perpich lieutenant governor and governor staff, interview, May 19, 1998; *Star Tribune*, May 18, 1986, Lori Sturdevant.

2. Andrew Kozak, aide to Perpich when he was lieutenant governor, interview, April 30, 1999.

3. Deborah Howell, interview, July 16, 1998.

4. *Pioneer Press*, July 4, 1982, Bill Salisbury.

5. *The Daily Journal*, International Falls and other newspapers, Associated Press, Dec. 8, 1989.

6. *Pioneer Press*, Dec. 8, 1989, Salisbury.

Notes to Chapter 19

1. *Star Tribune*, July 21, Doug Grow.

2. *Star Tribune*, July 21, Doug Grow interview with Perpich in Croatia,; *There Is No November*, Dave Hoium and Leon Oistad, 1991, Jeric Publications. Carlson e-mail, July 13, 2005.

3. *Pioneer Press*, Nov. 4, 1999.

4. *Star Tribune*, Oct. 9, 1990, author and Bill McAuliffe; Pioneer Press, Oct. 9, 1990, Bill Salisbury.

5. *Star Tribune*, Oct. 23, 1990, author, Dane Smith and Randy Furst.

6. Rosalie Wahl, interview, March 8, 2000; Nov. 11, 1999.

7. *Star Tribune*, Dec. 5, 1990, Robert Whereatt and author.

8.Saint Paul Pioneer Press, May 31, 1991; Press Advance by Mona Meyer & McGrath, June 3, 1991.

9. Donald Wozniak, interview, January 8, 1999.

10. *Star Tribune*, editorial, Oct. 28, 1990; *Star Tribune*, Nov. 11, Lou Gelfand.

11. Jack Fena, interview, May 9, 1999.

12. A. M. (Sandy) Keith, interview, December, 1998.

13. Rosalie Wahl also believed Popovich told Perpich immediately that Keith was absent from the court deliberations, before Fena brought it up in his visit with Perpich at the governor's residence after the election. She, too, felt it was inappropriate for Popovich to talk to reporters as he did the night the decision was filed.

14. *Star Tribune*, Dec. 5, 1990.

15. Minnesota Department of Finance forecast, November, 1990; Pioneer Press, Nov. 29, 1990; Star Tribune, Nov. 29; Star Tribune, March 19, 1991; Department of Finance forecast, March, 1991.

16. *The Washington Post*, Jan. 14, 1999, Gwen Ifill.

17. Robert Vanasek, interview, April 30, 1999.

18. *Pioneer Press*, Dec. 2, 1990.

19. "The Amazing Survival of Jon Grunseth," Nov. 4, 1999, Channel 4000, a Web site anchored by WCCO-TV and WCCO-Radio.

Notes to Chapter 21

1. for details on the pension issue, see Press release, Feb. 21, 1991, State Auditor Mark Dayton; *Star Tribune*, Feb. 22, 1991, Gregor W. Pinney; *Star Tribune*, June 9, 1994, Conrad deFiebre and Kevin Diaz;; *Pioneer Press*, June 9, 1994, Don Ahern; *Pioneer Press*, Feb. 22, 1991, Gary Dawson; *Star Tribune*, Feb. 22, 1991, Gregor W. Pinney; *Pioneer Press*, April 12, 1991; *Star Tribune*, June 10, 1994, Conrad deFiebre; *Pioneer Press*, Jan. 14, 1994, Bill Salisbury.

2. Joseph Perpich, interview, July 15, 1998.

3. *Pioneer Press*, July 15, 1993.

4. Ron Jerich, interview, fall of 1993. He said Perpich thought he could win in a three-way race. "He will be probably the only decent Pro Life candidate," said Jerich, who added that Perpich was meeting

that weekend with friends in Hibbing to discuss the election.

5. *Twin Cities Reader*, Feb. 2-8, 1994.

6. Robert Vanasek, interview, April 30, 1999.

7. *Pioneer Press*, April 7, 1994, Salisbury.

8. *Red Wing Republican Eagle*, July 18, 1999.

9. Douglas Johnson, interview, Nov. 20, 1998.

10. David Jennings, interview, March 15, 1999.

11. Joseph Perpich, interview , July 15, 1998.

Notes for Chapter 22

1. *Star Tribune*, Sept. 23, 1995, Patricia Lopez Baden and Doug Grow.

2. Donald Wozniak, interview, January, 1999.

3. Roger Moe, interview, Jan. 20, 1999.

4. Michael Hatch, interview, Dec. 11, 1999.

Jorgenson, Jack 114

K

Keefe, Steve 188, 189
Keith, A.M. (Sandy) 25-8, 32, 37,
    38, 43, 44, 89, 90, 92, 103,
    104, 117, 121, 125, 126,
    143, 144, 224, 225, 229,
    250, 251, 254-5, 278, 280,
    287, 288, 291, 292, 294, 300
Keith, Marion 126
Keller, Kenneth 202
Kelley, Doug 231, 235
Kelm, Tom 66, 78, 79, 222, 289,
    294
Kennedy, Ted 22
Kennedy, William (Bill) 90
Kiedrowski, Jay 205
Klobuchar, Jim 27, 48, 71, 126,
    284, 285, 286, 290
Knaak, Fritz 202
Knutsen, Oscar 46
Knutson, Coya 98
Kosiak, Dr. William 35
Kough, Tom 168
Kozak, Andrew 54
Krenik, Lauris 126

L

Lahammer, Gene 112
Lane, Wes 89
Lansing, Harriet 92, 133
Larsen, Libby 191
Latimer, George 114, 125, 155,
    161, 168, 171, 173-8, 180-4,
    195, 199, 200, 223,
Leary, D.J. 201, 297
Lebedoff, David 63, 203, 293
Lehr, Lewis 146, 156
Lehto, Arlene 120
LeVander, Harold 28, 30, 40, 103
Levi, Connie 153, 156, 162
Levine, Leonard 189, 223, 293

Levy, Roberta 89
Likins, Vera 74
Lindau, James 127, 161, 164, 183,
    184
Lindstrom, Ernest 79
Lindstrom, Elmer 50
Long, Dee 221
Lord, Jim 88
Lord, Miles 85, 86, 87, 88, 114
Ludeman, Cal 169, 178, 179, 180,
    183, 184, 186, 247

M

MacGregor, Clark 42
MacKay, Harvey 81
MacMillan, Whitney 239
Marty, John 269
Matonich, Ed 47
Mattson, Robert 87, 88, 92, 245
Maxwell, Robert 228, 238-240,
    258, 259, 262, 263, 264
Mayo, DR. Charles 35
McCarthy, Eugene 30, 34, 35, 36,
    41, 42, 43, 55, 65, 127, 128
McCormick, John 236
McCutcheon, William 104
McGovern, George 55, 56
McLaughlin, Harry 89
Menning, Mike 169, 178, 179
Merritt, Grant 36, 85
Minge, Dave 280
Minnesota Citizens Concerned for
    Life 60, 69, 105, 251
Moe, Don 196, 273
Moe, Richard 45
Moe, Roger 58, 59, 114, 157, 163,
    164, 167, 170, 171, 189,
    192, 194, 195, 196, 197,
    210, 218, 219, 230-3, 267,
    273, 279, 299, 301
Mondale, Walter 32, 35, 38, 42, 43,
    63, 64, 65, 72, 96, 98, 101,
    114, 124, 149, 188, 199,